Beginning Microsoft® Small Basic

A Computer Programming Tutorial

Illustrated Color Edition v1.0

BY PHILIP CONROD & LOU TYLEE

Kidware Software
PO Box 701
Maple Valley, WA 98038

http://www.computerscienceforkids.com
http://www.kidwaresoftware.com

Published by Kidware Software LLC
PO Box 701
Maple Valley, Washington 98038
1.425.413.1185
www.kidwaresoftware.com
www.computerscienceforkids.com

Printed in the United States of America

ISBN-13: 978-1-937161-54-5 (Color - 2nd Print Edition 2014)
ISBN-13 978-1-937161-21-7 (Glassbook PDF)

Illustrations: Kevin Brockschmidt
Copy Editor: Stephanie Conrod
Compositor: Michael Rogers

This guide was developed for the course, "Beginning Microsoft Small Basic," produced by Kidware Software, Maple Valley, Washington. It is not intended to be a complete reference to the Small Basic language. Please consult the Microsoft website for detailed reference information.

This guide refers to several software and hardware products by their trade names. These references are for informational purposes only and all trademarks are the property of their respective companies and owners.

Microsoft, Visual Studio, Small Basic, Visual Basic, Visual J#, and Visual C#, IntelliSense, Word, Excel, MSDN, and Windows are all trademark products of the Microsoft Corporation. Java is a trademark product of the Oracle Corporation. JCreator is a trademark product of XINOX Software

The example companies, organizations, products, domain names, e-mail addresses, logos, people, places, and events depicted are fictitious. No association with any real company, organization, product, domain name, e-mail address, logo, person, place, or event is intended or should be inferred.

This book expresses the author's views and opinions. The information in this book is distributed on an "as is" basis, without and expresses, statutory, or implied warranties.

Praise For Beginning Microsoft Small Basic – First Edition

"The Beginning Microsoft Small Basic Programming Tutorial by Philip Conrod and Lou Tylee is a fun read and covers all the fundamentals of Small Basic programming. I would recommend it to all my friends who want to learn Small Basic. They do a great job explaining Small Basic programming in an easy to read self-paced tutorial. I liked it so much, I got one for myself!" - **Vijaye Raji, Creator of Microsoft Small Basic**

"This book is an excellent guide to getting started with this language. There are plenty of excellent illustrations and example snippets of code for the student to enter and try out. The first couple of chapters provide an excellent introduction for a student who knows the essentials of Windows and the PC but has no prior programming experience. New concepts are introduced in a logical way. First, the standard text window is discussed, then simple looping and subroutines are covered, and this leads to the graphics window and how events, like clicking the mouse or pressing a key, are handled. Techniques of animation are covered, because most kids are in love with games. By reading the text and following the coding examples, students will be able to create their own simple games. What better way for kids to learn programming than to use it to create something they love! One chapter contains the code for 9 interactive programs to show how all of these programming structures and features can be combined to create really interesting programs, and the final chapter takes sample programs and shows the code for these programs in five popular programming languages: Small Basic, Visual Basic, Visual C#, Java, and a generic Basic. The book covers it all, from a great introduction to what programming is all about to the specific syntax and structure of a Small Basic program. The advice and suggestions given in the book are spot on. I think this book is valuable in two ways. For a self-motivated student who wants to learn a nice beginning programming language, the book provides an excellent tutorial. Everything the student will need to create and run text window or graphics window programs is here. Secondly, this book can be used as a complete curriculum for teaching students about introductory programming. I currently am using the book to teach programming to middle-school students (ages 11-14), and the book is also excellent in that regard. Microsoft does make freely available a "curriculum" consisting of a series of PowerPoint slides, but I don't believe that using these slides would be as effective as using this book. All teachers know that kids learn best when they are having fun. This book helps put the fun in this new language from Microsoft, and it is an excellent and valuable resource.
- **Donald M. Shepherd, Teacher, Louisville, Kentucky**

"It is easy to use and takes you step by step through writing a code for different applications. I loved how much fun my girls were having and I loved how much they were enjoying learning. They enjoyed this program so much that during non-school hours they would be in the Small Basic application trying to write new programs based on the coding they had previously learned. Sometimes they would go back to an older lesson and expand the program to include coding ideas from their current lesson. Thoughts from Tailorbear (14 Years Old, 8th grade): I have... wondered about computer programming for a long time, but I never found the materials needed for doing it. I liked this curriculum. It taught me how to do cool programs that make it like you're actually "talking to" something! Put your name into a paragraph, or sentence, (input) and the computer responds! Over all this program teaches me the basic computer programming language! Thoughts from daughter Turtlegirl (15 Years Old, 10th Grade), " I have really wanted to try computer programming, so I was thrilled when we got this. The Classes were easy to understand (except for some typos) and I really enjoyed doing this. I like how they encourage you to play around with the programs and experiment. I enjoyed typing the code and seeing what it would do as a program. I had a lot of fun using this program. For the most part, it's simple and easy. They start you off with the most basic of the basics and then start introducing more difficult concepts. I highly recommend this for those who wish to begin their study of computer programming." Thoughts from Boobear (17 Years Old, 12th Grade): " I enjoy giving the computer commands and seeing them followed. It is very satisfying to see that I made that. This curriculum makes it very easy to understand how this particular computer language works. It is also interesting to know the history behind it as well. I like creating things and seeing that they are successful, and work. It is fascinating to create programs and this curriculum makes it easy to do." "I was afraid this program would have been too simplistic or young for my teenagers; however, it has been an excellent fit. Challenging enough because it's new material but simple enough that they are having fun and building their confidence. Each of them has stated that they want to learn more about computer programming and learn more computer programming languages!" - **Tess**

"Hayden (age 13) was excited to try out this course! Hayden was able to sit right down and begin the first lesson without any help from me whatsoever. Hayden was so excited that he actually made something work! He came running downstairs jumping up and down and couldn't wait to show me! His enthusiasm and interest in the course began to skyrocket. He thought that was pretty cool. He has not encountered any difficulties or problems in completing the first 4 chapters, and he told me it has been really easy to use and follow. I love that he can complete this course independently. I think the cost of the downloadable course is very reasonable, and with the enjoyment he's gotten from using it so far I can definitely envision purchasing the next semester course when he finishes with this one. I would definitely recommend this course to others!" - **Kelly B.**

"So far we have found working in the Small Basic environment easy and that ease relates right back to the straight forward and uncomplicated methods that are taught in Beginning Microsoft Small Basic. Each concept is thoroughly explained and examples are given throughout the material. From the download of the material to working with the material we have had no problems, glitches, etc. So far I would have to say our favorite lesson has been 5, Debugging, Decisions, Random Numbers. This chapter has taught us what causes Syntax, Run-Time, and Logic Errors. Off and on I will get Run-Time Errors on my computer. Now we know the basics of why that might happen. I think Beginning Microsoft Small Basic is a great product that students can learn much from and the economical price helps too. - **Diane K.**

"Having the chance to test drive Beginning Microsoft Small Basic has been one of the highlights of our spring semester. This is a super easy to use, easy to succeed at, beginning programming course for your homeschool student! I've been looking for something like this for a long time and was not disappointed! Both Feeche (12th grade)and Cub (7th grade), with no previous programming experience have spent hours delving into this curriculum. If your kids are like mine, go ahead and purchase both at once; they'll love it, cruise through it, and beg for more! A must have for any conscientious homeschooling family. Content- excellent, Organization – excellent, Presentation – excellent." - **Lisa N.**

"I used this tutorial with my ten year old son. This tutorial was very easy to use and very easy to follow. Computers can be intimidating, especially if you have no programming experience, but the Beginning Microsoft Small Basic tutorial made it quite joyful to learn. My son and I really enjoyed using the Beginning Microsoft Small Basic tutorial together; this was our mother/son time in the evenings. Even though my son was on the younger end of the age spectrum for this product, I feel he did really well with it.. I feel that this is an excellent, thorough, beginner's course for computer programming. We plan to continue this course and then look into other courses that Computer Science For Kids offers." - **Sarah Avila**

"I knew Charles (my 12 year old) would have an interest in learning basic programming. He took off through the lessons. There were times when he did even more than two lessons for the week. The lessons were easy for him to comprehend for the most part. He worked through entirely self-directed. Despite the amount of reading, he has had only good things to say about the program. He's very excited about all he's learning. And he often chooses to do the program even if I haven't assigned it for the day. This has definitely been successful for us, and I'm glad we've had the opportunity to use it. - **Leah Courtney**

"Your Small Basic books are great!"- **Neil Kendall, United Kingdom**

"Liz quickly became very comfortable with the lessons and completed them all by herself and called me {constantly} to come see her fun little creations.   I was impressed with this narrative. She likes the "games." She likes the control and learning how changing just one letter or character can change the whole program. Her analytical mind at work! I love that she is learning about computers.   It's great help to her in math since she has to calculate the size of shapes or borders within the graphics. She was all proud of herself and showing me all these little "games" she wrote. It's like a new toy! - **Jennifer Lambert**

"If you have been thinking about adding programming to your lessons this year, I would highly recommend that you check out all the courses that Computer Science For Kids offers. - **Eddie D.**

"Captain C is 13 and this is perfect for him. I don't have to sit with him and do it all, but he does it at the kitchen table so I can be close by to help if needed. C is really enjoying it and I'm glad we got to review this. I think the price is very fair considering the quality of the lessons. Kids these days have such a bend towards video games and computers so I'm thrilled to have found this where he can still have that outlet, but be learning and building too. - **Leslie E.**

"My son is 10.5 and he is interested in computers and anything "techie". He is right at the beginning target market for this tutorial, which is ages 10 and up. The tutorial is self-paced which is great for a child just entering into the programming world. Just when I would think he was going to complain or be confused, he'd amaze me with his understanding." - **Heather H.**

"We recently were able to use the Beginning Microsoft Small Basic program (recommended ages 10 plus) for our 11 year old son with great success. I really like this hands-on approach as it speaks to my learning style and I think my son was able to grasp the material without having too much further instruction. All in all we enjoyed using Computer Science For Kids and discovering what Microsoft Small Basic could do. I would recommend using this program to get your youngster started as a computer programmer or at least give them the exposure and knowledge that there's more to that pretty little icon that sits on your desktop." - **Michele P.**

"Like many children today, Luke has a strong interest in programming. He's had some experience with different programming languages, and seems to have a knack for it. Luke enjoyed working through the program and I was glad to have him work through a systematic course, since much of what he has learned in the realm of computer programming is self-taught." - **Courtney L.**

"For us the books were very easy to follow. Yes, I say us. I couldn't help but do this along with my son. Learning like this is so fun that it doesn't even feel like learning. Isn't that how it should be?" -**Alyson Brown**

""When he finished any programs he wrote, he was very quick to show me. He was super excited that he was able to do it all by himself. A few times, him and daddy had a great time playing around to see what different options she could come up with! Lessons are not super long, so he usually does a couple at a time. He is almost completed with the whole book. He just has so much fun, he sometimes plays with certain lessons more than others! This was a great program for him to do, and get to see a bit more inside look of what a computer programmer does. Monkey Man really enjoyed the program. He had lots of fun creating things, and showing off his work. He also liked that it was not long and drawn out. I think that was one of the main things that kept his attention. I have been reading the e-book when he is not using it. I must tell you just browsing over that I have learned a lot. I actually have considered giving myself a shot at it, see how bad I do. It's a pretty neat program!!!" - **Monica B.**

"This curriculum has been super easy to implement and has required almost no effort from me. Yay! I've been impressed with his ability to learn the concepts being taught and immediately implement them into his own programs. He hasn't been copying the sample programs, but synthesizing the new information and creating something purely his own. We like Beginning Microsoft Small Basic and recommend it (without reservation) for kids (and adults) ages 10 and up who want to learn about programming."- **Susan A.**

"I must to confess; I was very nervous prior to this review as I have no programming experience and was unsure how well I would cope with overseeing this program. I am glad to say it was much easier than I imagined :) Don't let the fear of programming put you off - this is a wonderfully easy curriculum to use and it has given Lilly great confidence and encouraged her to experiment more with our computer. - **Zelda A.**

" I know, you are thinking WHAT, computer programming??? Don't despair, this curriculum isn't as complicated as the name lets on. In fact, you don't even need to have any previous computer programming experience. One of the biggest things he was impressed with was the ease of use. He said everything was clearly laid out and not once did he ever become confused on what he was to do." -**Jenn P.**

"I was very impressed with the amount of information packed into each chapter. I like that the instructions are mixed within the reading, making the reading more interesting and keep Joey's focus. I am definitely leaving this program as part of Joey's weekly schoolwork. Who knows what he may start creating? The price also makes it a very affordable option for families to use." - **Renita Kuehner**

"Beginning Microsoft Small Basic is a computer programming course that starts right at the very beginning. It is intended for kids aged 10 and up, but my nine-year old had no problem sitting down and working it on his own without any instruction or help or previous experience in programming. He just opened both the lesson file and the Small Basic program and worked through the lesson. It was so simple and easy to use this program that he did it completely and totally on his own. He would spend 30 minutes to an hour (as long as I would let him, really) and would do from half a lesson to a lesson in a sitting. I am not a techie person, but Nate had many a conversation with his dad about what he was learning and my husband was quite impressed. Nate had so much fun with this program! He loved learning what to type to make things happen: background colors changing; a turtle drawing shapes; writing words; making fractals; and then watching them happen. Nate loved this program well enough that he asked to use it several times a day. And I always had to wrestle him back off of it. He was quick to remind me that he needed to do it, because it was, after all, school, and not just playing on the computer. He has not completely finished the program, but rest assured, he will make sure that he does complete it. I loved that his dad and I were able to relax and let him work on Small Basic because he is not just playing around, but is learning a useful and even vital skill that he can use the rest of his life. We are pleased with the start that Small Basic gave him into the programming world." - **Laura Hoggard.**

"Beginning Microsoft Small Basic is a computer programming course that teaches the basics of computer programming codes and language. There is no prior computer programming experience needed to begin this course! Which I was happy to find out because I have none:)   The first lesson really got her engaged in learning about the history of computers. One of the things that she commented about was how she loved the author's style of writing. It surprised her that it was written in a lively way. Michelle had a preconceived notion that learning the codes of programming would be boring and to the point, just letters and numbers. Which was one of the reasons that delayed her interest in the world of computer programming. When it got time to learning the codes and playing the games I haven't seen her off of the computer since. Michelle has made it through seven chapters during the review period and if life was just about computer programming I am sure she would have completed it all the way. DJ and Ken have also had a blast and can't wait to get their turn to participant in this independent study of computer programming since they have watched alongside Michelle coding games. Some of the things I like about this course is that it can be done independently, each lesson builds on the previous lesson, and the program promotes self correcting. As soon as I can I will also start to do this course myself too, I'll be sure to update you all when that time comes." - **Michelle**

"I was pleasantly surprised that it was simple enough for my 11 year old daughter to use AND simple enough for me to use! My daughter is a lot like me (not really interested in techie stuff) so we were both starting from the absolute beginning which is where this program starts. I believe short daily lessons of this (rather than trying to rush through) would be the best way to use this when you are starting at the beginning like my daughter and I did.   I would recommend this curriculum to others interested in learning about computer science because it really is easy to use. The suggested age is 10 and up and that would be my recommendation also." - **Joy Capps**

"My son had programmed in Visual Basic, which is a similar language, before. So he found parts of the program easy, especially at the beginning. He enjoyed using the program and found it very user friendly. I like the fact that the curriculum covers more than just simple concepts. It introduces arrays and looping, which are crucial for more complicated programs. It also covers graphics, which of course is fun for the kids. We both thought this curriculum provides an excellent introduction to computer programming that isn't overly difficult for a beginner, but still provides plenty of challenge." - **Anne G.**

"I often say that I have a love/hate relationship with technology. As stated above I am not a techy girl, I had no trouble understand the lessons and even found them to be engaging instead of dull. I was able to write my first program using the lessons provided and I was so excited that I did it all by myself! My poor husband had no idea what I was talking about, but he got that I was pretty excited! The price of the Beginning Small Basic Tutorial is very reasonable, I feel for a course this detailed. " - **Aurie Good**

"The program is written in easy to follow terms. My son that used this program is a high school Junior so he worked on his own.   He has enjoyed working through the program and getting to learn how to do some Basic programming. It has been very well explained and he didn't have any trouble following the directions. He has come and told me numerous times that he thinks this program is really cool. He is looking forward to getting through the rest of the program." - **Dana B.**

"She had a blast & every little bit she would holler at everyone to see what she had done. Beginning Microsoft Small Basic programming tutorial teaches very basic programming and is written for children ages 10 and up or adults who have never tried their hand at computer programming. The directions were very easy for her to understand. Amber loves working with the small basic program and she is already asking for more. This is a great program for a beginner programmer. It was easy enough for her to use & she was very excited with the results of her work." - **Lisa McClanahaan**

"I have to say, I have been pleasantly surprised. Microsoft Small Basic is a computer programming course; but, it is more like a guided road map through computer programming. The kids have been enjoying it because they like being able to tell the computer how to 'do math' for them. For my high school age kids, this course is going to be listed as Computer Programming on their transcripts. Until now, I just had them go through basic keyboarding skills. This takes their computer knowledge to an entirely new level. I recommend Microsoft Small Basic for anyone, pre-teen through adult, who wants to learn about how computer programs are put together and how to create basic computer programs. It is easy to follow, although, as with most computer things, there is a learning curve. You will learn terminology and skills that are incredibly useful in our computerized world." - **Sarah Dugger**

"My daughter has been doing this program 3 days a week. She is really enjoying herself. I haven't had to step in and help her at all. The one time she asked for help I leaned over her shoulder to see what she was doing and she figured it out before I was even able to read two lines of what she typed. she works on her lessons and then calls me over when she is finished so I can watch what she has accomplished. I do recommend this program. With the dependency on computers it would be beneficial for your children to have an understanding of basic computer language and programming."- **Lori L.**

"River is enjoying working through the tutorial. The logic of computer programming – you get what you code – is such a great concept for him to learn. When creating the few programs he already has, he sees the importance of taking the time to decide exactly what he wants the program to do before coding it, because What you see is what you get" (WYSIWYG). Although the concentration is in the Small Basic environment, the course is presented in such an easy to understand manner that removes the fear of learning some stronger and more advanced programming languages, like Visual Basic and Java, which are introduced in the last chapter. I think that this is going to be a great springboard for him as he moves into some of those other languages. Computer Science for Kids also offers tutorials in those areas. Conrod and Tylee have created a curriculum that has opened the doors to programming for the young programmer." - **Jennifer S.**

"Joshua worked completely independently on this program. Joshua says he loved the program. He can't wait to finish up and to move on to bigger programs and projects. I loved the idea that working with the basic program would afford him the effort to work on practical logic when he ran into a problem. It also helps to encourage him to work carefully and how to proof-read before he runs the program to avoid errors to begin with. Additionally, the simple and easy to use programs helped Joshua to think about how those programs could be used in everyday life. Perhaps these simple programs may inspire him to explore money-making projects or a personal saving program. The fact that Joshua could work through the material on his own was helpful to me because it gave me time to work one-on-one with Hannah on other school material. Also, it help him discover the need to plan his own work time effectively. It was really interesting to hear about how working through the program is leading to an interest in further programming instruction."- **Karen M.**

About The Authors

Philip Conrod has been programming computers since 1978. Since then, he has authored, co-authored and edited many beginning computer programming tutorials and books for kids, teens and adults. Philip also holds a BS in Computer Information Systems and a Master's certificate in the Essentials of Business Development from Regis University. Philip has also held various Information Technology leadership roles in companies like Sundstrand Aerospace, Safeco Insurance Companies, FamilyLife, Kenworth Truck Company, and PACCAR. Today, Philip serves as the Chief Information Officer for a large manufacturing company based in Seattle, Washington. In his spare time, Philip serves as the President of Kidware Software, LLC. He makes his home with his lovely wife and three beautiful and "techie" daughters in Maple Valley, Washington.

Lou Tylee holds BS and MS degrees in Mechanical Engineering and a PhD in Electrical Engineering. Lou has been programming computers since 1969 when he took his first Fortran course in college. He has written software to control suspensions for high speed ground vehicles, monitor nuclear power plants, lower noise levels in commercial jetliners, compute takeoff speeds for jetliners, locate and identify air and ground traffic and to let kids count bunnies, learn how to spell and do math problems. He has written several on-line texts teaching Visual Basic, Visual C# and Java to thousands of people. He taught a beginning Visual Basic course for over 15 years at a major university. Currently, Lou works as an engineer at a major Seattle aerospace firm. He is the proud father of five children and proud husband of his special wife. Lou and his family live in Seattle, Washington.

Acknowledgements

I would like to thank my three wonderful daughters - Stephanie, Jessica and Chloe, who helped with various aspects of the book publishing process including software testing, book editing, creative design and many other more tedious tasks like textbook formatting and back office administration. I could not have published this book without all your hard work, love and support. I also want to thank my best friend Jesus who always stands by my side providing me wisdom and guidance.

Last but definitely not least, I want to thank my multi-talented co-author, Lou Tylee, for doing all the real hard work necessary to develop, test, and debug, all the 'kid-friendly' applications, games and base tutorial text found in this book. Lou has tirelessly poured his heart and soul into so many previous versions of this tutorial and there are so many beginners who have benefited from his work over the years. Lou is by far one of the best application developers and tutorial writers I have ever worked with.   Thanks Lou for collaborating with me on this book project.

Philip Conrod
Maple Valley, Washington

Contents

Introduction vii
Course Description vii
System Requirements... viii
Installing and Using the Downloadable Solution Files........................ viii
Course Rerequisites ix
How To Take the Course ix
Forward by Alan Payne, A Computer Science Teacher......................... x

1. Introducing Small Basic

Preview 1-1
Why Learn Small Basic?... 1-2
A Brief History of Small Basic 1-4
Let's Get Started.. 1-10
Downloading and Installing Small Basic.. 1-12
Starting Small Basic... 1-16
Opening a Small Basic Program 1-19
Running a Small Basic Program 1-21
Stopping Small Basic 1-23
Summary 1-24

2. Small Basic Program Basics

Review and Preview 2-1
The Welcome Program (Revisited).. 2-2
Some Rules of Small Basic Programming 2-5
Creating Small Basic Programs 2-7
Saving Small Basic Programs... 2-12
Small Basic Files.. 2-15
Summary 2-16

3. Your First Small Basic Program

Review and Preview 3-1
Creating a Small Basic Program 3-2
Small Basic - The First Lesson 3-6
    Variables..3-6
    Variable Names 3-7
    Variable Types 3-8
    Assignment Statement..3-10
    Arithmetic Operators 3-11
    String Concatenation 3-15
    Comments 3-16
    Program Output 3-17
Program - Sub Sandwich Party..3-21
    Program Design...3-21
    Program Development..3-22
    Run the Program..3-25
    Other Things to Try 3-26
Summary 3-28

4. Small Basic Program Design, Input Methods

Review and Preview 4-1
Program Design...4-2
Small Basic – The Second Lesson 4-4
    Mathematical Functions 4-4
Program Input Methods 4-9
    Input Methods Example 4-10
Program – Savings Calculator 4-14
    Program Design...4-14
    Program Development..4-15
    Run the Program..4-18
    Other Things to Try 4-20
Summary 4-22

5. Debugging, Decisions, Random Numbers

Review and Preview 5-1
Debugging a Small Basic Program 5-2
    Syntax Errors 5-3
    Run-Time Errors 5-6
    Logic Errors 5-9
Small Basic – The Third Lesson 5-10
    Logical Expressions 5-10
    Comparison Operators...5-11
    Logical Operators..5-14
    Decisions – The If Statement..5-19
    Random Number Generator 5-24
Program – Guess the Number Game 5-27
    Program Design..5-27
    Program Development...5-28
    Run the Program...5-31
    Other Things to Try 5-32
Summary 5-34

6. Small Basic Looping, Subroutines

Review and Preview 6-1
Small Basic – The Fourth Lesson 6-2
    Small Basic Loops 6-2
A Brief Interlude – Guess the Number Game (Revisited) 6-12
Small Basic – The Fourth Lesson (Continued)....................................6-14
    Small Basic Subroutines 6-14
Program – Lemonade Stand 6-18
    Program Design..6-19
    Program Development...6-20
    Run the Program...6-27
    Other Things to Try 6-29
Summary 6-30

7. More Small Basic Looping, Arrays

Review and Preview 7-1
Small Basic – The Fifth Lesson..7-2
    Small Basic For Loops 7-2
    Variable Arrays 7-6
"Shuffle" Method 7-11
Program – Card Wars 7-18
    Program Design...7-18
    Program Development 7-19
    Run the Program...7-27
    Other Things to Try 7-29
Summary 7-30

8. Small Basic Graphics, Mouse Methods

Review and Preview 8-1
Graphic User Interfaces (GUI) 8-2
Small Basic Graphics..8-7
    Graphics Window..8-7
    Colors 8-9
    Pen Object 8-10
    Graphics Coordinates 8-11
    DrawLine Method 8-12
    DrawRectangle Method 8-16
    Brush Object 8-19
    FillRectangle Method 8-19
    Clear Method 8-22
Small Basic – The Sixth Lesson...8-23
    Mouse Events 8-23
    MouseDown Event...8-23
    Mouse Properties..8-26
    MouseMove Event 8-30
Program – Blackboard Fun 8-33
    Program Design...8-33
    Program Development 8-34
    Run the Program...8-44
    Other Things to Try 8-46
Summary 8-49

9. Timers, Animation, Keyboard Methods

Review and Preview 9-1
Timer Object 9-2
Small Basic – The Final Lesson...9-10
  DrawText Method...9-10
  Animation 9-12
  Object Disappearance 9-21
  Border Crossing 9-24
  Object Erasure 9-28
  Collision Detection 9-29
  Keyboard Methods...9-34
  KeyDown Event 9-34
Program – Balloons 9-39
  Program Design...9-39
  Program Development..9-40
  Run the Program..9-56
  Other Things to Try 9-58
Sharing a Small Basic Program 9-60
Summary 9-69

10. More Programs

Preview..10-1
Program 1 – Computer Stopwatch...10-2
Program 2 – Loan Calculator 10-5
Program 3 – Units Conversion 10-8
Program 4 – Times Tables..10-11
Program 5 – State Capitals 10-14
Program 6 – Dice Rolling 10-20
Program 7 – Memory Game 10-24
Program 8 – Tic-Tac-Toe..10-30
Program 9 – Decode 10-35

11. Porting Small Basic Computer Games

Preview 11-1
Program 1 – EVEN WINS 11-7
   Small Basic 11-8
   Visual Basic 11-11
   Visual C# 11-21
   Java 11-27
   BASIC 11-31
Program 2 – MUGWUMP 11-34
   Small Basic 11-35
   Visual Basic 11-38
   Visual C# 11-45
   Java 11-50
   BASIC 11-54

Appendix I. Small Basic Colors

Introduction

Microsoft Small Basic is a wonderful programming environment for beginners. Small Basic is very easy and approachable for both kids and adults. The aim of this book is to teach you the fundamentals of programming with Microsoft Small Basic by using the free Microsoft Small Basic Development Environment. You will learn the features of the Small Basic language, and then use them to build applications running on the Microsoft Windows operating system. Beginning Microsoft Small Basic consists of 11 chapters explaining (in simple, easy-to-follow terms) how to build a Small Basic application. You learn about program design, text window applications, graphics window applications and many elements of the Small Basic language. Numerous examples are used to demonstrate every step in the building process. The tutorial also includes several detailed computer programs to illustrate the fun of Small Basic.

Beginning Microsoft Small Basic is presented using a combination of over 400 pages of course notes and actual Small Basic examples. In the final chapter, we list out three classic computer games that were originally published by David H. Ahl, the founder of Creative Computing Magazine. We list the source code to each of these games in Microsoft Small Basic, Visual Basic, Visual C#, Java, and BASIC. This allows you to easily compare and contrast the Small Basic source code against several different computer programming languages that you may or may not know. If you are new to programming this will help you understand how these games would be developed in another more sophisticated programming language.   Kidware Software also produces beginning programming tutorials for several other programming languages like Visual Basic, Visual C#, and Java. Please visit our website for more information on our beginning programming tutorials: http://www.computerscienceforkids.com. If you are learning Microsoft Small Basic after learning a different programming language, the final chapter of this tutorial can help you leverage your existing programming knowledge in that specific programming language to help you better understand Microsoft Small Basic.

By the time you complete this book; you will have a thorough understanding of Microsoft Small Basic and will have used it to build several applications and games that can be published on the internet.

System Requirements

You will need Microsoft Windows XP-SP3, Vista, 7 or 8 to complete the exercises in this book: You will also need Microsoft Small Basic v1.0.

Installing and Using the Solution Files

If you purchased this textbook directly from the Kidware Software website there will be a companion download compressed .zip emailed directly to you.   If you purchased this textbook through a 3rd Party Book Store, the source code solutions and the associated multimedia files for the Beginning Microsoft Small Basic Tutorial are included in a compressed .zip file that is available for download from our website at http://www.kidwaresoftware.com/BMSB-Color-Registration.htm

Please complete the online web form with the bookstore name, your order confirmation number, and the last 4 digits of the credit card that was used to purchase your textbook from the Book Store.   After you download the Source Code Solutions compressed .zip file, use your favorite 'unzipping' application to write all files to your computer. The course is included in the folder entitled BeginSB.   The BSB Code folder includes all the Small Basic program solutions developed during the course.

Course Prerequisites

To use the Beginning Microsoft Small Basic programming tutorial, you should be comfortable working within the Windows (or other operating system) environment, knowing how to find files, move windows, resize windows, etc. No programming experience is needed. You will also need the ability to view and print documents saved in Microsoft Word format. This can be accomplished in one of three ways. The first, and easiest, is that you already have Microsoft Word (or a compatible equivalent) on your computer. The second way is that you can download the Microsoft Word Viewer. This is a free Microsoft product that allows viewing and printing Word documents - it is available for download at all the major shareware internet sites and from our website.

Finally, and most obvious, you need to have Microsoft Small Basic. This is a FREE product that can be downloaded from the Microsoft Small Basic website:

http://www.smallbasic.com

How To Take the Course

The Beginning Microsoft Small Basic Tutorial is a self-paced course. The suggested approach is to do one chapter a week for ten weeks. This assumes that you can dedicate 45-60 minutes a day reading through the tutorial chapter and completing the exercises. Each week's class should require about 3 to 6 hours of your time to grasp the concepts completely. If you didn't purchase our physical book and you are reading the downloaded eTutorial, open the class notes file for that week and print it out prior to doing a particular week's work, then, work through the chapters at your own pace. Try to do each example as they are encountered in the tutorial. Work through all the programs. If you need any help, all completed programs are included in the BSB Code folder.

Forward by Alan Payne, A Computer Science Teacher

What is "Beginning Microsoft Small Basic" and how it works.

These lessons are a highly organized and well-indexed set of lessons in the Microsoft Small Basic programming environment. Small Basic is a simplified version of the many BASIC (**B**asic **A**ll-Purpose **S**ymbolic **I**nstruction **C**ode) programming languages of the past. Small Basic has only 14 keywords (premised upon pre-existing classes) – each providing their own set of commands (methods) and variants (overloads).

The Small Basic language is simple enough to allow programs to be written with keyboard driven input and text-only output, but powerful enough to create eye-catching graphical user interface (GUI) applications where input may come from a keyboard, a mouse, or even a touch-screen.

The Small Basic programming environment is very user-friendly – providing a context-sensitive command reference, so that the user learns the commands while typing. Each command has help on the side-bar providing an explanation of the syntax and the options available in order to complete the command. While the Small Basic environment is ideal for the youngest programmer, these tutorials are written to provide the best foundation to learn programming concepts in computer science – regardless of the language.

The tutorials provide the benefit of completed real-world applications - fully documented projects from the teacher's point of view. That is, while full solutions are provided for the teacher's (and learner's) benefit, projects are presented in an easy-to-follow set of lessons explaining concepts fundamental to all languages – data types, input and output, decision making, looping, built-in functions, the different types of errors (syntax versus logical), logical expressions, comparison operators, random numbers, arrays, and finally, and finally the GUI features of the language. An experienced teacher would recognize all of the above as a substantive list of topics in any *first* computer science course – whether for elementary, middle or secondary school students.

The learner may follow the tutorials at their own pace while focusing upon context relevant information. Every bit of the lesson is remembered as it contributes to the final solution to a real-life application. The finished product is the reward, but the student is fully engaged and enriched by the process. This kind of learning is often the focus of teacher training. Every computer science teacher knows what a great deal of work is required for projects to work in this manner, and with these tutorials, the work is done by an author who understands the classroom experience. That is extremely rare!

Graduated Lessons for Every Project ... Lessons, examples, problems and projects. Graduated learning. Increasing and appropriate difficulty... Great results.

With these projects, there are lessons providing a comprehensive background on the programming topics to be covered. Once understood, concepts are easily applicable to a variety of applications. Then, specific examples are drawn out so that a learner can practice with the Small Basic commands. Finally, a summative program for the chapter is presented. Problems are broken down into manageable parts – the logical solution to the problem, the design of the user-interface and supporting sub-routines (code modules) come together in the finished product.

By presenting lessons in this graduated manner, students are fully engaged and appropriately challenged to become independent thinkers who can come up with their own project ideas, design their own text-only or graphical user interfaces, and do their own coding. Once the process is learned, then student engagement is unlimited! I have seen student literacy improve dramatically as they cannot get enough of what is being presented.

Indeed, lessons encourage *accelerated* learning - in the sense that they provide an enriched environment to learn computer science, but they also encourage *accelerating* learning because students cannot put the lessons away once they start! Computer Science provides this unique opportunity to challenge students, and it is a great testament to the authors that they are successful in achieving such levels of engagement with consistency.

My history with the Kidware Software products.

I have used single license or shareware versions for over a decade to keep up my own learning. By using these lessons, I am able to spend time on things which will pay off in the classroom. I do not waste valuable time ensconced in language reference libraries for programming environments and help screens which can never be fully remembered! These projects are examples of how student projects should be as final products - thus, the pathway to learning is clear and immediate in every project.

By following these lessons, I was able to come up with my own projects - An Equation Solver which allows a student to solve any equation that they are likely to encounter in high school, a dice game of Craps, a Financial Calculator covering all grade 12 Financial Math applications, and finally, the game of Mastermind - where I presently have a "Mastermind Hall of Fame" for the best solutions by students over the years. I have made several applications for hardware interfacing in Computer Technology class. I could do all of this only because of these lessons by Kidware Software!

The exciting thing is that all of the above could also be done in other BASIC or Visual Studio languages – such as QBasic, Small Basic, Visual C# or Visual C++, though I first learned to do the programming using Kidware Software's "*Learn Visual Basic*". For me to go from one language to another is now an inevitable outcome!

With these lessons, I am able to concentrate on the higher order thinking skills presented by the problem, and not be chained to a language reference in order to get things done! In the *Beginning Small Basic* tutorial, the authors have provided a final chapter where 2 popular programs are presented in Small Basic, Visual Basic, Visual C#, Java and QBasic - just to emphasize how concepts and ideas are transferable from one language to another.

If I want to use or expand upon some of the projects for student use, then I take advantage of site-license options. I have found it very straight forward to emphasize the fundamental computer science topics that form the basis of these projects when using them in the classroom.

Quick learning curve for teachers! How teachers can use the product:

Having projects completed ahead of time can allow the teacher to present the design aspect of the project FIRST, and then have students do all of their learning in the context of what is required in the finished product. This is a much faster learning curve than if students designed all of their own projects from scratch. Lessons concentrating on a unified outcome for all make for much more streamlined engagement for first-time students of computer programming, as they complete more projects within a short period of time and there is a context for everything that is learned.

Meet Different State and Provincial Curriculum Expectations and More

Different states and provinces have their own curriculum requirements for computer science. With the Kidware Software products, you have at your disposal a series of projects which will allow you to pick and choose from among those which best suit your curriculum needs. Students focus upon design stages and sound problem-solving techniques from a computer-science perspective. In doing so, they become independent problem-solvers, and will exceed the curricular requirements of elementary, middle and secondary schools everywhere.

Useable projects - out of the box!

The specific projects covered in the Beginning Microsoft Small Basic tutorials are suitable for Grade 6 and above:

Sub Sandwich Party
Savings Calculator
Guess the Number Game
Lemonade Stand
Card Wars
Blackboard Fun
Balloons
Computer Stopwatch
Loan Calculator
Units Conversion
Times Tables
State Capitals
Dice Rolling
Memory Game
Tic-Tac-Toe
Decoder/Encoder

and classic games such as

Even Wins
Mugwump

As you can see, there is a high degree of care taken so that projects are age-appropriate.

You can begin teaching the projects on the first day. It's easy for the teacher to have done their own learning by starting with the solution files. Then, they will see how all of the parts of the lesson fall into place. Even a novice teacher could make use of the accompanying lessons. The lessons will provide more than just the coding of the solution - they will provide the correct context for the coding decisions which were made, and provide help in the investigation of related functions. Students then experiment with projects of their own making.

How to teach students to use the materials.

Teachers can introduce the style of presentation *(lesson, examples, end-of-chapter problems)* to the students in such a way that they quickly grasp how to use the lessons on their own. The lessons are provided so that students may trust the order of presentation in order to have sufficient background information for every project. But the lessons are also highly indexed, so that students may pick and choose projects if limited by time.

How to mark the projects.

In a classroom environment, it is possible for teachers to mark student progress by asking questions during the various design and coding stages. Teachers can make their own written quizzes easily from the reference material provided, but I have found the requirement of completing projects (mastery) sufficient for gathering information about student progress - especially in the later grades.

Lessons encourage your own programming extensions.

Once concepts are learned, it is difficult to NOT know what to do for your own projects.

Once having done my own projects in one language, such as Small Basic, I know that I could easily adapt them to other languages once I have studied the Kidware Software tutorials. *I do not believe there is any other reference material out there which would cause me to make the same claim! In fact, I know there is not as I have spent over a decade looking!*

Having used Kidware Software tutorials for the past decade, I have to say that I could not have achieved the level of success which is now applied in the variety of many programming environments which are currently of considerable interest to kids! I thank Kidware Software and its authors for continuing to stand for what is right in the teaching methodologies which work with kids - even today's kids where competition for their attention is now so much an issue.

Regards,

Alan Payne
Computer Science Teacher
T.A. Blakelock High School
Oakville, Ontario
http://chatt.hdsb.ca/~paynea

1

Introducing Small Basic

Preview

You are about to start a new journey. Writing programs that ask a computer to do certain tasks is fun and rewarding. Like any journey, you need to prepare before starting. In this first class, we do that preparation. You will learn why you might want to learn Small Basic. You will see the historical lineage of Small Basic. You will download and install the Small Basic development software that will help you create Small Basic programs. Once the preparation is done, you will run your first Small Basic application to check that you have prepared properly. Let's get started.

Why Learn Small Basic?

We could very well just ask the question – **Why Learn a Programming Language?** A programming language is used to provide instructions to a computer to do specific tasks. There are several reasons for doing this. First, if you know how to program, you will have a better understanding of just how computers work. Second, writing programs is good exercise for your thinking skills – you must be a very logical thinker to write computer programs. You must also be something of a perfectionist – computers are not that smart and require exact, perfect instructions to do their jobs. Third, computer programmers are in demand and you can make a good living. And, last, writing computer programs is fun. It's rewarding to see your ideas for a certain computer program come to life on the computer screen.

So, why learn **Small Basic**? One big reason is that it's free from Microsoft. Another reason for learning Small Basic is that it is one of the easiest languages to learn. Small Basic is a simple language. There are many built-in elements that make your work simpler and the language itself is very simple – only 14 reserved keywords and 2 operators. But, just because it is a simple language doesn't mean it lacks capabilities. You will see throughout these notes that you can build some fairly complex programs.

Because of its simplicity, you can learn to write Small Basic programs very quickly. But, just because you can write your first program quickly doesn't mean you'll learn everything there is to know about Small Basic. This course just introduces Small Basic. There's still a lot to learn – there's always a lot to learn. So, consider this course as a first step in a journey to becoming a proficient computer programmer.

And, once you've mastered Small Basic, you can graduate to its more capable big brother **Visual Basic**, another Microsoft product used to develop **GUI** (graphical user interface) based applications. These are applications with menus, toolbars, buttons, scroll bars, and other controls which depend on the computer mouse for input. Examples of GUI applications you may have used are word processors, spreadsheet programs and computer games.

A Brief History of Small Basic

We're almost ready to get started. But, first I thought it would be interesting for you to see just where the **Small Basic** language fits in the history of some other computer languages and, in particular, with Microsoft products.

Most programming in the early days of programming was done in such cryptic languages by engineers and mathematicians. Two professors at Dartmouth College wanted to explain programming to "normal" people and developed the **BASIC** (Beginner's All-Purpose Symbolic Code) language to help in that endeavor. BASIC was meant to be a simple language with just a few keywords to allow a little math and a little printing.

In the later 1960's, timeshare computing, where a user could sit at a terminal and interact with the computer, became popular. The primary language used in these interactive sessions was BASIC. The Dartmouth BASIC was not sufficient for the many applications being developed, so many extensions and improvements were made in the BASIC language. Many of the first computer games were written on timeshare terminals using BASIC. The first complete game I wrote was on an HP-1000 Timeshare Basic system using a ASR-33 paper tape.

In the summer of 1969, Bill Gates and Paul Allen began writing BASIC programs at Lakeside High School in Seattle using this same kind of teletype terminal.

Bill continued programming and started little business ventures until January 1975 when this magazine appeared on the stands:

On the cover is an Altair 8800 computer. It must have been really expensive – note the 'Save Over $1000' line. About all the computer could do was flash some lights according to a program written by the user. But, it was the first home computer. Bill Gates and Paul Allen saw the potential. They developed a BASIC language for the Altair computer and marketed it through their new company – Microsoft. Yes, the first product sold by Microsoft was the BASIC computer language. It sold for $350 and was distributed on a cassette tape.

Then, in the late 1970's and early 1980's, it seems there were computers everywhere with names like Radio Shack TRS-80, Commodore 64, Texas Instruments 99/4A, Atari 400, Coleco Adam, Timex Sinclair and the IBM PC-Jr. Stores like Sears, JC Penneys and even K Mart sold computers. One thing all these machines had in common was that they were all programmed in some version of Microsoft's BASIC. Each computer had its own fans and its own magazines. Computer users would wait each month for the next issue of a magazine with BASIC programs you could type into your computer and try at home. My computer of choice at that time was the TRS-80 Color Computer:

Like Microsoft's first product, our first learning programs and games were distributed on audio cassette tapes.

This was a fun and exciting time for the beginning programmer, but the fun times ended with the introduction of the IBM-PC in the early 1980's. Bigger and faster computers brought forth bigger languages and more complicated development environments. These new languages were expensive to purchase and difficult for the beginning programmer to grasp. Which brings us to **Small Basic**, which I would call a close relative of the early, original BASIC language. Small Basic was developed by Vijaye Raji, a developer at Microsoft, in 2008 in response to an article written in September 2006 by David Brin called, "Why Johnny can't code". It would be best to let Vijaye tell the story of how Small Basic was born. The following Small Basic History was copied from Vijaye's Blog dated October 23, 2008 entitled "Hello World".

"It all happened in August of 2007 when someone sent me a pointer to the article Why Johnny Can't Code and it got me thinking. After all, when I was a kid, I started programming in ZX Spectrum with a built in Sinclair BASIC interpreter and did so until I ran into Turbo BASIC. To me that transformation was groundbreaking and was the single most important reason why I chose to write software for a living, for the rest of my life.

An informal poll along the corridors in Microsoft revealed that most developers within Microsoft had started programming in some variant of BASIC. It had all the good characteristics of a good beginner programming language - simplicity, minimal ceremony, instant gratification and ubiquity. It helped them "get" programming and assisted them with understanding the need for more advanced concepts.

When I asked them how they're going to teach programming to their children, they were stumped. Almost everyone wanted to, they just didn't know how. Some said KPL, Python and Ruby. Some said Alice and Scratch. But they all felt that none of these have the charm of BASIC. Of course there were some that took the Dijkstra's stand, but they were few.

Of the numerous programming languages, BASIC, from its inception in the 1960s has undergone some major transformations. Even among Microsoft's BASIC offerings, the language and the environment (VS) has been repeatedly updated to include more powerful features with every release. On the one hand this makes the language and the environment very powerful and capable, but on the other hand, it makes it daunting for a beginner.

That got me thinking as to why isn't there a "Small" variant of BASIC that brings the simplicity of the original language to the modern day. And after a year, here we are, announcing Small Basic. Small Basic is a project that will help make programming easy and approachable for beginners. Now, that's a pretty big claim - let's see how Small Basic does it.

Make programming approachable

Small Basic starts with a really simple programming language that gathers inspiration from the original BASIC language. It has no more than 15 keywords and is strictly imperative. There are no classes, scopes, generics, lambdas, etc. - just pure imperative code. The language is typeless and all variables are dynamic and global all the time. The code gets compiled to IL and runs on the .Net Framework.

It comes with a set of libraries that can be accessed from within a Small Basic program. Since the language itself is .Net based, new libraries can be created or the existing libraries modified using any .Net programming language.

Next, it combines the features of the language and the libraries into a very simple and friendly programming environment. This environment gives beginners, access to professional features like Intellisense(TM) and Instant context sensitive help. It makes writing programs and executing them a breeze.

The development of Small Basic was a several year by Vijaye Raj to rekindle the exciting days when just about anyone could sit down at a computer and write a simple program using the BASIC language. Those of you who wrote programs on those old "toy" computers will recognize the simplicity of the Small Basic language and the ease of its use. And, you will also notice Small Basic is a great environment for writing and testing code, something missing in the early 1980's. Let's get started now. For those of you new to programming, I hope you can feel the excitement we old timers once had. For the old timers, I hope you rekindle your programming skills with this new product."

Let's Get Started

Learning how to use **Small Basic** to write a computer program (like learning anything new) involves many steps, many new terms, and many new skills. We will take it slow, describing each step, term, and skill in detail. Before starting, we assume you know how to do a few things:

* You should know how to start your computer and use the mouse.

* You should have some knowledge on working with your particular operating system (Windows 8, 7, Vista or XP). In these notes, we use Windows Vista. If you are using another operating system, your screens may appear different than those shown here.

* You should know how to resize and move windows around on the screen.

* You should know how to run an application on your computer by using the **Start Menu** or some other means.

* You should know how to fill in information in dialog boxes that may pop up on the screen.

* You should know about folders and files and how to create and find them on your computer.

* You should know what file extensions are and how to identify them. For example, in a file named **Example.ext**, the three letters **ext** are called the extension.

* You should know how to click on links to read documents and move from page to page in such documents. You do this all the time when you use the Internet.

* You should know how to access the Internet and download files.

You have probably used all of these skills if you've ever used a word processor, spreadsheet, or any other software on your computer. If you think you lack any of these skills, ask someone for help. They should be able to show you how to do them in just a few minutes. Actually, any time you feel stuck while trying to learn this material, never be afraid to ask someone for help. We were all beginners at one time and people really like helping you learn.

Let's get going. And, as we said, we're going to take it slow. In this first class, we will learn how to install Small Basic and its documentation on your computer, how to load a Small Basic program, how to run the program, and how to stop the program. It will be a good introduction to the many new things we will learn in the classes to come.

Note: At this update, Microsoft was offering Version 1.0 of Small Basic. That is the version used in these notes.

Downloading and Installing Small Basic

To write and run programs using Small Basic, you need the **Small Basic** program. This is a free product that you can download from the Internet. This simply means we will copy a file onto our computer to allow installation of Small Basic.

Start up your web browser (Internet Explorer, Netscape or other). Small Basic is hosted at **Kid's Corner** in Microsoft's **Beginner Development Learning Center**:

http://www.smallbasic.com

This web site has lots of useful programming information. As you become more proficient in your programming skills, you will go to this site often for answers to programming questions, interaction with other programmers, and lots of sample programs. Though it's hosted at a 'kid' site, Small Basic is appropriate for all ages.

On the Small Basic web page, you should see a button that allows to download Small Basic:

Click the download button. This window will appear:

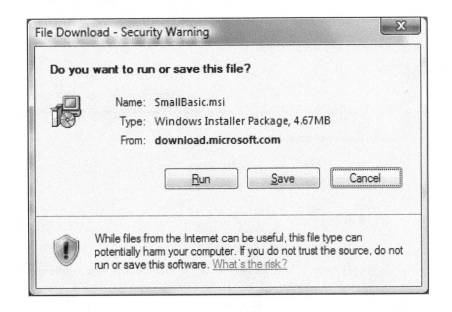

Click **Run** and the download of the installer begins:

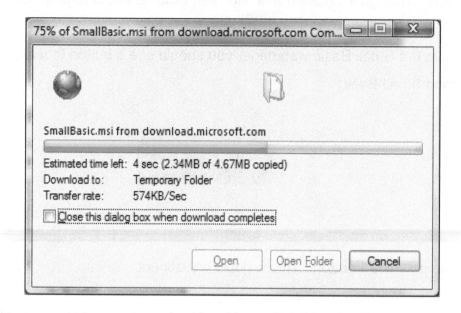

When complete, you should see:

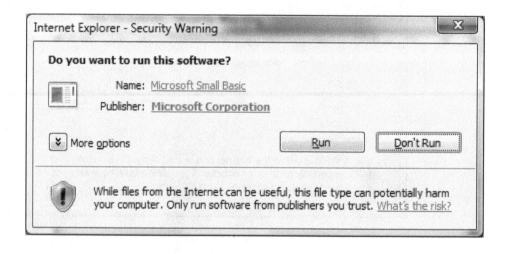

Again, click **Run** to see the Setup Wizard:

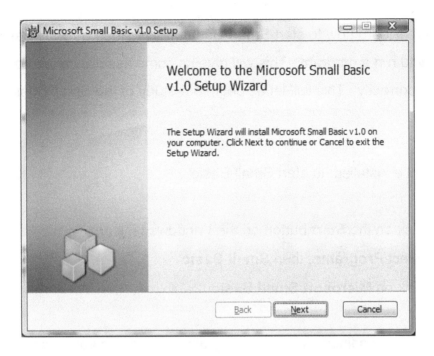

Click **Next** to start the installation process. Accept the licensing agreement. Then, for each screen afterwards, accept the default choice by clicking **Next**. When done you should see a screen announcing a successful installation.

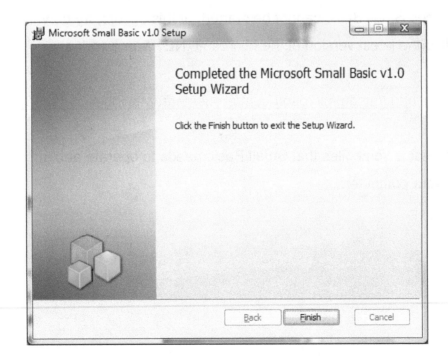

Starting Small Basic

We'll learn how to start **Small Basic**, how to load a Small Basic program, and how to run a program. This will give us some assurance we have everything installed correctly. This will let us begin our study of the Small Basic programming language.

Once installed, to start Small Basic:

* Click on the **Start** button on the Windows task bar
* Select **Programs**, then **Small Basic**
* Click on **Microsoft Small Basic**

(Some of the headings given here may differ slightly on your computer, but you should have no trouble finding the correct ones.) The Small Basic program should start. Several windows will appear on the screen.

After installation and trying to start, you may see an error message that announces Small Basic cannot be started. If this occurs, try downloading and installing the latest version of the Microsoft .NET framework at:

http://msdn.microsoft.com/en-us/netframework/aa569263.aspx

This contains some files that Small Basic needs to operate and such files may not be on your computer.

Upon starting, my screen shows:

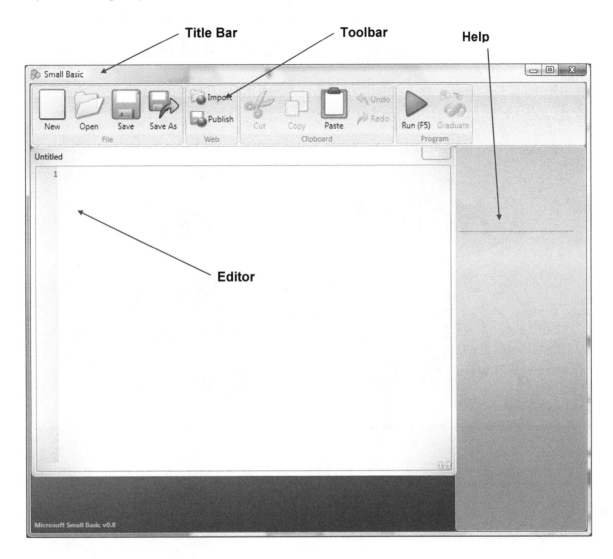

This window displays the **Small Basic Development Environment**. We will learn a lot more about this in Class 2. Right now, we're just going to use it to test our Small Basic installation and see if we can get a program up and running. There are many windows on the screen. At the top of the window is the **Title Bar**. The title bar gives us information about what program we're using and what Small Basic program we are working with. Below the title bar is a **Toolbar**. Here, little buttons with pictures allow us to control Small Basic. Almost all Windows applications (spreadsheets, word processors, games) have toolbars that help us do different tasks. This is the purpose of the Small Basic toolbar. It will help us do most of our tasks. In the middle of the screen is the **Editor**. This is where we will write our Small Basic programs. To the right is a **Help** area. Small Basic has great help features when writing programs. This area will display hints and tips while we write code.

Opening a Small Basic Program

What we want to do right now is **open a program**. Included with these notes are many Small Basic programs you can open and use. Let's open one now. Make sure **Small Basic** is running. We will open a program using the toolbar. Follow these steps:

- Click the **Open Program** button:

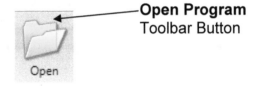

Open Program
Toolbar Button

- An **Open Program** window will appear:

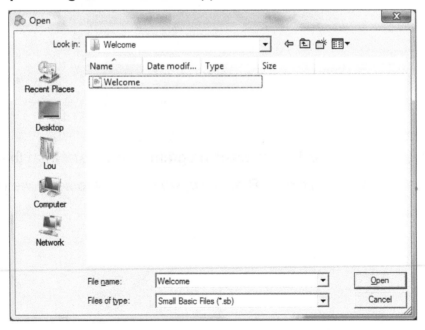

- Find the folder named **BeginSB** (stands for **Beginning Small Basic**). This is the folder that holds the notes and programs for this course. Open that folder.

- Find and open the folder named **BSB Code**. This folder holds all the programs for the course

Remember how you got to this folder. Throughout the course, you will go to this folder to open programs you will need. Open the program folder named **Welcome**. Note there is one file in **Welcome** named **Welcome**. Select that file and click **Open**.

This should appear in the Small Basic editor:

```
Welcome.sb - C:\BeginSB\BSB Code\Welcome\Welcome.sb                        [x]
1 TextWindow.Title = "Welcome Program"
2 TextWindow.WriteLine("Welcome to Beginning Small Basic!")
3
4
5
6
7
8
9
```

You now finally see your first Small Basic program: We'll learn what these few lines of code do in the next class. Right now, we just want to see if we can get this program running.

Running a Small Basic Program

After developing a Small Basic program, you want to start or run the program. This gets the program started and allows the computer do its assigned tasks. We can also run a program also using the toolbar. Look for a button that looks like the **Play** button on a VCR, CD player, or cassette tape player:

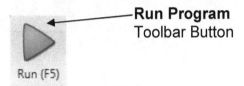

Run Program
Toolbar Button

- Click this button to run the **Welcome** program (the program we opened previously).

You can also run a program by pressing the **<F5>** function key.

A window should open and you should see the following Welcome message:

If you've gotten this far, everything has been installed correctly. If you don't see the Welcome message, something has not been installed correctly. You should probably go back and review all the steps involved with installing Small Basic and Small Basic and make sure all steps were followed properly.

To stop this program, press any key or click the boxed **X** in the upper right corner of the window.

Stopping Small Basic

It's been a lot of work just to get to this point. We finally have our first Small Basic program running and now we're just going to stop it and move on. We'll dig into many more details in Class 2.

When you are done working with a Small Basic program, you want to leave the Small Basic environment. To stop Small Basic, click on the close button in the upper right hand corner of the main window. It's the button that looks like an **X**. Stop Small Basic now. Small Basic will close all open windows and you will be returned to the Windows desktop. You may be asked if you would like to save the program modifications (in case any were made):

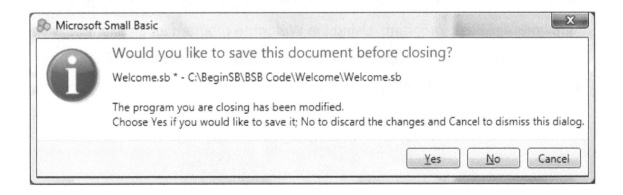

If you are asked such a question, answer **No** so the Welcome program remains unchanged.

We covered a lot of new material here. As we said earlier, you learned a lot of new words and concepts. Don't worry if you don't remember everything we talked about here. You will see the material many times again. It's important that you just have some concept of what goes into a Small Basic program. You also know how to start and stop the Small Basic environment.

In summary, we installed the Small Basic environment. Using Small Basic, we learned how to open a Small Basic program. We learned how to run a program. In the next class, you will learn (in detail) what each of these steps really means. And, you will begin to acquire the skills that allow you to start building your own Small Basic program. Using the **Welcome** program as an example, you will learn about important concepts related to a Small Basic program. Then, in Class 3, you will actually build your first program!

2

Small Basic Program Basics

Review and Preview

In the first class, we spent all of our time just preparing our computer for creating and running Small Basic programs. In this second class, we will look further into some of the tasks we have done. We will reexamine the Welcome program from Class 1. We will learn some of the basic rules for writing Small Basic programs. We will create and save a program using Small Basic. This will give us the skills needed to create our first Small Basic program in Class 3.

The Welcome Program (Revisited)

Start **Small Basic** and open the **Welcome** program we looked at in Class 1 Here's the code you will see in the editor:

```
'
'  Welcome Program
'  Beginning Small Basic
'
TextWindow.Title = "Welcome Program"
TextWindow.WriteLine("Welcome to Beginning Small Basic!")
```

A program is made up of many **statements**. Every line is a statement and every statement instructs the computer to do something.. Let's go through this code line by line to explain its structure and see what each line does.

The first several lines of the program are:

```
'
'  Welcome Program
'  Beginning Small Basic
'
```

These lines are **comments**. They simply provide some information about what the program is and provides some contact information. The comment begins with a single apostrophe (**'**). These lines are also known as a **program header**. It's a good idea to always put a header on your Small Basic programs to give someone an idea of what your program does and who wrote it. When running a program, Small Basic ignores any comments – their only use is provide explanation.

The first non-comment statement is:

```
TextWindow.Title = "Welcome Program"
```

Remember the Welcome program back in Class 1? When you ran the program, you saw this window:

Notice the words **Welcome Program** in the title bar of the window. The above line of code displays that title. In this line, **TextWindow** is an **object** built into Small Basic – it is the window that displays the output of the program. Small Basic has a number of such objects available for our use. We will use the **TextWindow** object extensively in our first few programs. Objects have both **properties** and

methods. Properties describe objects, while methods do things to objects. In this single line of code, we are setting the **Title** property of the **TextWindow** object to the text string "**Welcome Program**". The dot (**.**) and assignment operator (**=**) are punctuations that must be placed appropriately for the computer to understand your intent. This line of code literally says "set the **Title** property of the **TextWindow** object to **Welcome Program**."

The other statement in this short program is:

```
TextWindow.WriteLine("Welcome to Beginning Small Basic!")
```

Notice in the text window of the running program, there is a message that says **Welcome to Beginning Small Basic!** . The above line of code printed that message. This line of code uses the TextWindow **WriteLine** method to perform the task. We say the text "Welcome to Beginning Small Basic!" is passed to the **WriteLine** method – the input is placed in parentheses – which then results in the input text being written in the text window.

Though this is a very short, very simple program, it illustrates some major components in a Small Basic program. We want a program header and appropriate comments. Using properties and methods, we can display information using the built-in Small Basic object, the **TextWindow**.

Some Rules of Small Basic Programming

Let's look at the **Welcome** code one more time to point out some basic rules of Small Basic programming. Here's that code:

```
'
'  Welcome Program
'  Beginning Small Basic
'
TextWindow.Title = "Welcome Program"
TextWindow.WriteLine("Welcome to Beginning Small Basic!")
```

And, here's the rules:

- Small Basic code requires perfection. All keywords must be spelled correctly. If you type **WriteLne** instead of **WriteLine**, a human may know what you mean, but a computer won't.
- Small Basic is <u>not</u> case-sensitive, meaning upper and lower case letters are considered to be the same characters. That means **writeline** and **WriteLine** are the same. But, even though Small Basic is not case-

sensitive, it is good practice to use accepted case conventions in programming.

- Small Basic ignores any "**white space**" such as blanks. We will often use white space to make our code more readable to humans.

- To set an object property, we use this 'dot' convention:

```
ObjectName.PropertyName = PropertyValue
```

where **ObjectName** is the object, **PropertyName** the property and **PropertyValue** the value you want to establish.

To invoke an object method, use this convention:

```
ObjectName.MethodName(MethodInputs)
```

where **ObjectName** is the object, **MethodName** the method and **MethodInputs** the inputs needed by the method.

We'll learn a lot more Small Basic programming rules as we progress.

Creating Small Basic Programs

In Class 3, we will begin learning the Small Basic language and start writing our own Small Basic programs. In preparation for this, you'll need to know how to create a new program with Small Basic. Let's do that now. What we'll do is re-create the **Welcome** program.

If it's not already running, start **Small Basic**. Click the **New Program** button in the toolbar:

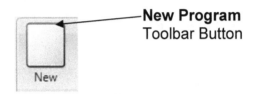

New Program
Toolbar Button

An empty editor will appear:

Click in this window and start typing in the code for the **Welcome** program.

Type one line at a time, paying close attention that you type everything as shown (pay attention to the rules seen earlier). After each line, press the <Enter> key. Here, again, is the code.

```
'
'  Welcome Program
'  Beginning Small Basic
'
TextWindow.Title = "Welcome Program"
TextWindow.WriteLine("Welcome to Beginning Small Basic!")
```

After typing the four comment lines and starting to type the first line of code you will notice this popup appears:

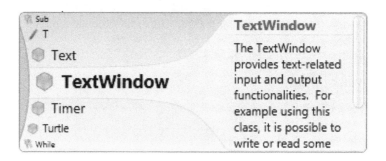

Small Basic has a feature called "intellisense" that helps you type your programs faster. When this list appears, you move through the list using the up/down arrow keys and make a selection by pressing <Enter>. It will appear for object names, properties and methods. Give it a try!

Also notice as soon as you type **TextWindow**, this appears in the help area of the Small Basic environment:

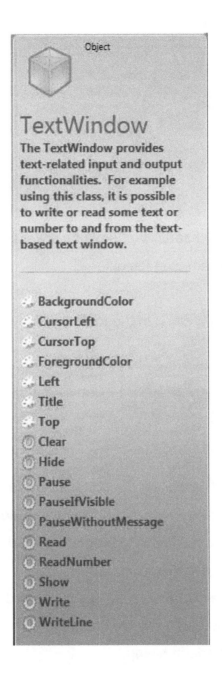

Small Basic provides "context-sensitive" help. The help area will always display information it deems is important to the user at the appropriate time. In this case, information concerning the properties (marked by painter's palette icon) and methods (marked by gear icon) for the TextWindow object are displayed. And, once you select a property or method, a help description for that selection appears. For example, once you type **Title**, you will see this help screen describing the property and how its used:

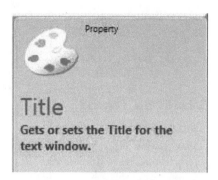

With intellisense and context-sensitive help, you always have on-line information to help you with your programming tasks.

Notice these editing buttons in the toolbar:

If you've ever used a word processor, these tasks are familiar to you. When typing code, you can **Cut**, **Copy** and **Paste**. And you can **Undo** and **Redo** tasks. These tasks make typing code (especially long programs) much easier in the Small Basic environment. Another thing to notice is that the editor uses different colors for different things in the code. Comments, objects, method names and data used by objects are all colored differently. This coloring sometimes helps you identify mistakes you may have made in typing.

When done typing, you should see:

Try running your program. Use the toolbar run program button (or press <**F5**>).

You should once again see the **Welcome to Beginning Small Basic!** Message:

You should also see that it's really kind of easy to get a Small Basic program up and running.

Saving Small Basic Programs

Before leaving Small Basic, we need to discuss how to save programs we create. Each program should be saved in its own folder. You decide where you want to store this folder. There are two buttons on the toolbar used to save programs. To save a new program, click the **Save Program** button:

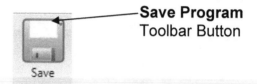

Save Program
Toolbar Button

A dialog box will appear:

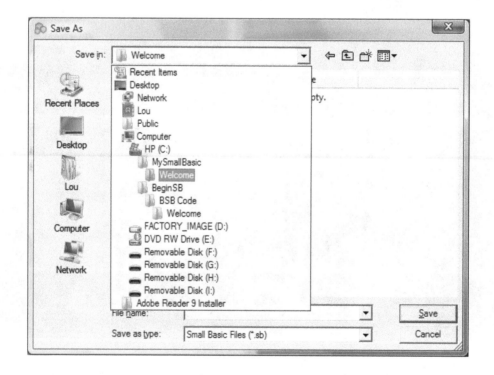

Create the folder you want to save the program in. In this example, I have created a folder named **Welcome** in a **MySmallBasic** folder.

Select a name for your program. Here I have selected **Welcome**:

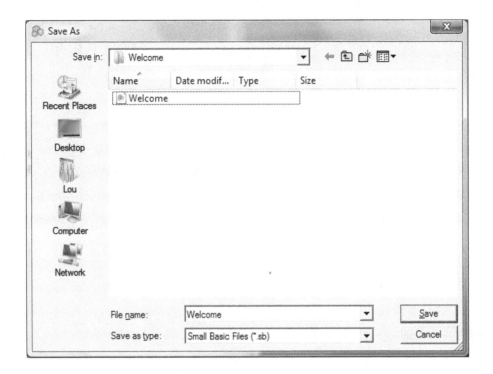

Click **Save** and the program is saved. From this point on, whenever you reopen this program and make modifications, if you click the **Save** toolbar button, the program will be automatically saved with the same name in the same folder. We suggest you do this occasionally while modifying a program.

If you wish to assign a different name to or create a different folder for the modified program, use the **Save As** toolbar button:

Save Program
Toolbar Button

Use the resulting dialog boxes to name and locate your program.

If you try to exit Small Basic and have not saved programs, Small Basic will pop up a dialog box to inform you of such and give you an opportunity to save files before exiting. An example dialog is:

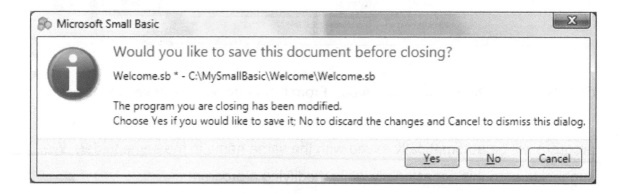

Make the appropriate choice. Click "Yes" to save your program if you want to keep the changes you have made to it.

Small Basic Files

When you save a Small Basic program in a particular folder, files other than the file listing your code are saved. These files are needed by the Small Basic environment to keep track of things.

Using My Computer or Windows Explorer in Windows, go to the folder containing the **Welcome** program you just built and ran. You should see the following files:

Name	Date modified	Type	Size
SmallBasicLibrary.dll	2/3/2010 11:56 PM	Application Extens...	238 KB
Welcome	3/19/2010 8:04 AM	Application	3 KB
Welcome.pdb	3/19/2010 8:04 AM	PDB File	12 KB
Welcome	3/19/2010 8:03 AM	Small Basic Progra...	1 KB

The file named **Welcome** with type **Small Basic Program** is the source code that appears in the editor of Small Basic. The **Welcome** file marked **Application** is a 'compiled' version of the code and is the 'executable' code. If you double-click this file, the Welcome program will run independent of the Small Basic environment. Try it if you like. Later we will learn how to use this file to let your friends run your programs on their computers or even on the Internet! The **Welcome.pdb** file is a database file with information needed by your program and lastly, **SmallBasicLibrary.dll** is called a run-time library. It contains files that help your program run.

We describe these files so you are aware of their presence. Do not modify or delete any of these files outside of the Small Basic environment.

After all the downloading and installing done in the first class, this second class must have seemed like a breeze. In this class, we looked at several important concepts that will let us start building our own Small Basic programs.

In this class, we studied the structure of a program, knowing it is built using objects, properties and methods. We learned how to use Small Basic to create and run a new program. We looked briefly at some of the rules used in writing Small Basic code and we saw how to save a program. In the next class, we finally get started learning the Small Basic language. And, we'll write and run our first Small Basic program.

3

Your First Small Basic Program

Review and Preview

In the first two classes, you've learned about the structure of a Small Basic program, some rules for typing code, and how to run a Small Basic program. Do you have some ideas of programs you would like to build using Small Basic? If so, great. Beginning with this class, you will start to develop your own programming skills. In each class to come, you will learn some new features of the Small Basic language. In this class, you will write your first Small Basic program. To do this, you first need to learn about some of the basic components of the Small Basic language. You will learn about variables, assignment statements and some simple operators.

Creating a Small Basic Program

Recall from Class 2 that a **Small Basic statement** does something. In the **Welcome** example, we saw a statement that printed some information ("Welcome to Beginning Small Basic!"). Each program we build in this class will be made up of many Small Basic statements for the computer to process. Creating a computer program using Small Basic (or any other language) is a straightforward process. You have a particular task you would like the computer to do for you. You tell the computer in a logical, procedural set of steps how to accomplish that task.

It's relatively easy to write out solution steps to a problem in our language (English, in these notes). The difficult part is you have to talk to the computer in its own language. It would be nice if we could just write "Hey computer, here's two numbers – add them together and tell me the sum." A human might understand these instructions, but a computer won't. Why? First, the computer needs to be told how to do tasks in very specific, logical steps. For this little addition example, the steps would be:

1. Give a value to the first number.
2. Give a value to the second number.
3. Add the first number to the second number, resulting in the sum, a third number.
4. Tell me the sum.

Next, we need to talk to the computer in its own language. We translate each solution step into a statement (or statements) in the computer's language. And, in this course, the computer's language is **Small Basic**. To be able to tell the computer how to do any task, you need to have a thorough understanding of the

Small Basic language. Your understanding of Small Basic will allow you to translate your programming steps into a language the computer can understand.

Another thing to remember as you write Small Basic programs is that you need to be logical and exact. A computer will follow your instructions – even if they're wrong! So, as you learn Small Basic, we will emphasize the need to be exact. Once you write exact and logical Small Basic code, the computer is very good and fast at doing its job. And, it can do some pretty amazing things. Let's look at a couple of other examples of writing out a programming task as a series of steps to illustrate some things a computer can do.

What if the local school principal asks you to average the test scores of the 352 students in the school? Those steps are:

1. Determine the score of each student.
2. Add up the 352 scores to get a sum.
3. Divide the sum by 352 to get the average value.
4. Tell the principal the average.

Not too hard, huh? Notice here that the second step can be further broken down into smaller steps. To add up 352 scores, you would:

1. Start with the first score.
2. Add in the second score, then the third score, then the fourth score, etc.
3. Stop when all scores have been added.

In these steps, the computer would do the same task (adding a number) 352 times. Computers are very good at repeating tasks – we will see that this process of repetition is called **looping**. You will build code for this example in Class 7.

Computers are also very good at playing games with you (that's why video games are so popular). Have you ever played the card game "War?" You and another player take a card from a standard playing deck. Whoever has the 'highest' card wins the other player's card. You then each get another card and continue the comparison process until you run out of cards. Whoever has the most cards once the game stops is declared the winner. Playing this game would require steps similar to these:

1. Shuffle a deck of cards.
2. Give a card to the first player.
3. Give a card to the second player.
4. Determine which card is higher and declare a winner.
5. Repeat the process of giving cards to players until you are out of cards.

Things are a bit more complicated here, but the computer is up to the task. The first step requires the computer to shuffle a deck of cards. How do you tell a computer how to do this? Well, before this course is over, you will know how. For now, just know that it's a series of several programming steps. We will put the Small Basic program for such a specific task in its own area called a **subroutine**. This makes the program a little easier to follow and also allows use this code in other programs. Notice Step 4 requires the computer to make a **decision** – determining which card is higher. Computers are very good at making decisions. Finally, Step 5 asks us to repeat the handing out of cards – another example of **looping**. You will also build this program in Class 7.

If all of these concepts are not clear at the moment, that's okay. They will become clearer as you progress through this course. I just wanted you to have some idea of what you can do with Small Basic programs.

Just remember, for every Small Basic program you create, it is best to first write down a series of logical steps you want the computer to follow in performing the tasks needed by your program. Then, converting those steps into the Small Basic language will give you your Small Basic program – it's really that simple. This class begins instruction in the elements of Small Basic. And, in subsequent classes, you learn more and more Small Basic, adding to your Small Basic vocabulary. We'll start slow. By the end of this course, you should be pretty good at "talking Small Basic."

Small Basic - The First Lesson

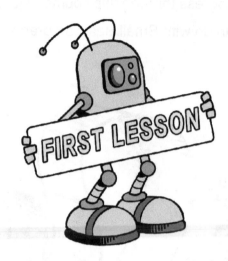

At long last, we are ready to get into the heart of a Small Basic program - the Small Basic language. In this class, we will discuss variables (name and type), assignments, arithmetic operations, and techniques for working with a particular type of variable called strings. In each subsequent class in this course, you will learn something new about the Small Basic language.

Variables

All computer programs work with information of one kind or another. Numbers, text, dates and pictures are typical types of information they work with. Computer programs need places to store this information while working with it. What if we need to know how much ten bananas cost if they are 25 cents each? We would need a place to store the number of bananas, the cost of each banana, and the result of multiplying these two numbers together. To store such information, we use something called **variables**. They are called variables because the information stored there can change, or vary, during program execution. Variables are the primary method for moving information around in a Small Basic program. And, certain rules must be followed in the use of variables.

Variable Names

You must **name** every variable you use in your program. Rules for naming variables are:

- Can only use letters, numbers, and the underscore (_) character (though the underscore character is rarely used).
- The first character must be a letter. It is customary, though not required, in Small Basic that this first letter be upper case
- You cannot use a word reserved by Small Basic (for example, you can't have a variable named **WriteLine** or one named **TextWindow**).

If a variable name consists of more than one word, the words are joined together, and each word after the first begins with an uppercase letter

The most important rule is to use variable names that are meaningful. You should be able to identify the information stored in a variable by looking at its name. As an example, in our banana buying example, good names would be:

Quantity	Variable Name
Cost of each banana	BananaCost
Number of bananas purchased	NumberBananas
Cost of all bananas	TotalBananaCost

As mentioned in an earlier class, the Small Basic language is <u>not</u> case sensitive. This means the names **BananaCost** and **bananacost** refer to the <u>same</u> variable. Try to be consistent in how you write variable names. And make sure you assign unique names to each variable. A nice feature of the Small Basic intellisense feature is that as you add variables to your program, the variable names are added to the list of choices available in the intellisense drop-down menu.

Variable Types

We need to know the **type** of information stored by each variable. Does it contain a number? Does the number have a decimal point? Does it just contain text information? Let's look at some variable types.

The first variable type is the **integer** type. This type of variable is used to represent whole, non-decimal, numbers. Examples of such numbers are:

1   -20   4000

Notice you write 4,000 as 4000 in Small Basic – we can't use commas in large numbers. In our banana example, **NumberBananas** would an **integer** type variable.

What if the variable you want to use will have decimal points. In this course, such variables will be of **floating** type (the decimal point being the thing that "floats"). All you need to know about floating type variables is that they are numbers with decimal points. Examples of such numbers:

-1.25   3.14159   22.7

In our banana example, the variables **BananaCost** and **TotalBananaCost** would be **floating** type variables.

The next variable type is a **string** variable. A **string** variable is just that – one that stores a string (list) of various characters. A string can be a name, a string of numbers, a sentence, a paragraph, any characters at all. And, many times, a string will contain no characters at all (an empty string). We will use lots of strings in Small Basic, so it's something you should become familiar with. Strings are always enclosed in quotes ("). Examples of strings:

"I am a Small Basic programmer"   "012345"   "Title   Author"

One last variable type is the **boolean** variable. It takes its name from a famous mathematician (Boole). It can have one of two values: **true** or **false**. Many languages have **true** and **false** as reserved words for use with Boolean variables. Small Basic does not have such reserved words. In Small Basic, we will use string values of "**true**" and "**false**" to provide a representation for boolean variables. We will see that such variables are at the heart of the computer's decision making capability. If wanted to know if a banana was rotten, we could name a boolean variable **IsBananaRotten**. If this was "true", the banana is indeed rotten.

With all the different variable types, we need to be careful not to improperly mix types. We can only do mathematical operations on numbers (integer and floating types). String types must only work with other string types. Boolean types are used for decisions.

Assignment Statement

The simplest, and most widely used, statement in Small Basic is the **assignment** statement. Such a statement appears as:

```
VariableName = VariableValue
```

Note that only a single variable can be on the left side of the assignment operator (**=**). Some simple assignment examples using our "banana" variables:

```
NumberBananas = 22
BananaCost = 0.27
IsBananaRotten = "false"
MyBananaDescription = "Yes, we have no bananas!"
```

The actual values assigned to variables here are called **literals**, since they literally show you their values.

You may recognize the assignment operator as the equal sign used in arithmetic, but it's not called an equal sign in computer programming. Why is that? Actually, the right side (**VariableValue** in this example) of the assignment operator is not limited to literals. Any legal Small Basic expression, with any number of variables or other values, can be on the right side of the operator. In such a case, Small Basic computes **VariableValue** first, then assigns that result to **VariableName**. This is an important programming concept to remember – "evaulate the right side, assign to the left side." Let's start looking at some operators that help in evaluating Small Basic expressions.

Arithmetic Operators

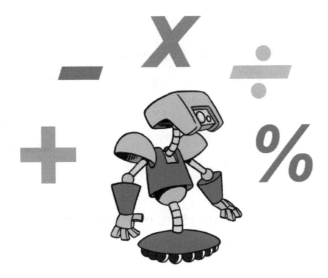

One thing computer programs are very good at is doing arithmetic. They can add, subtract, multiply, and divide numbers very quickly. We need to know how to make our Small Basic programs do arithmetic. There are four **arithmetic operators** we will use from the Small Basic language.

Addition is done using the plus (**+**) sign and **subtraction** is done using the minus (**-**) sign. Simple examples are:

Operation	Example	Result
Addition	7 + 2	9
Addition	3 + 8	11
Subtraction	6 - 4	2
Subtraction	11 - 7	4

Multiplication is done using the asterisk (*) and **division** is done using the slash (/). Simple examples are:

Operation	Example	Result
Multiplication	8 * 4	32
Multiplication	2 * 12	24
Division	12 / 2	6
Division	42 / 6	7

I'm sure you've done addition, subtraction, multiplication, and division before and understand how each operation works.

What happens if an assignment statement contains more than one arithmetic operator? Does it make any difference? Look at this example:

7 + 3 * 4

What's the answer? Well, it depends. If you work left to right and add 7 and 3 first, then multiply by 4, the answer is 40. If you multiply 3 times 4 first, then add 7, the answer is 19. Confusing? Well, yes. But, Small Basic takes away the possibility of such confusion by having rules of **precedence**. This means there is a specific order in which arithmetic operations will be performed. That order is:

1. Multiplication (*) and division (/)
2. Addition (+) and subtraction (-)

So, in an assignment statement, all multiplications and divisions are done first, then additions and subtractions. In our example (7 + 3 * 4), we see the multiplication will be done before the addition, so the answer provided by Small Basic would be 19.

If two operators have the same precedence level, for example, multiplication and division, the operations are done left to right in the assignment statement. For example:

24 / 2 * 3

The division (24 / 2) is done first yielding a 12, then the multiplication (12 * 3), so the answer is 36. But what if we want to do the multiplication before the division - can that be done? Yes - using the Small Basic **grouping operators** - parentheses **()**. By using parentheses in an assignment statement, you force operations within the parentheses to be done first. So, if we rewrite our example as:

24 / (2 * 3)

the multiplication (2 * 3) will be done first yielding 6, then the division (24 / 6), yielding the desired result of 4. You can use as many parentheses as you want, but make sure they are always in pairs - every left parenthesis needs a right parenthesis. If you nest parentheses, that is have one set inside another, evaluation will start with the innermost set of parentheses and move outward. For example, look at:

((2 + 4) * 6) + 7

The addition of 2 and 4 is done first, yielding a 6, which is multiplied by 6, yielding 36. This result is then added to 7, with the final answer being 43. You might also want to use parentheses even if they don't change precedence. Many times, they are used just to clarify what is going on in an assignment statement.

As you improve your programming skills, make sure you know how each of the arithmetic operators work, what the precedence order is, and how to use parentheses. Always double-check your assignment statements to make sure they are providing the results you want.

Some examples of Small Basic assignment statements with arithmetic operators:

```
TotalBananaCost = NumberBananas * BananaCost
NumberOfWeeks = NumberOfDays / 7
AverageScore = (Score1 + Score2 + Score3) / 3.0
```

Notice a couple of things here. First, notice the parentheses in the **AverageScore** calculation forces Small Basic to add the three scores <u>before</u> dividing by 3. Also, notice the use of "white space," spaces separating operators from variables. This is a common practice in Small Basic that helps code be more readable. We'll see lots and lots of examples of assignment statements as we build programs in this course.

String Concatenation

We can apply arithmetic operators to numerical variables. String variables can also be operated on. Many times in Small Basic programs, you want to take a string variable from one place and 'tack it on the end' of another string. The fancy word for this is **string concatenation**. The concatenation operator is a plus sign (**+**) and it is easy to use. As an example:

```
NewString = "Beginning Small Basic " + "is Fun!"
```

After this statement, the string variable **NewString** will have the value "Beginning Small Basic is Fun!".

Notice the string concatenation operator is identical to the addition operator. We always need to insure there is no confusion when using both. String variables are a big part of Small Basic. As you develop as a programmer, you need to become comfortable with strings and working with them.

Comments

You should always follow proper programming rules when writing your Small Basic code. One such rule is to properly comment your code. You can place non-executable statements (ignored by the computer) in your code that explain what you are doing. These **comments** can be an aid in understanding your code. They also make future changes to your code much easier.

To place a comment in your code, use the comment symbol, a single apostrophe ('). Anything written after the comment symbol will be ignored by the computer. You can have a comment take up a complete line of Small Basic code, like this:

```
' Set number of bananas
NumberBananas = 14
```

Or, you can place the comment on the same line as the assignment statement:

```
NumberBananas = 14 ' Set number of bananas
```

You, as the programmer, should decide how much you want to comment your code. We will try in the programs provided in this course to provide adequate comments.

Program Output

You're almost ready to create your first Small Basic program. But, we need one more thing. We have ways to name variables and ways to do math with them, but once we have results, how can those results be displayed? In this class, we will use the method seen in our little Welcome program, the Small Basic **WriteLine** method that works with the **TextWindow** object. What this method does is print a string result on a single line:

```
TextWindow.WriteLine(StringValue)
```

In this expression, **StringValue** could be a string variable that has been evaluated somewhere (perhaps using the concatenation operator) or a literal (an actual value). In the Welcome example, we used a literal:

```
TextWindow.WriteLine("Welcome to Beginning Small Basic!")
```

And saw that **Welcome to Beginning Small Basic!** was output to the text window.

What if you want to output numeric information? It's really quite easy. The **WriteLine** method will automatically convert a numeric value to a string for output purposes. For example, look at this little code segment:

```
NumberBananas = 45
TextWindow.WriteLine(NumberBananas)
```

If you run this code, a **45** will appear on the output screen. Go ahead and start Small Basic and try it. This is one fun thing about Small Basic. It is an easy environment to try different ideas.

I started a new program in Small Basic and typed these lines in the editor:

```
1  NumberBananas = 45
2  TextWindow.WriteLine(NumberBananas)
3
4
```

When I run this code, I see (I resized the window):

```
C:\Users\Lou\AppData\Local\Temp\tmp9BA.tmp.exe
45
Press any key to continue...
```

You can also combine text information with numeric information using the concatenation operator. For example, this code:

```
NumberBananas = 45
TextWindow.WriteLine("Number of Bananas is " + NumberBananas)
```

will print **Number of Bananas is 45** on the output screen:

```
C:\Users\Lou\AppData\Local\Temp\tmpD16.tmp.exe
Number of Bananas is 45
Press any key to continue...
```

The numeric data (**NumberOfBananas**) is converted to a string before it is concatenated with the text data.

So, it's pretty easy to output text and numeric information. Be aware one slight problem could occasionally arise though. Recall the concatenation operator is identical to the arithmetic addition operator. Look at this little segment of code:

```
NumberBananas = 32
NumberApples = 22
TextWindow.WriteLine("Pieces of fruit " + NumberBananas +
NumberApples)
```

You might think you are printing out the total number of fruit (numberBananas + numberApples = 54) with this statement. However, if you run this code, you will get **Pieces of fruit 3222**:

What happens is that Small Basic converts both pieces of numeric data to a string before the addition can be done. Then, the plus sign separating them acts as a concatenation operator yielding the 3222. To print the sum, we need to force the numeric addition by using parentheses:

```
NumberBananas = 32
NumberApples = 22
TextWindow.WriteLine("Pieces of fruit " + (NumberBananas +
NumberApples))
```

In this case, the two numeric values are summed before being converted to a string and you will obtain the desired output of **Pieces of fruit 54**:

```
C:\Users\Lou\AppData\Local\Temp\tmpD85.tmp.exe
Pieces of fruit 54
Press any key to continue...
```

So, we see the **WriteLine** method offers an easy-to-use way to output both text and numeric information, but it must be used correctly.

Notice one other thing about this example. The last line of code looks like it's two lines long! This is solely because of the word wrap feature of the word processor being used. In an actual Small Basic program, this line will appear as, and should be typed as, one single line. Always be aware of this possibility when reading these notes. Let's build a program.

Program – Sub Sandwich Party

Your family has decided to have a party. Two very long submarine sandwiches are being delivered and it is your job to figure out how much each person can eat. Sure, you could do this with a calculator, but let's use Small Basic!! This program is saved in the **Sandwich** folder in the course programs folder (**\BeginSB\BSB Code**).

Program Design

Assume you know the length of each submarine sandwich. To make the cutting easy, we will say that each person will get a whole number of inches (or centimeters) of sandwich (no decimals). With this information, you can compute how many people can be fed from each sandwich. If the total number is more than the people you have in your family, everyone eats and things are good. If not, you may have to make adjustments. The program steps would be:

1. Set a value for the number of inches a person can eat.
2. Determine length of both sandwiches.
3. Determine how many people can eat from each sandwich.
4. Increase or decrease the number of inches until the entire family can eat.

Let's translate each of these steps into Small Basic code as we build the program. Since this is your first program, we'll review many steps (creating a new program) and we'll type and discuss the code one or two lines at a time.

Program Development

Start **Small Basic**. Click the **New Program** button in the toolbar. A blank editor will appear. Immediately save the program as **Sandwich** in a folder of your choice.

First, type the following header information as a multi-line comment and add a title to the text window:

```
'   Sub Sandwich Program
'   Beginning Small Basic
'
TextWindow.Title = "Sub Sandwich Party"
```

We will use five variables in this program: one for how much each person can eat (**InchesPerPerson**), two for the sandwich lengths (**LengthSandwich1**, **LengthSandwich2**), and two for how many people can eat from each sandwich (**Eaters1**, **Eaters2**). These will all be numeric variables. Values for Eaters1 and Eaters2 must be whole numbers since you can't have a fraction of a family member. Set values for some of the variables (also include a comment about what you are doing):

```
'   set values
InchesPerPerson = 5
LengthSandwich1 = 114
LengthSandwich2 = 93
```

These are just values we made up, you can use anything you like. Notice we assume each person can eat 5 inches of sandwich.

Next, we compute how many people can eat from each sandwich using simple division:

```
'  determine how many people can eat each sandwich
Eaters1 = Math.Floor(LengthSandwich1 / InchesPerPerson)
Eaters2 = Math.Floor(LengthSandwich2 / InchesPerPerson)
```

We have used something not seen yet – the **Math.Floor** function. Small Basic provides a **Math** library that contains a large number of functions for our use (we will look at more of these in the next class). The Math.Floor function returns the whole number part of a decimal number – in this case it insures a whole number person is eating.

Also, notice when you start type the line computing Eaters1, the intellisense drop-down now includes added variables like **LengthSandwich1**:

Display the results using the **WriteLine** method:

```
'  write results
TextWindow.WriteLine("Letting each person eat " + InchesPerPerson
+ " inches")
TextWindow.WriteLine((Eaters1 + Eaters2) + " people can eat these
two sandwiches!")
```

Notice how each of the string concatenations works. Notice, too, that we sum the number of people before printing it.

The finished code in Small Basic should look like this:

```
'
'  Sub Sandwich Program
'  Beginning Small Basic
' TextWindow.Title = "Sub Sandwich Party"
'  set values
InchesPerPerson = 5
LengthSandwich1 = 114
LengthSandwich2 = 93
'  determine how many people can eat each sandwich
Eaters1 = Math.Floor(LengthSandwich1 / InchesPerPerson)
Eaters2 = Math.Floor(LengthSandwich2 / InchesPerPerson)
'  write results'  write results
TextWindow.WriteLine("Letting each person eat " + InchesPerPerson
+ " inches")
TextWindow.WriteLine((Eaters1 + Eaters2) + " people can eat these
two sandwiches!")
```

Double-check to make sure each line is typed properly.

Run the Program

Save your program (click the **Save** toolbar button). Run your program by clicking the **Run** toolbar button or it by pressing <**F5**>. If the program doesn't run, any errors encountered are listed below the editor. Double-check your code is exact – no misspellings, no missing quotes, no missing punctuation. When it runs, the text window should show this:

This says 40 people can eat from this particular set of sandwiches. Congratulations – you have written your very first Small Basic program!!

Other Things to Try

For each program in this course, we will offer suggestions for changes you can make and try. In this above run, we saw 40 people can eat. What if you need to feed more or less? Adjust the **InchesPerPerson** variable and determine the numbers of people who can eat for each value. After each adjustment, you will need to rerun the program. Assume the sandwiches cost so much per inch. Modify the program so it also computes the cost of the sandwiches. Determine how much each person would have to contribute to pay for their lunch. Give it a try!

Since we require each person to eat an whole number of inches, there might be leftover amounts in each sandwich. Can you figure out how to compute this amount? It's a neat little application of the **Remainder** function (returns the remainder when two whole numbers are divided) in the **Math** library. There are just a couple of code modifications. A new variable **InchesLeftOver** will be used to compute the leftover amount.

Now, the code that computes that value:

```
'   compute Leftovers
InchesLeftOver = Math.Remainder(LengthSandwich1, InchesPerPerson)
+ Math.Remainder(LengthSandwich2, InchesPerPerson)
TextWindow.WriteLine("There are " + InchesLeftOver + " inches left
over.")
```

Add this code to your program and rerun. Do you see that there are a total of 7

inches remaining?

Can you see why in computing **InchesLeftOver**, we just don't add both

sandwiches length together before using the remainder operator?

Again, congratulations are due for completing your first Small Basic program. You learned a lot about the Small Basic statements and assignments and how to do a little bit of arithmetic. You should be comfortable with starting a new program with Small Basic. In subsequent classes, we'll learn a little more Small Basic and write increasingly more detailed Small Basic programs.

4

Small Basic Program Design, Input Methods

Review and Preview

You should now be fairly comfortable with creating and running simple Small Basic programs. In this class, we continue learning new Small Basic topics to expand our programming knowledge. We'll look at some program design ideas, some mathematical functions and at ways to get input from users of your programs. And, we'll build a savings calculator program.

Program Design

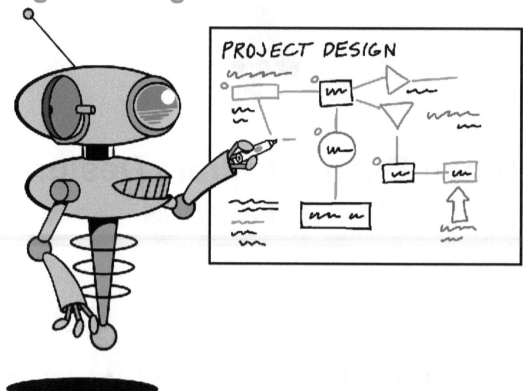

PROJECT DESIGN

You are about to start developing fairly detailed programs using Small Basic. We will give you programs to build and maybe you will have ideas for your own programs. Either way, it's fun and exciting to see ideas end up as computer programs. But before starting a program, it's a good idea to spend a little time thinking about what you are trying to do. This idea of proper **program design** will save you lots of time and result in a far better program.

Proper program design is not really difficult. The main idea is to create a program that is easy to use, easy to understand, and free of errors. That makes sense, doesn't it? Spend some time thinking about everything you want your program to do. What information does the program need? What information does the computer determine? Decide what programming steps you need to follow to accomplish desired tasks.

Make the Small Basic code in your methods readable and easy to understand. This will make the job of making later changes (and you will make changes) much easier. Follow accepted programming rules - you will learn these rules as you learn more about Small Basic. Make sure there are no errors in your program. This may seem like an obvious statement, but many programs are not error-free.

The importance of these few statements about program design might not make a lot of sense right now, but they will. The simple idea is to make a useful, clearly written, error-free program that is easy to use and easy to change. Planning carefully and planning ahead helps you achieve this goal. For each program built in this course, we will attempt to give you some insight into the program design process. We will always try to explain why we do what we do in building a program. And, we will always try to list all the considerations we make.

One other consideration in program design is to always build your program in stages. Don't try to build your entire Small Basic program and test it all at once. This just compounds the possibility of errors. We suggest always building your program in stages. Write a little code. Test that little bit of code making sure it works correctly. Slowly add more and more code. Run and test each code addition. Continue this approach until your program is complete. You will find that this "go slow" approach to creating a Small Basic program will make your programming task much simpler. Give it a try in programs we build.

Small Basic - The Second Lesson

We covered a lot of Small Basic in the last class. This was necessary to introduce you to many basic concepts so you could write your first program. In this briefer second lesson, we look at some mathematical functions.

Mathematical Functions

In Class 3, we saw the Small Basic arithmetic operators that allow us to perform the basics of addition, subtraction, multiplication and division. Like other computer programming languages, Small Basic also has the capability of doing very power mathematical computations. Small Basic's built-in mathematical **functions** (also called **methods**) are often used in these computations. We used a couple of these functions in the Sub Sandwich program (**Math.Floor** and **Math.Remainder**)

We don't expect you to be a mathematical genius to work through these notes, so we will only look at three mathematical functions. First, just what is a **function**? A function is a routine that computes some value for you, given some information. The format for using a function is:

```
FunctionValue = FunctionName(ArgumentList)
```

FunctionName is the name of the function and **ArgumentList** is a list of values (**inputs**, separated by commas) provided to the function so it can do its work. In this assignment statement, FunctionName uses the values in ArgumentList to compute a result and assign that result to the variable we have named **FunctionValue**.

How do you know what Small Basic mathematical functions exist, what type of information they provide and what the arguments are? Check various Small Basic references and the Microsoft Small Basic website. Or, just type the word **Math** in the Small Basic code window and the help area will display all the functions:

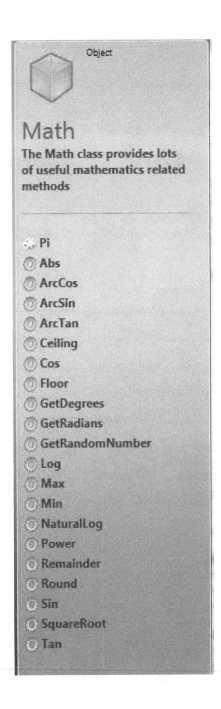

Then, choose a function name and the help window will tell you how to use it. Here is information on the first function we look at (**Abs**):

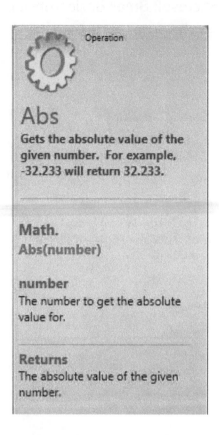

As mentioned, we will look at three mathematical functions here. The methods that support mathematical functions are implemented in the Small Basic class named **Math**. Hence, to refer to a particular function, you write **Math**, then a period, then the function name.

The first function we examine is the **absolute value** function. In math, the absolute value is the positive part of a number. The Small Basic function is:

```
Math.Abs(Argument)
```

where **argument** is number we want the absolute value of. The argument can be either an **int** or **double** type and the returned value will be the same type as the argument. Some examples:

Example	Result
Math.Abs(7)	7
Math.Abs(-11)	11
Math.Abs(-3.14)	3.14
Math.Abs(72.1)	72.1

Have you ever needed the **square root** of a number? A square root is a number that when multiplied by itself gives you the original number. For example, the square root of 4 is 2, since 2 times 2 is four. There's a button on your calculator ($\sqrt{}$) that will do this for you. In Small Basic, the square root function is:

```
Math.SquareRoot(Argument)
```

where **Argument** is number we want the square root of. The argument must be a non-negative number. Some examples:

Example	Result
Math.SquareRoot(4)	2
Math.SquareRoot(36)	6
Math.SquareRoot(72.1)	8.491

The last function we will use in this class is the **exponentiation** method. In exponentiation, a number is multiplied times itself a certain number of times. If we multiply a number by itself 4 times, we say we raise that number to the 4th power. The Small Basic function used for exponentiation is:

```
Math.Power(Argument1, Argument2)
```

Notice the **Power** function has two arguments. **Argument1** is the number we are multiplying times itself **Argument2** times. In other words, this function raises Argument1 to the Argument2 power. Some examples:

Example	Result
Math.Power(4, 2)	16
Math.Power(-3, 3)	-27
Math.Power(10, 2)	10000

In each example here, the arguments have no decimal parts. We have done this to make the examples clear. You are not limited to such values. It is possible to use this function to compute what happens if you multiply 7.654 times itself 3.16 times!! (The answer is 620.99, by the way.)

For the more mathematically inclined reader, you should know that there are many more Small Basic functions available for your use. You might want to look into using them. There are trigonometric functions and inverse trig functions, functions to convert from radians to degrees and vice versa, functions to find extreme values, functions for rounding, logarithm and inverse logarithm functions and a built-in value for pi. (If none of this means anything to you, don't worry – we won't be using them in this class).

Program Input Methods

In the example (Sub Sandwich Program) we built in the last class, we established variable values in code and ran the program to see the results. The results were printed by the Small Basic output method **WriteLine**. If we want to use different values, we need to change the code and rerun. This is a pain! It would be nice, in such a program, to allow a user to type in values while the program is running and have the computer do the computations based on the inputs. This way no code changes or recompiling would be needed to get a new answer. We need such capabilities in our programs.

The Small Basic language has two general methods that supports typed input. The methods are part of the **TextWindow** object we have been using. The first input method (**ReadNumber**) allows reading numeric (integer and floating) inputs. Its usage is:

```
ReturnedValue = TextWindow.ReadNumber()
```

where **ReturnedValue** is the number input by the user.

The other method (**Read**) returns a line of text (string information) input by the user. Its usage is:

```
ReturnedValue = TextWindow.Read()
```

where **ReturnedValue** is the text input by the user.

With either of these methods, the user types the requested input and presses the **<Enter>** key to have the computer accept the value.

Input Methods Example

Start **Small Basic**. Click the **New Program** button in the toolbar. A blank editor will appear. Immediately save the program as **InputExample** in a folder of your choice. Type these lines in the editor

```
UserAge = TextWindow.ReadNumber()
TextWindow.WriteLine("You input " + UserAge)
```

In this code, we ask for a user to input their age, then write it in the text window.

Run the program (click the **Run** button or press **<F5>**). You should see:

```
C:\Users\Lou\AppData\Local\Temp\tmp12F0.tmp.exe
What is your age?
```

Notice how the prompt appears. Type in a value and press **<Enter>**. Once the number is input, it is assigned to the variable **UserAge** and the **WriteLine** method displays the entered value:

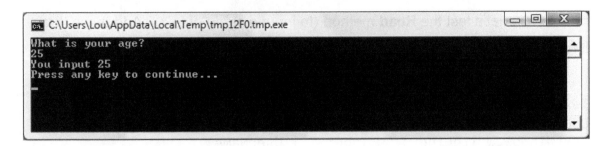

Notice the input value appears on a separate line after the prompting question. Most times, you would like this value to be on the same line as the prompt. This can be done by using a different **TextWindow** method. The **WriteLine** method appends a new line character to the output text, hence subsequent information goes to that new line. The Write method does not begin a new line. Modify the first line of code with the shaded changes (change the WriteLine method to Write and add a space after the question mark):

```
TextWindow.Write("What is your age? ")
```

Rerun the program. Now when you type your age, it appears next to the prompting question:

```
C:\Users\Lou\AppData\Local\Temp\tmpA745.tmp.exe
What is your age? 25
You input 25
Press any key to continue...
```

Run the program again and try to enter non-numeric characters – you won't be able to. The **ReadNumber** method only accepts numeric data (the digits 0 through 9, a leading minus sign, or a single decimal point).

Now, let's test the **Read** method (to input a string of text). Add these three lines of code that ask for a user's name in a manner similar to requesting the age:

```
TextWindow.Write("What is your name? ")
UserName = TextWindow.Read()
TextWindow.WriteLine("You input " + UserName)
```

Run the program again. Type your age, press <Enter> and you will see the prompt asking for your name:

Enter a string (any characters at all can be typed) and press <Enter> to see:

It seems the input methods are working just fine. Did you notice how building a program in stages (adding a few lines of code at a time) is good? Always follow such a procedure. Before leaving this example and building another program, let's take a quick look at one other useful Small Basic concept. In the text window above, it would be nice if there was a blank line between each input request. This just makes your output appear a little cleaner, a quality of a well designed Small Basic program. To insert a blank line in the output, just use a **WriteLine** method with a blank argument:

```
TextWindow.WriteLine("")
```

Add the shaded line to the current code:

```
TextWindow.Write("What is your age? ")
UserAge = TextWindow.ReadNumber()
TextWindow.WriteLine("You input " + UserAge)
TextWindow.WriteLine("")
TextWindow.Write("What is your name? ")
UserName = TextWindow.Read()
TextWindow.WriteLine("You input " + UserName)
```

Run the program again and answer the prompts. Notice the new blank line.

This program has been saved in the **InputExample** folder in the course programs folder (**\BeginSB\BSB Code**).

Program – Savings Calculator

In this program, we will build a savings account calculator. We will input how much money we can put into an account each month and the number of months we put money in the account. The program will then compute how much we saved. This program is saved in the **Savings** folder in the course programs folder (**\BeginSB \BSB Code**).

Program Design

The steps needed to do this calculation are relatively simple:

1. Obtain an amount for each month's deposit.
2. Obtain a number of months.
3. Multiply the two input numbers together.
4. Output the product, the total savings.

We will use the **ReadNumber** method to get user input. The **WriteLine** and **Write** methods will be used to output the savings amount. We'll throw in an additional step to ask for the user's name (an example of using the **Read** method).

Program Development

Start **Small Basic**. Click the **New Program** button in the toolbar. A blank editor will appear. Immediately save the program as **Savings** in a folder of your choice.

First, type the following header information and code that adds a window title:

```
'

'  Savings Program
'  Beginning Small Basic
'

TextWindow.Title = "Savings Calculator"
```

We will use four variables in this program: one for the user's name (**YourName**), one for the deposit amount (**Deposit**), one for the number of months (**Months**) and one for the total amount (**Total**). Type these lines to initialize the variables:

```
YourName = ""
Deposit = 0.0
Months = 0
Total = 0.0
```

Now, we start the code, using the steps outlined under Program Design. At any time, after typing some code, you might like to stop and run just to see if things are going okay. That is always a good approach to take. First, ask the user his/her name using this code:

```
'  ask user name
TextWindow.Write("Hello, what is your name? ")
YourName = TextWindow.Read()
```

Next, determine how much will be deposited in the savings account each month:

```
TextWindow.WriteLine("")
' get deposit amount
TextWindow.Write("How much will you deposit each month? ")
Deposit = TextWindow.ReadNumber()
```

Notice the insertion of a blank line before printing the prompt. Finally, obtain the number of months:

```
TextWindow.WriteLine("")
' get number of months
TextWindow.Write("For how many months? ")
Months = TextWindow.ReadNumber()
```

With this information, the total deposit can be computed and displayed using a WriteLine method:

```
TextWindow.WriteLine("")
'  compute and display total
Total = Deposit * Months
TextWindow.WriteLine(yourName + ", after " + months + " months,
you will have $" + total + " in your savings.")
TextWindow.WriteLine("")
```

Save your program by clicking the **Save** button.

The finished code in the Small Basic editor should appear as:

```
'

' Savings Program
' Beginning Small Basic
'
TextWindow.Title = "Savings Calculator"
'   initialize variables
YourName = ""
Deposit = 0.0
Months = 0
Total = 0.0

'  ask user name
TextWindow.Write("Hello, what is your name? ")
YourName = TextWindow.Read()
TextWindow.WriteLine("")
' get deposit amount
TextWindow.Write("How much will you deposit each month? ")
Deposit = TextWindow.ReadNumber()
TextWindow.WriteLine("")
' get number of months
TextWindow.Write("For how many months? ")
Months = TextWindow.ReadNumber()
TextWindow.WriteLine("")
'  compute and display total
Total = Deposit * Months
TextWindow.WriteLine(yourName + ", after " + months + " months,
you will have $" + total + " in your savings.")
TextWindow.WriteLine("")
```

Run the Program

Run your program. If the program does not run successfully, try to find out where your errors are using any error messages that may appear. We will cover some possible errors in the next class.

When the program runs successfully, you will see:

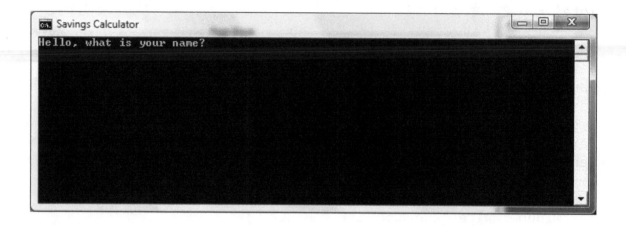

Type in your name, a deposit amount and a number of months. Your total will be given to you in a nicely formatted string output. Notice how the name, deposit, months and total are all put together (concatenated) in a single sentence, along with a dollar sign ($). Make sure the answer is correct. Remember, a big step in program design is making sure your program works correctly! If you say you want to save 200 dollars a month for 10 months and your computer program says you will have a million dollars by that time, you should know something is wrong somewhere!

When I tried the program, I got:

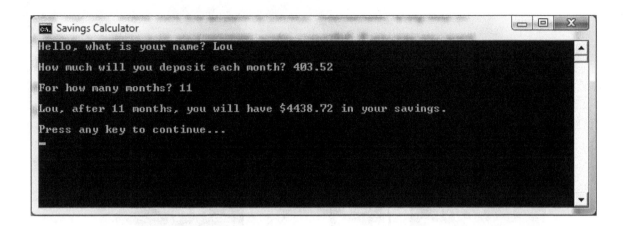

Notice if I deposit 403.52 (you don't, and can't, enter the dollar sign) for 11 months, the program tells me I will have $4438.72 in my savings account.

This program may not seem all that complicated. And it isn't. After all, we only multiplied two numbers together. But, the program demonstrates steps that are used in every Small Basic program. Valuable experience has been gained in recognizing how to read input values, do the math to obtain desired results, and output those results to the user.

Other Things to Try

Most savings accounts yield interest, that is the bank actually pays you for letting them use your money. This savings account program has ignored interest. But, it is fairly easy to make the needed modifications to account for interest - the math is just a little more complicated. We will give you the steps, but not show you how, to change your program. Give it a try if you'd like:

- Define a variable **Interest** to store the yearly savings interest rate. Interest rates are floating decimal numbers.
- Add additional statements to allow the user to input an interest rate.
- Modify the code to use Interest in computing **Total**. The code for that computation is (get ready - it's messy looking):

```
Total = 1200 * (Deposit * (Math.Power((1 + Interest / 1200),
Months) - 1) / Interest)
```

Make sure you type this all on one line – as often happens, the word processor has made it look like it is on two. As we said, this is a pretty messy expression, but it's good practice in using parentheses and a mathematical function (**Power**).

The number '1200' is used here to convert the interest from a yearly value to a monthly value.

Now, run the modified program. Type in values for deposit, months, and interest. Make sure you get reasonable answers. (As a check, if you use a deposit value of 300, a months value of 14, and an interest value of 6.5, the total answer should be $4351.13. Note you'd have $4200 without interest, so this makes sense). Save your program.

I told a little lie, I didn't get $4351.13 in the above example with interest. I actually got $4351.1272052172923076923076923!!!:

I rounded the answer. In such cases, the number should just be displayed with two numbers after the decimal. It is possible to do this using Small Basic but beyond the scope of our discussion at the moment.

Notice the programs are getting a little more detailed as you learn more Small Basic. In this class, you learned about proper program design, mathematical functions and how to add input capabilities to your Small Basic programs. You built a little savings account program. And, an important concept to remember as you continue through this course is to always try to build your programs a few lines of code at a time. A good mantra is "code a little, test a little." You will introduce fewer errors in your programs using this approach.

5

Debugging, Decisions, Random Numbers

Review and Preview

We continue our journey through the world of Small Basic. Hopefully, creating and running a Small Basic program is getting easier for you. In this class, you will examine how to find and eliminate errors in your programs, how you can make decisions using Small Basic, and look at a fun function, the random number generator. You will build a 'Guess the Number' game program.

Debugging a Small Basic Program

No matter how well you plan your program and no matter how careful you are in implementing your ideas in Small Basic code, you will make mistakes. Errors, or what computer programmers call **bugs**, do creep into your program. You may have already encountered a few in the programs we've built so far. Perhaps you spelled a keyword wrong, forgot a punctuation mark or misspelled a variable name. These are all examples of program bugs. You, as a programmer, need to have a strategy for finding and eliminating those bugs. The process of eliminating bugs in a program is called **debugging**. Unfortunately, there are not a lot of hard, fast rules for finding bugs in a program. Each programmer has his or her own way of attacking bugs. You will develop your ways. We can come up with some general strategies, though, and that's what we'll give you here.

Program errors, or bugs, can be divided into three types:

- **Syntax** errors
- **Run-time** errors
- **Logic** errors

Syntax errors occur when you make an error typing a line of Small Basic code. Something is misspelled or something is left out that needs to be there. Your program won't run if there are any syntax errors. **Run-time errors** occur when you try to run your program. It will stop abruptly because something has happened beyond its control. **Logic errors** are the toughest to find. Your program will run okay, but the results it gives are not what you expected. Let's examine each error type and address possible debugging methods.

Syntax Errors

Syntax errors are the easiest to identify and eliminate. The JCreator development environment is a big help in finding syntax errors. Syntax errors will occur as you're writing Small Basic code.

Start Small Basic. We'll type in a few snippets of code to see how different bugs are identified. Let's look at some typical errors. In the editor, type these two lines of code:

```
MyNumber = 7
TextWindow.WriteLine(MyNmber)
```

We've misspelled the assigned variable name (**MyNumber**) in the **WriteLine** statement.

Try running this and below the editor you will see the message:

Sorry, we found some errors...	Close
2,22: The variable 'MyNmber' is used, but its value is not assigned. Are you sure you have spelled it correctly?	

The 2,22 implies there is an error in Line 2, Column 22. It tells you it does not recognize the variable **MyNmber** and asks if you misspelled it. We did. Small Basic is pretty smart!

Correct that error, but misspell **WriteLine** as **WriteLne**:

```
MyNumber = 7
TextWindow.WriteLne(MyNumber)
```

Try running and Small Basic will tell you the problem:

> **Sorry, we found some errors...**
> 2,12: Cannot find operation 'WriteLne' in 'TextWindow'.

Correct your error. But, change the first line as shown (leave out the assignment operator):

```
MyNumber   7
TextWindow.WriteLine(MyNumber)
```

Try running and you'll get this error message:

> **Sorry, we found some errors...**
> 1,11: Unrecognized statement encountered.

You are being told this (line 1 again) is not a recognized statement and the problem is somewhere around Column 11. You should immediately see the problem and be able to fix it. Fix the error.

Let's try one other example. Change the second line by adding an additional parenthesis at the end of the **WriteLine** method:

```
MyNumber = 7
TextWindow.WriteLine(MyNumber))
```

Try running and you receive this message:

Sorry, we found some errors...
2,31: Unexpected token) found.

The problem is clear – you have one too many right parentheses.

So when you try to run with syntax errors, the Small Basic environment will kindly point out your errors to you so you can fix them. Note that syntax errors usually result because of incorrect typing, either misspellings, additions or omissions - another great reason to improve your typing skills, if they need it.

Run-Time Errors

Once you have written your code and eliminated all identified syntax errors, obtaining a successful compilation, you try to run your program. If the program runs, great! But, many times, your program may stop and tell you it found an error - this is a run-time error. You need to figure out why it stopped and fix the problem. At this writing, the Small Basic environment does not give you much useful information when a run-time error occurs. Many times, the program will just stop.

Let's look at a couple of examples. Type these lines in the editor:

```
MyNumber = 7
MyOtherNumber = 0
TextWindow.WriteLine(MyNumber / MyOtherNumber)
```

Yes, I know we'll get a divide by zero (a classic run-time error), but that's the point here – to illustrate potential errors. The program should not run, giving you some indication you are dividing by zero. If you run the program, it runs without error, printing a zero as the division result:

This needs to be corrected in future Small Basic versions.

Another common run-time error occurs when using one of Small Basic's built-in functions. Errors result if you use the wrong type or value as one of the arguments. Try these two lines of code:

```
MyNumber = -7
TextWindow.WriteLine(Math.SquareRoot(MyNumber))
```

We attempt to take the square root of a negative number (not allowed). When we run the program, we get some indication that something is wrong, but it is not very explicit:

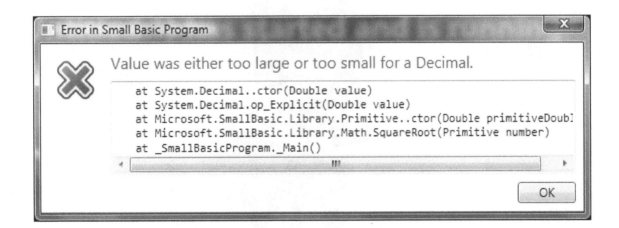

Click **OK** and the program just stops:

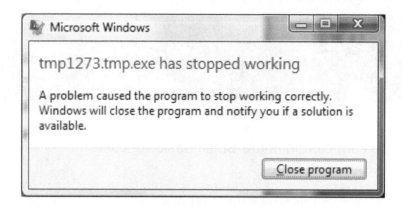

We've seen just a couple of possible run-time errors. There are others and you'll see them as you start building programs. And, unfortunately, the current Small Basic program is not very helpful in pointing out where errors are. Hopefully, this situation will change with future versions. One last thing about run-time errors. Small Basic will not find all errors at once. It will stop at the first run-time error it encounters. After you fix that error, there may be more. You have to fix run-time errors one at a time.

Logic Errors

Logic errors are the most difficult to find and eliminate. These are errors that don't keep your program from running, but cause incorrect or unexpected results. The only thing you can do at this point, if you suspect logic errors exist, is to dive into your program and make sure everything is coded exactly as you want it. Finding logic errors is a time-consuming art, <u>not</u> a science. There are no general rules for finding logic errors. Each programmer has his or her own particular way of searching for logic errors.

With the example we have been using, a logic error would be setting a variable to an incorrect value. Or, perhaps you add two numbers together when you should have subtracted. Logic errors are mistakes you have inadvertently introduced into your Small Basic code. And, unfortunately, these errors are not pointed out to you. Hence, eliminating logic errors is not always easy.

Advanced programming languages use something called a **debugger** that helps in the identification of logic errors. Using a debugger lets you examine variable values, stop your code wherever and whenever you want, and run your program line-by-line. Small Basic does not offer a debugger. So, for now, you need to learn to eliminate logic errors by paying close attention to your code. And, the best approach is to be so careful that you don't have any logic errors to worry about.

Small Basic - The Third Lesson

In the Small Basic lesson for this class, we learn about one of the more useful capabilities of a computer program - decision making. We will discuss expressions and operators used in decisions and how decisions can be made. We will also look at a new Small Basic mathematical function - the random number generator. Such a function is at the heart of every computer game.

Logical Expressions

You may think that computers are quite smart. They appear to have the ability to make amazing decisions and choices. Computers can beat masters at chess and help put men and women into space. Well, computers really aren't that smart - the only decision making ability they have is to tell if something is **true** or **false**. But, computers have the ability to make such decisions very quickly and that's why they appear smart (and because, unlike the True or False tests given in schools, computers <u>always</u> get the right answer!). To use Small Basic for decision making, we write all possible decisions in the form of **true or false?** statements, called **logical expressions**. We give the computer a logical expression and the computer will tell us if that expression is true or false. Based on that decision, we can take whatever action we want in our computer program.

Say in a computer program we need to know if the value of the variable **A** is larger than the value of the variable **B**. We would ask the computer (by writing some Small Basic code) to provide an answer to the true or false? statement: "A is larger than B." This is an example of a logical expression. If the computer told us this was true, we could take one set of Small Basic steps. If it was false, we could take another. This is how decisions are done in Small Basic.

To make decisions, we need to know how to build and use logical expressions. The first step in building such expressions is to learn about comparison operators.

Comparison Operators

In the Class 3, we looked at one type of Small Basic operator - arithmetic operators. In this class, we introduce the idea of a **comparison operator**. Comparison operators do exactly what they say - they compare two values, with the output of the comparison being either **true** or **false**. Comparison operators allow us to construct logical expressions that can be used in decision making.

There are six comparison operators. The first is the "**equal to**" operator represented by an equal (**=**) sign. This operator tells us if two values are equal to each other. Examples are:

Comparison	Result
6 = 7	false
4 = 4	true

There is also a "**not equal to**" operator represented by a **<>** (you need to type two characters to form this symbol). Examples of using this operator:

Comparison	Result
6 <> 7	true
4 <> 4	false

There are other operators that let us compare the size of numbers. The "**greater than**" operator (**>**) tells us if one number (left side of operator) is greater than another (right side of operator). Examples of its usage:

Comparison	Result
8 > 3	true
6 > 7	false
4 > 4	false

The "**less than**" operator (**<**) tells us if one number (left side of operator) is less than another (right side of operator). Some examples are:

Comparison	Result
8 < 3	false
6 < 7	true
4 < 4	false

The last two operators are modifications to the "greater than" and "less than" operators. The "**greater than or equal to**" operator (**>=**) compares two numbers. The result is true if the number on the left of the operator is greater than or equal to the number on the right. Otherwise, the result is false. Examples:

Comparison	Result
8 >= 3	true
6 >= 7	false
4 >= 4	true

Similarly, the "**less than or equal to**" operator (**<=**) tells us if one number (left side of operator) is less than or equal to another (right side of operator). Examples:

Comparison	Result
8 <= 3	false
6 <= 7	true
4 <= 4	true

Comparison operators have equal precedence among themselves, but are lower than the precedence of arithmetic operators. This means comparisons are done after any arithmetic. Comparison operators allow us to make single decisions about the relative size of values and variables. What if we need to make multiple decisions? For example, what if we want to know if a particular variable is smaller than one number, but larger than another? We need ways to combine logical expressions - logical operators can do this.

Logical Operators

Logical operators are used to combine logical expressions built using comparison operators. Using such operators allows you, as the programmer, to make any decision you want. As an example, say you need to know if two variables named A and B are <u>both</u> greater than 0. Using the "greater than" comparison operator (>), we know how to see if A is greater than zero and we know how to check if B is greater than 0, but how do we combine these expressions and obtain one result (true or false)?

Small Basic supports two logical operators. The first is the **And** operator. The format for using this operator is (using two logical expressions, **X** and **Y,** each either true or false):

X **And** Y

This expression is asking the question "are X <u>and</u> Y both true?" That's why it is called the And operator. The And operator will return a true value only if both X <u>and</u> Y are true. If either expression is false, the And operator will return a false. The four possibilities for **And** are shown in this **logic table**:

X	Y	X And Y
true	true	true
true	false	false
false	true	false
false	false	false

Notice the And operator would be used to solve the problem mentioned in the beginning of this section. That is, to see if the variables A and B are both greater than zero, we would use the expression:

A > 0 And B > 0

The other logical operator we will use is the **Or** operator. The format for using this operator is:

X **Or** Y

This expression is asking the question "is X <u>or</u> Y true?" That's why it is called the Or operator. The Or operator will return a true value if either X <u>or</u> Y is true. If both expressions are false, the Or operator will return a false. The four possibilities for **Or** are:

X	Y	X Or Y
true	true	true
true	false	true
false	true	true
false	false	false

The Or operator is second in precedence to the And operator (that is, And is done before Or), and all logical operators come after the comparison operators in precedence. Use of comparison operators and logical operators to form logical expressions is key to making proper decisions in Small Basic. Make sure you understand how all the operators (and their precedence) work. Let's look at some examples to help in this understanding.

In these examples, we will have two variables A and B, with values:

A = 14, B = 7

What if we want to evaluate the logical expression:

A > 10 And B > 10

Comparisons are done first, left to right since all comparison operators share the same level of precedence. A (14) is greater than 10, so A > 10 is true. B (7) is not greater than 10, so B > 10 is false. Since one expression is not true, the result of the And operation is false. This expression 'A > 10 And B > 10' is false. What is the result of this expression:

A > 10 Or B > 10

Can you see this expression is true (A > 10 is true, B > 10 is false; true Or false is true)?

There is no requirement that a logical expression have just one logical operator. So, let's complicate things a bit. What if the expression is:

A > 10 Or B > 10 And A + B = 20

Precedence tells us the arithmetic is done first (A and B are added), then the comparisons, left to right. We know A > 10 is true, B > 10 is false, A + B = 20 is false. So, this expression, in terms of Boolean comparison values, becomes:

true Or false And false

How do we evaluate this? Precedence says the And is done first, then the Or. The result of 'false And false' is false, so the expression reduces to:

true Or false

which has a result of true. Hence, we say the expression 'A > 10 Or B > 10 And A + B = 20' is true.

Parentheses can be used in logical expressions to force precedence in evaluations. What if, in the above example, we wanted to do the Or operation first? This is done by rewriting using parentheses:

(A > 10 Or B > 10) And A + B = 20

You should be able to show this evaluates to false (do the Or first). Before, without parentheses, it was true. The addition of parentheses has changed the value of this logical expression! It's always best to clearly indicate how you want a logical expression to be evaluated. Parentheses are a good way to do this. Use parentheses even if precedence is not affected. If we moved the parentheses in this example and wrote:

A > 10 Or (B > 10 And A + B = 20)

the result (true) is the same as if the parentheses were not there since the And is done first anyway. The parentheses do, however, clearly indicate the And is performed first. Such clarity is good in programming.

Comparison and logical operators are keys to making decisions in Small Basic. Make sure you are comfortable with their meaning and use. Always double-check any logical expression you form to make sure it truly represents the decision logic you intend. Use parentheses to add clarity, if needed.

Decisions - The If Statement

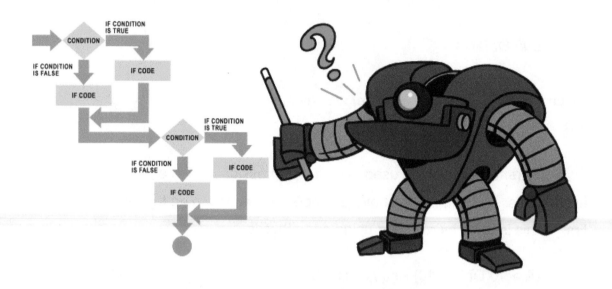

We've spent a lot of time covering comparison operators and logical operators and discussed how they are used to form logical expressions. But, just how is all this used in computer decision making? We'll address that now by looking at the Small Basic **If** statement. Actually, the If statement is not a single statement, but rather a group of statements that implements some decision logic. It is conceptually simple.

The If statement checks a particular logical expression. It executes different groups of Small Basic statements, depending on whether that expression is true or false. The Small Basic structure for this logic is:

```
If (Expression) Then
  ' Small Basic code to be executed if Expression is true
Else
  ' Small Basic code to be executed if Expression is false
EndIf
```

Let's see what goes on here. We have some logical **Expression** (enclosed by parentheses) which is formed from comparison operators and logical operators. **If** Expression is true, **Then** the first group of Small Basic statements is executed.

Else (meaning Expression is not true, or it is false), the second group of Small Basic statements is executed. The If statement group is ended with an **Endlf** statement (all **If** statements require a matching **Endlf** statement). Whether Expression is true or false, program execution continues with the first line of Small Basic code after the EndIf statement.

The Else keyword and the statements between Else and EndIf are optional. If there is no Small Basic code to be executed if Expression is false, the If structure would simply be:

```
If (Expression) Then
  ' Small Basic code to be executed if Expression is true
EndIf
```

Let's try some examples.

Pretend a neighbor kid just opened a lemonade stand and you want to let the computer decide how much she should charge for each cup sold.

Define a variable **Cost** (cost per cup in cents - our foreign friends can use some other unit here) and another variable **Temperature** (outside temperature in degrees F - our foreign friends would, of course, use degrees C). We will write an

If/EndIf structure that implements a decision process that establishes a value for Cost, depending on the value of Temperature.

Look at the Small Basic code:

```
If (Temperature > 90) Then
  Cost = 50
Else
  Cost = 25
EndIf
```

We see that if Temperature > 90 (a warm day, hence we can charge more), a logical expression, is true, the Cost will be 50, else (meaning Temperature is not greater than 90) the Cost will be 25. Not too difficult. Notice that we have indented the lines of Small Basic code following the If and Else statements. This is common practice in writing Small Basic code. It clearly indicates what is done in each case and allows us to see where an If structure begins and ends (with the EndIf statement). The Small Express environment will actually handle the indenting for you.

We could rewrite this (and get the same result) without the Else statement. Notice, this code is equivalent to the above code:

```
Cost = 25
If (Temperature > 90) Then
  Cost = 50
EndIf
```

Here, before the If/EndIf structure, Cost is 25. Only if Temperature is greater than 90 is Cost changed to 50. Otherwise, Cost remains at 25. Even though, in these examples, we only have one line of Small Basic code that is executed for each decision possibility, we are not limited to a single line. We may have as many lines of Small Basic code as needed in If/EndIf structures.

What if, in our lemonade stand example, we want to divide our pricing structure into several different Cost values, based on several different Temperature values. The If/EndIf structure can modified to include an **ElseIf** statement to consider multiple logical expressions. Such a structure is:

```
If (Expression1) Then
   ' Small Basic code to be executed if Expression1 is true
ElseIf (Expression2) Then
   ' Small Basic code to be executed if Expression2 is true
ElseIf (Expression3) Then
   ' Small Basic code to be executed if Expression3 is true
Else
   ' Small Basic code to be executed if Expression1, Expression 2,
and Expression3 are all false]
EndIf
```

Can you see what happens here? It's pretty straightforward - just work down through the code. If Expression1 is true, the first set of Small Basic code is executed. If Expression1 is false, the program checks to see if Expression2 (using the ElseIf) is true. If Expression2 is true, that section of code is executed. If Expression2 is false, Expression3 is evaluated. If Expression3 is true, the corresponding code is executed. If Expression3 is false, and note by this time, Expression1, Expression2, and Expression3 have all been found to be false, the code in the Else section (and this is optional) is executed.

You can have as many ElseIf statements as you want. You must realize, however, that only one section of Small Basic code in an If/EndIf structure will be executed. This means that once Small Basic has found a logical expression that is true, it will execute that section of code then leave the structure and execute the first line of code following the EndIf statement. For example, if in the above example, both Expression1 and Expression3 are true, only the Small Basic statements associated with Expression1 being true will be executed. The rule for If/EndIf structures is: only the statements associated with the first true expression will be executed.

How can we use this in our lemonade example? A more detailed pricing structure is reflected in this code:

```
If (Temperature > 90) Then
  Cost = 50
ElseIf (Temperature > 80) Then
  Cost = 40
ElseIf (Temperature > 70) Then
  Cost = 30
Else
  Cost = 25
EndIf
```

What would the Cost be if Temperature is 85? Temperature is not greater than 90, but is greater than 80, so Cost is 40. What if this code was rewritten as:

```
If (Temperature > 70) Then
  Cost = 30
ElseIf (Temperature > 80) Then
  Cost = 40
ElseIf (Temperature > 90) Then
  Cost = 50
Else
  Cost = 25
EndIf
```

This doesn't look that different - we've just reordered some statements. But, notice what happens if we try to find Cost for Temperature = 85 again. The first If expression is true (Temperature is greater than 70), so Cost is 30. This is not the result we wanted and will decrease profits for our lemonade stand! Here's a case where the "first true" rule gave us an incorrect answer - a logic error.

This example points out the necessity to always carefully check any If/EndIf structures you write. Make sure the decision logic you want to implement is working properly. Make sure you try cases that execute all possible decisions and that you get the correct results. The examples used here are relatively simple. Obviously, the If/EndIf structure can be more far more complicated. Using multiple variables, multiple comparisons and multiple operators, you can develop very detailed decision making processes. In the remaining class programs, you will see examples of such processes.

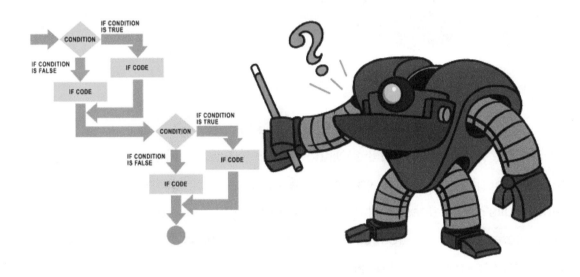

Random Number Generator

Let's leave decisions for now and look at a fun concept - the random number. Have you ever played the Windows solitaire card game or Minesweeper or some similar game? Did you notice that every time you play the game, you get different results? How does this happen? How can you make a computer program unpredictable or introduce the idea of "randomness?"   The key is the random number generator. This generator simply produces a different number every time it is referenced.

Why do you need random numbers? In the Windows solitaire card game, the computer needs to shuffle a deck of cards. It needs to "randomly" sort fifty-two cards. It uses random numbers to do this. If you have a game that rolls a die, you need to randomly generate a number between 1 and 6. Random numbers can be used to do this. If you need to flip a coin, you need to generate Heads or Tails randomly. Yes, random numbers are used to do this too.

Small Basic has a random generator of whole numbers (integers). The generator uses **GetRandomNumber** method of the Small Basic **Math** class.

So, whenever you need a random integer value, use this method:

```
Math.GetRandomNumber(Limit)
```

This statement generates a random integer value that is between 1 and **Limit**. For example, the method:

```
Math.GetRandomNumber(5)
```

will generate random numbers from 1 to 5. The possible values will be 1, 2, 3, 4 and 5.

Let's see how this all works by building a quick application. Start **Small Basic**. Type this little code snippet:

```
'  Random Test
'  Beginning Small Basic
TextWindow.WriteLine("Random number " + Math.GetRandomNumber(10))
```

This code simply generates a random integer between 1 and 10 (**GetRandomNumber** uses a limit of 10) and prints it. Run the program. Some number should print in the text window. Here's my first run:

Stop the program and run it again. Most likely a different number will be printed; it could print the same number again, after all it is random. Continue stopping and running to see how each run results in a random result. The number printed should always be between 1 and 10.

So, the random number generator can be used to introduce randomness in a program. This opens up a lot of possibilities to you as a programmer. Every computer game, video game, and computer simulation, like sports games and flight simulators, use random numbers. A roll of a die can produce a number from 1 to 6. To use **GetRandomNumber** to roll a die, we would write:

```
DieNumber = Math.GetRandomNumber(6)
```

For a deck of cards, the random integers would range from 1 to 52 since there are 52 cards in a standard playing deck. Code to do this:

```
CardNumber = Math.GetRandomNumber(52)
```

If we want a number between 0 and 100, we would use:

```
YourNumber = Math.GetRandomNumber(101) - 1
```

Check the examples above to make sure you see how the random number generator produces the desired range of integers. Now, let's move on to a program that will use this generator.

Program - Guess the Number Game

As we mentioned in Class 1, discussing the history of Small Basic, back in the early 1980's, the first computers intended for home use appeared. Brands like Atari, Coleco, Texas Instruments, and Commodore were sold in stores like Sears and Toys R Us (sorry, I can't type the needed 'backwards' R). These computers didn't have much memory, couldn't do real fancy graphics, and, compared to today's computers, cost a lot of money. But, these computers introduced a lot of people to the world of computer programming. Many games appeared at that time and the program you will build here is one of those classics. This program is saved in the **Number** folder in the course programs folder (**\BeginSB\BSB Code**).

Program Design

You've all played the game where someone said "I'm thinking of a number between 1 and 10" (or some other limits). Then, you try to guess the number. The person thinking of the number tells you if you're right or wrong, low or high, or provides some other clue and, sometimes, you guess again. We will develop a computer version of this game here. The computer will pick a number between 1 and 10 (using the random number generator). You will try to guess the number. Based on your guess, the computer will tell you if you are correct, too low or too high and tell you the answer. You only get one chance to guess it!!

The steps needed to do play this game are:

1. Computer picks a number between 1 and 10.
2. Computer asks your guess.
3. Computer analyzes your guess and outputs the result.

We will use the **ReadNumber** input method to get user input. The **WriteLine** method will be used to output the result of your guess.

Program Development

Start **Small Basic**. Click the **New Program** button in the toolbar. A blank editor will appear. Immediately save the program as **Number** in a folder of your choice.

First, type the following header information and title information:

```
'
'  Number Program
'  Beginning Small Basic
'

TextWindow.Title = "Guess the Number Game"
```

We will use two variables in this program: one for the computer's number (**ComputerNumber**) and one for your guess (**YourGuess**).

Now, we start writing the code, following the steps listed in Program Design. Again, after typing some code, you might like to stop and run just to see if things are going okay. First, have the computer pick and print its random number:

```
'  get the computer's number between 1 and 10
ComputerNumber = Math.GetRandomNumber(10)
TextWindow.WriteLine("I'm thinking of a number between 1 and 10.")
'  get your guess
```

Notice how the number selected is between 1 and 10.

Next, you input your guess using the **ReadNumber** method:

```
' get your guess
TextWindow.Write("What do you think it is? ")
YourGuess = TextWindow.ReadNumber()
```

With this information, your guess is next analyzed for correctness using a Small Basic **If** structure:

```
' analyze guess and print results
If (YourGuess = ComputerNumber) Then
  ' you got it
  TextWindow.WriteLine("You got it!! That's my number!")
ElseIf (YourGuess < ComputerNumber) Then
  ' too low
  TextWindow.WriteLine("You are too low!! My number was " +
ComputerNumber)
Else
  ' too high
  TextWindow.WriteLine("You are too high!! My number was " +
ComputerNumber)
EndIf
```

You should be able to see how this works. Save your program by clicking the **Save** button.

The finished code in the Small Basic editor should appear as:

```
'
'  Number Program
'  Beginning Small Basic
'
TextWindow.Title = "Guess the Number Game"
'  get the computer's number between 1 and 10
ComputerNumber = Math.GetRandomNumber(10)
TextWindow.WriteLine("I'm thinking of a number between 1 and 10.")
'  get your guess
TextWindow.Write("What do you think it is? ")
YourGuess = TextWindow.ReadNumber()
'  analyze guess and print results
If (YourGuess = ComputerNumber) Then
  '  you got it
  TextWindow.WriteLine("You got it!! That's my number!")
ElseIf (YourGuess < ComputerNumber) Then
  '  too low
  TextWindow.WriteLine("You are too low!! My number was " +
ComputerNumber)
Else
  '  too low
  TextWindow.WriteLine("You are too high!! My number was " +
ComputerNumber)
EndIf
```

Run the Program

Run the program. Eliminate any syntax, run-time or logic errors you may encounter. You should now see (I resized the text window a little):

```
Guess the Number Game
I'm thinking of a number between 1 and 10.
What do you think it is? _
```

Enter your guess and make sure the computer provides the correct analysis. Here's the results of my guess:

```
Guess the Number Game
I'm thinking of a number between 1 and 10.
What do you think it is? 4
You are too low!! My number was 8
Press any key to continue...
_
```

Run the program again and again until you know it can determine if a guess is correct, too low or too high. You should always thoroughly test your program to make sure all options work. Save your program if you needed to make any changes.

Other Things to Try

A good modification would be to offer more informative messages following a guess. Have you ever played the game where you try to find something and the person who hid the item tells you, as you move around the room, that you are freezing (far away), cold (closer), warm (closer yet), hot (very close), or burning up (right on top of the hidden item)? Try to modify the **Guess the Number** game to give these kind of clues. That is, the closer you are to the correct number, the warmer you get. To make this change, you will need the Small Basic **absolute value** function, **Math.Abs**. Recall this function returns the value of a number while ignoring its sign (positive or negative).

In our number guessing game, we can use **Math.Abs** to see how close a guess is to the actual number. One possible decision logic is:

```
If (YourGuess = ComputerNumber) Then
  ' Small Basic code for correct answer
ElseIf (Math.Abs(YourGuess - ComputerNumber) <= 1) Then
  ' Small Basic code when burning up - within 1 of correct answer
ElseIf (Math.Abs(YourGuess - ComputerNumber) <= 2) Then
  ' Small Basic code when hot - within 2 of correct answer
ElseIf (Math.Abs(YourGuess - ComputerNumber) <= 3) Then
  ' Small Basic code when warm - within 3 of correct answer
Else
  ' Small Basic code when freezing - more than 3 away
EndIf
```

I'm sure you noticed it was kind of a pain to only get one guess at the computer's number. A great modification to this program would be to add the capability of entering another guess, based on the computer's analysis. Then, you could see how many guesses it takes to "hone in" on the correct answer. To do this requires capability we haven't discussed yet in this course. But, don't worry, this idea of **looping** is covered in the next class. With looping, or the capability to repeat code, we will modify the Guess the Number game to allow repeated guesses until correct.

Adding the ability to enter improved guesses opens up a number of additional modifications you could make to this little game. One suggestion is to allow the user to input the upper range of numbers that can be guessed. That way, the game could be played by a wide variety of players. Use a maximum value of 10 for little kids, 1000 for older kids. Implement the "hot, warm, cold" If logic discussed above. Or, perhaps make the program into a math game, and tell the guesser "how far away" the guess is. I'm sure you can think of other ways to change this game. Have fun doing it.

In this class, you learned a lot of new material. You discovered there are three types of errors that try to attack your hard work: syntax errors, run-time errors and logic errors. You learned about a key part of Small Basic programming - decision making. You learned about logical expressions, comparison operators, logical operators, and If structures. And, you had fun with random numbers in the Guess the Number game. You are well on your way to being a Small Basic programmer.

6

Small Basic Looping, Subroutines

Review and Preview

The programs we build are becoming more detailed, especially with the capability to make decisions using the If structure. In this class, you learn about another very important programming concept – looping, which allows you to repeat blocks of code. You also learn about subroutines, which are self-contained blocks of code that accomplish given tasks. And, you will build a Lemonade Stand simulation as your program.

Small Basic - The Fourth Lesson

In the Guess the Number program built in Class 5, we noted it would be nice if we could continue to make guesses until we got the correct number. To do this requires the ability to repeat segments of code. In this Small Basic lesson, we learn how to add this looping capability to our Small Basic programs. We will also learn about subroutines, which allow us to write better, more compact programs.

Small Basic Loops

Many (in fact, most) Small Basic programs require repetition of certain code blocks. For example, as just noted, the Guess the Number game we built could really use it. Or, you may want to roll a die (simulated die of course) until it shows a six. Or, you might generate some math results until a value has been achieved. This idea of repeating code is called iteration or **looping**.

In Small Basic, one way of looping is with the **While** loop:

```
While (Expression)
  ' Small Basic code block to repeat while Expression is true
EndWhile
```

In this structure, all code between While and EndWhile is repeated **while** the given logical **Expression** is **true**.

Notice a while structure looks a lot like a simple **If** structure:

```
If (Expression) Then
  ' Small Basic code block to process if Expression is true
EndIf
```

What's the difference? In the If structure, the code block is processed just once if Expression is true. In the While structure, the code block is continually processed as long as Expression remains true.

Note a **While** loop structure will not execute even once if Expression is false the first time through. If we do enter the loop (Expression is true), it is assumed at some point Expression will become false to allow exiting. Once this happens, code execution continues at the statement following the EndWhile statement. This brings up a very important point about loops – if you get in one, make sure you get out at some point. In the While loop, if Expression is always true, you will loop forever – something called an infinite loop.

Let's look at a couple of examples. First, here is a loop that can be used in a rocket countdown. It repeats as long as (while) the variable **Counter** (starting at 10) is greater than or equal to 0:

```
Counter = 10
While (counter >= 0)
  TextWindow.WriteLine("Counter is " + Counter)
  Counter = Counter - 1
EndWhile
TextWindow.WriteLine("Blastoff!!")
```

Start Small Basic and type in this code. Run it and you will see:

```
C:\Users\Lou\AppData\Local\Temp\tmpCC40.tmp.exe
Counter is 10
Counter is 9
Counter is 8
Counter is 7
Counter is 6
Counter is 5
Counter is 4
Counter is 3
Counter is 2
Counter is 1
Counter is 0
Blastoff!!
Press any key to continue...
```

Another example:

```
Rolls = 0
Counter = 0
While (Counter < 10)
  '  Roll a simulated die
  Roll = Roll + 1
  TextWindow.WriteLine("Roll Number " + Roll)
  If (Math.GetRandomNumber(6) = 6) Then
    Counter = Counter + 1
    TextWindow.WriteLine("That's " + Counter + " sixes!")
  EndIf
EndWhile
```

This loop repeats while the **Counter** variable remains less than 10. The counter variable is incremented (increased by one) each time a simulated die rolls a 6. The **Roll** variable tells you how many rolls of the die were needed to roll 10 sixes. Theoretically, it should take 60 rolls since there is a 1 in 6 chance of rolling a six. Type this code in the Small Basic editor and run it. You will see something like this:

In this case, it took 63 rolls. Because you are using random numbers, you will see different results.

As mentioned, if the logical expression used by a While loop is false the first time the loop is encountered, the code block in the While loop will not be executed. This may be acceptable behavior – it may not be. We can build a loop that will always be executed at least once. To do this we need to introduce the Small Basic **Goto** statement. A Goto allows you to transfer code execution to anywhere in your code. A Goto requires a **label**. A label is like a bookmark – it can be named anything you want. A label name is always followed by a colon. An example is:

```
MyLabel:
```

Anytime we want to transfer program execution to this label statement, we use a Goto:

```
Goto MyLabel
```

You do not write the colon in the Goto statement. Using these new concepts in a loop, we have what we'll call a **Goto loop**:

```
MyLabel:
  ' Small Basic code block to process
If (Expression) Then
  Goto MyLabel
EndIf
```

The code block repeats as long as **Expression** is true. Unlike the While loop, this loop is always executed at least once. Somewhere in the loop, Expression should be changed to false to allow exiting.

Let's look at examples of the **Goto** loop. What if we want to keep adding three to a **Sum** until the value exceeds 50. This loop will do it:

```
Sum = 0
SumLoop:
  Sum = Sum + 3
  TextWindow.WriteLine("Sum is " + sum)
If (Sum <= 50) Then
  Goto SumLoop
EndIf
```

Try this code in Small Basic and you should see:

Or, another dice example:

```
Sum = 0
Roll = 0
SumLoop:
  '  Roll a simulated die
  Die = Math.GetRandomNumber(6)
  Sum = Sum + Die
  Roll = Roll + 1
  TextWindow.WriteLine("After Roll #" + Roll + ", the sum is " +
Sum)
If (Sum <= 30) Then
  Goto SumLoop
EndIf
```

This loop rolls a simulated die (**Die**) while the **Sum** of the rolls does not exceed 30. It also keeps track of the number of rolls (**Roll**) needed to achieve this sum. Try this in Small Basic and you will see something like this (again, due to random numbers, your results will be different):

```
C:\Users\Lou\AppData\Local\Temp\tmp98F6.tmp.exe
After Roll #1, the sum is 5
After Roll #2, the sum is 8
After Roll #3, the sum is 12
After Roll #4, the sum is 17
After Roll #5, the sum is 22
After Roll #6, the sum is 26
After Roll #7, the sum is 32
Press any key to continue...
```

You need to decide which of the loop structures (While, Goto) fits your program. Recall the major difference is that a Goto loop is always executed at least once; a While loop may never be executed. And, make sure you can always get out of a loop. In both looping structures, this means that, at some point, the checking logical expression must become false to allow exiting the loop. When you exit a While loop, processing continues at the next Small Basic statement after the EndWhile. In a Goto loop, processing continues at the Small Basic statement after the If structure checking whether the loop should repeat.

If, at some point in the code block of a loop, you decide you need to immediately leave the loop, a **Goto** statement can also do this. You just need a label statement at the end of the loop. When the **Goto** statement is encountered, processing is immediately transferred to the labeled statement. As an example:

```
Sum = 0
Roll = 0
SumLoop:
  '  Roll a simulated die
  Die = Math.GetRandomNumber(6)
  If (die = 5) Then
    TextWindow.WriteLine("Rolled a 5 - we're stopping!")
    Goto EndLoop
  EndIf
  Sum = Sum + Die
  Roll = Roll + 1
  TextWindow.WriteLine("After Roll #" + Roll + ", the sum is " +
Sum)
If (sum <= 30) Then
  Goto SumLoop
EndIf
EndLoop:
```

This is a modified version (new code is shaded) of the dice example we just looked at. In this example, the Die value is added to the Sum, unless the die rolls a 5. In that case, the loop is immediately exited via a Goto statement. When I run this code in Small Basic, I get:

```
C:\Users\Lou\AppData\Local\Temp\tmp269E.tmp.exe
After Roll #1, the sum is 4
After Roll #2, the sum is 5
After Roll #3, the sum is 9
After Roll #4, the sum is 10
After Roll #5, the sum is 12
After Roll #6, the sum is 18
After Roll #7, the sum is 21
Rolled a 5!
Press any key to continue...
```

Some times, we may not want to leave a loop completely but only skip statements not yet executed in the loop and immediately return to the beginning of the loop. In a While loop, this means control returns to the While statement. In a Goto loop, control is returned to the label starting the loop. In either case, a Goto statement (you will need to add a label if using a While) will do the job. Let's try this with the dice example (modified code is shaded):

```
Sum = 0
Roll = 0
SumLoop:
  ' Roll a simulated die
  Die = Math.GetRandomNumber(6)
  If (Die = 5) Then
    TextWindow.WriteLine("Rolled a 5!")
    Goto SumLoop
  EndIf
  Sum = Sum + Die
  Roll = Roll + 1
  TextWindow.WriteLine("After Roll #" + Roll + ", the sum is " +
Sum)
If (sum <= 30) Then
  Goto SumLoop
EndIf
EndLoop:
```

In this case, if a 5 is rolled (Die = 5), that value is just not included in Sum and program control transfers to the SumLoop label. The big difference is that the loop continues. Running this in Small Basic, I got:

```
C:\Users\Lou\AppData\Local\Temp\tmp37EA.tmp.exe

After Roll #1, the sum is 4
After Roll #2, the sum is 6
After Roll #3, the sum is 8
After Roll #4, the sum is 10
After Roll #5, the sum is 13
Rolled a 5!
After Roll #6, the sum is 14
After Roll #7, the sum is 16
Rolled a 5!
After Roll #8, the sum is 22
After Roll #9, the sum is 23
Rolled a 5!
After Roll #10, the sum is 29
After Roll #11, the sum is 35
Press any key to continue...
```

A Brief Interlude - Guess the Number Game (Revisited)

We'll return to our Small Basic lesson in a bit. But first, let's change the Guess the Number game from Class 5 so a user can have repeated guesses until getting the computer's number. It's a simple application of a **Goto** loop – we want to keep guessing as long as your guess does not equal the computer's number. Start Small Basic and open the Guess the Number game you built in Class 5. Resave the program (use the **Save As** toolbar button) as **Number2** in a folder of your choice. The modified code (changes are shaded) is:

```
'
'  Number Program
'  Beginning Small Basic
'
TextWindow.Title = "Guess the Number Game"
'  get the computer's number between 1 and 10
ComputerNumber = Math.GetRandomNumber(10)
TextWindow.WriteLine("I'm thinking of a number between 1 and 10.")

' Start loop here
StartLoop:
'  get your guess
TextWindow.Write("What do you think it is? ")
YourGuess = TextWindow.ReadNumber()
'  analyze guess and print results
If (YourGuess = ComputerNumber) Then
  '  you got it
  TextWindow.WriteLine("You got it!! That's my number!")
ElseIf (YourGuess < ComputerNumber) Then
  '  too low
  TextWindow.WriteLine("You are too low!!")
Else
  '  too high
  TextWindow.WriteLine("You are too high!!")
EndIf
If (YourGuess <> ComputerNumber) Then
  Goto StartLoop
EndIf
```

In this code, we have made a few changes. We have put the code asking for your guess and checking your guess within a loop (using the "not equals" operator in the If structure at the end). And, we have removed the display of the computer's number when you are too low or too high (that would make the game too easy). We have saved this modification in the **Number2** folder in the course programs folder (**\BeginSB\BSB Code**).

Once you have modified the code, run it. Here's one time I played:

```
Guess the Number Game
I'm thinking of a number between 1 and 10.
What do you think it is? 5
You are too low!!
What do you think it is? 8
You are too high!!
What do you think it is? 7
You got it!! That's my number!
Press any key to continue...
```

I think you will agree that this is a much better game. The loop has really improved this program. We often use our programming skills to improve programs we build. You can probably think of many more improvements. Maybe add another loop that, once one game ends, you are given the option to play again. With repeated guesses possible, you might like to extend the possible range for the computer's number (try it with 100). Maybe implement the "hot, warm, cold" logic outlined in Class 5. Have fun trying your own ideas!!

Now, back to the Small Basic lesson.

Small Basic - The Fourth Lesson (Continued)

The interlude is over. We finish this class' Small Basic lesson with a look at a very important Small Basic programming concept – the subroutine.

Small Basic Subroutines

In the looping discussion, we saw how code in one particular block could be repeated until some desired condition was met. Many times in Small Basic programs, we might have a need to repeat a certain block of code at several different points in the program. Why would you want to do this? Say we had a game that requires us to roll 5 dice and add up their individual values to yield a sum. What if we needed to do this at 10 different places in our program? We could write the code, then copy and paste it to the 10 different places. I think you can see problems already. What if you need to change the code? You would need to change it in 10 different places. What if you needed to put the code in another place in your program? You would need to do another 'copy and paste' operation. There's a better way. And that way is to use a Small Basic **subroutine**.

A subroutine allows you to write the code to perform certain tasks just once. Then, whenever you need to access the code in your program, you can "call it.," providing any information it might need to do its tasks. Subroutines are the building blocks of a Small Basic program. Using subroutines in your Small Basic programs can help divide a complex application into more manageable units of code. Just think of a subroutine as a code block you can access from anywhere in a Small Basic program. When you call the subroutine, program control goes to that subroutine, performs the assigned tasks and returns to the calling program. It's that easy.

Let's see how to create and call a subroutine. Subroutines go at the end of your '**main**' program code. A subroutine named **MySubroutine** would have the form (starts with a **Sub** keyword and ends with **EndSub**):

```
Sub MySubroutine
  ' Code to be executed in the subroutine
EndSub
```

You execute, or call, this subroutine using:

```
MySubroutine()
```

The parentheses are needed to tell the computer you are executing a subroutine. When the subroutine is called, the corresponding code is executed until the **EndSub** line is reached. At this point, program execution returns to the 'main' code after the line calling the subroutine. A subroutine can access and use any variable you use in your main program. Likewise, your main program can use any variables defined in your subroutines. In computer talk, we say the variables in a Small Basic program have **global scope**.

Let's try to make this clearer by looking at a few of subroutine examples. We'll do the dice example of rolling five dice and computing their sum. The subroutine that accomplishes this task is:

```
Sub RollDice
  Die1 = Math.GetRandomNumber(6)
  Die2 = Math.GetRandomNumber(6)
  Die3 = Math.GetRandomNumber(6)
  Die4 = Math.GetRandomNumber(6)
  Die5 = Math.GetRandomNumber(6)
  SumDice = Die1 + Die2 + Die3 + Die4 + Die5
EndSub
```

This subroutine is named **RollDice** and the variable **SumDice** has the resulting sum.

Using this subroutine, any time you need the sum of five dice in your program, you would use:

```
RollDice()
A = SumDice
```

After this code is executed, the variable **Sum** will have sum of five dice. Let's try it. Start Small Basic and type this code (just the two lines above with an added WriteLine statement and the subroutine): Notice the subroutine is placed after the 'main' code:

```
RollDice()
A = SumDice
TextWindow.WriteLine("Sum of five dice is " + A)

Sub RollDice
  Die1 = Math.GetRandomNumber(6)
  Die2 = Math.GetRandomNumber(6)
  Die3 = Math.GetRandomNumber(6)
  Die4 = Math.GetRandomNumber(6)
  Die5 = Math.GetRandomNumber(6)
  SumDice = Die1 + Die2 + Die3 + Die4 + Die5
EndSub
```

Run the code. When I do it, I get:

Notice we also have access to Die1, Die2, Die3, Die4 and Die5 if we want any of the individual dice values.

Now, we will build a subroutine that, given the length (**RectangleLength**) and width (**RectangleWidth**) of a rectangle, prints out the area of the rectangle. Here's that subroutine (yes, I know it's a very simple one):

```
Sub RectangleArea
  TextWindow.WriteLine("Your rectangle has an area of " +
RectangleWidth * RectangleHeight)
EndSub
```

To use this subroutine, you supply a value for the length variable and the width variable, then call the subroutine. Try this code in Small Basic:

```
RectangleWidth = 13
RectangleHeight = 15
RectangleArea()

Sub RectangleArea
  TextWindow.WriteLine("Your rectangle has an area of " +
RectangleWidth * RectangleHeight)
EndSub
```

Run this program and you should see:

As you progress in your Small Basic programming education, you will become more comfortable with using subroutines and see how useful they are. In the remainder of this course, we will use subroutines when needed. Study each example to help learn how to build and use subroutines.

Program – Lemonade Stand

A very powerful use of computers is to do something called **simulation**. Before building an actual airplane, companies "build" the plane on a computer and simulate its performance. This is much cheaper and far safer than testing actual airplanes. Engineers simulate how a building might react to an earthquake to help them design better buildings. And, businesses use computers to simulate how decisions could affect their profits. Based on computer results, they decide how and where to invest their money. In this program, we will build a small business simulation. We will simulate the operation of the neighborhood kids' backyard lemonade stand. Based on the temperature, they set a selling price for their lemonade (the hotter it is, the more they can charge). They will then be told how many cups were sold and how much money was made. If the kids are too greedy, asking too much for their product, they won't sell as much. If they're too nice, they won't make as much money. It's a tough world out there! This program is saved in the **Lemonade** folder in the course programs folder (**\BeginSB\BSB Code**).

Program Design

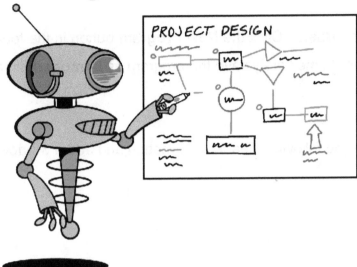

Lemonade will be sold for five days (simulated days). On each day, the temperature is reported. Based on this temperature, a price is set for a cup of lemonade. You will be told how many cups of lemonade were sold and how much money was made. The steps to follow on each day:

1. Computer picks a random temperature.
2. Assign a price for each cup of lemonade.
3. Computer analyzes the information and computes number of cups sold.
4. Sales are computed and displayed.

The first step is a straightforward use of the random number generator. In the second step, we will use the **ReadNumber** method to get the price. Step 3 is the difficult one – how does the computer determine cups sold? In this program, we will give you the code to do this (code we made up) in the form of a subroutine you can use. This is something done all the time in programming – borrowing and using someone else's code. In this subroutine, you provide the temperature and the price and the subroutine computes the number of cups sold. Finally, the **WriteLine** method will be used to output the results of each day's sales.

Program Development

Start **Small Basic**. Click the **New Program** button in the toolbar. A blank editor will appear. Immediately save the program as **Lemonade** in a folder of your choice.

First, type the following header information and add a window title:

```
'
'  Lemonade Stand
'  Beginning Small Basic
'

TextWindow.Title = "Lemonade Stand"
```

We will use several variables in this program. Notice with good naming practice, you can see what each variable is. We keep track of the current day (**DayNumber**), the temperature (**Temperature**), the price set for a cup of lemonade (**CupPrice**), the number of cups sold (**CupsSold**), the amount of money made in one day (**DaySales**) and the current total sales (**TotalSales**). One note – we will assume the **CupPrice** is an whole number value in cents, while **DaySales** and **TotalSales** are in dollars. For our foreign readers, there are 100 cents in a dollar. Feel free to change the units to anything you want.

Now, we write the code, following the previously defined programming steps. First, initialize the **DayNumber** and TotalSales and begin a **While** loop over the five days of sales:

```
'   start loop of five days
DayNumber = 1
TotalSales = 0.0
While (DayNumber < 6)
  ' go to next day
  DayNumber = DayNumber + 1
EndWhile
```

Each day begins with the computer selecting a random temperature (degrees F, you can change this if you want) between 61 and 100 degrees:

```
' pick a random temperature between 61 and 100
Temperature = Math.GetRandomNumber(40) + 60
```

Based on this, you set the price for each cup of lemonade:

```
' get price
TextWindow.Write("How many cents are charged for a cup of
lemonade? ")
CupPrice = TextWindow.ReadNumber()
```

With this information, the computer computes how many cups were sold and determines daily and total sales. The cups sold (**CupsSold**) will be computed in a subroutine named **GetSales**, with two inputs, **Temperature** and **CupPrice**. We will show you that subroutine soon. For now, just assume it is available so it can be called. The code to report sales is:

```
' get cups sold (from GetSales subroutine), provide sales report
GetSales()
DaySales = CupsSold * CupPrice / 100.0
TotalSales = TotalSales + DaySales
TextWindow.WriteLine("")
TextWindow.WriteLine(CupsSold + " cups of lemonade were sold,
earning $" + DaySales + ".")
If (dayNumber > 1) Then
  TextWindow.WriteLine("Total sales after " + DayNumber + " days
are $" + TotalSales + ".")
EndIf
```

You should be able to see what's going on here. We find the **CupsSold**, compute daily and total sales and report the results. Notice that **TotalSales** are only displayed for the second through the fifth day (since, on the first day, daily and total sales are the same). Next, increment the **DayNumber**, close out the **While** loop:

```
' go to next day
DayNumber = DayNumber + 1
EndWhile
TextWindow.WriteLine("")
TextWindow.WriteLine("The lemonade stand is now closed.")
```

The subroutine (**GetSales**) that computes the number of cups sold is placed after the final line of 'main' code. For this subroutine, we will just give you the code, so you can type it in. We will try to explain what's going on. Here is the complete subroutine. Type this in the editor, being careful to check that it is correct (note some lines are fairly long):

```
Sub GetSales
  '
  '  GetSales subroutine
  '  input temperature Temperature and price CupPrice
  '  output number of cups sold - CupsSold
  '
  '  find best price
  BestPrice = (Temperature - 60) * (46 - Math.GetRandomNumber(20))
/ 40 + 20
  ' find maximum sales
  MaxSales = (Temperature - 60) * (231 -
Math.GetRandomNumber(100)) / 40 + 20
  ' find sales adjustment
  Adjustment = 1.0 - Math.Abs((CupPrice - BestPrice) / BestPrice)
  If (Adjustment < 0.0) Then
    Adjustment = 0.0
  EndIf
  ' compute adjusted sales
  CupsSold = Math.Floor(Adjustment * MaxSales)
EndSub
```

Let me try to explain what I'm doing here. First, I assume there is a **BestPrice** (most that can be charged) for a cup of lemonade, based on the temperature (**Temperature**). More can be charged on hotter days. The equation used assumes this BestPrice ranges from 20 cents at 60 degrees to a random value between 45 and 65 cents at 100 degrees. Similarly, there is a maximum number of cups that can be sold (**MaxSales**) based on Temperature. More can be sold on hotter days. The equation used assumes MaxSales ranges from 20 cups at 60 degrees to a random value between 150 and 250 at 100 degrees. Before returning a number of cups, I compute an **adjustment** variable. This is used to adjust sales based on input price (**CupPrice**). If the "asking" price is more than the BestPrice, sales will suffer because people will think too much is being asked for the product. Sales will also suffer if too little is charged for lemonade! Why's that? Many people think if something doesn't cost enough, it may not be very good. You just can't win in the business world. So, adjustment is computed based on how far the set price (**CupPrice**) is from the **BestPrice**. Once the adjustment is found, it is multiplied times MaxSales to compute CupsSold:

```
CupsSold = Math.Floor(Adjustment * MaxSales)
```

You may not recognize the **Math.Floor** function being used here. This function converts the product (Adjustment * MaxSales) to a whole number. You can't sell a fraction of a cup! This brings up a good point. Many times, when using someone else's Small Basic code, you may see things you don't recognize. What do you do? The best thing is to consult some Small Basic reference (another Small Basic programmer, a textbook, the Microsoft website) and do a little research and self-study. This helps you learn more and helps you become a better Small Basic programmer.

Notice if you play this program as a game, you wouldn't know all the details behind the rules (how CupSales are computed). You would learn these rules as you play. That's what happens in all computer games – the games have rules and, after many plays, you learn what rules the programmers have included. If you can't follow all the math in the **GetSales** subroutine, that's okay. You don't really need to – just trust that it does the job. Actually, Small Basic programmers use subroutines all the time without an understanding of how they work (do you know how Small Basic finds the square root of a number?). In such cases, we rely on the subroutine writer to tell us what information is required (inputs) and what information is computed (outputs) and trust that the subroutine works. That's the beauty of subroutines – we get code without doing the work.

The finished code in the Small Basic editor should appear as (note the subroutine is at the end of the code:

```
'
'  Lemonade Stand
'  Beginning Small Basic
'
TextWindow.Title = "Lemonade Stand"
'  start loop of five days
DayNumber = 1
TotalSales = 0.0
While (DayNumber < 6)
  ' pick a random temperature between 61 and 100
  Temperature = Math.GetRandomNumber(40) + 60
  TextWindow.WriteLine("")
  TextWindow.WriteLine("Welcome to Day " + DayNumber + ", the
temperature is " + Temperature + " degrees.")
  ' get price
  TextWindow.Write("How many cents are charged for a cup of
lemonade? ")
  CupPrice = TextWindow.ReadNumber()
  ' get cups sold (from GetSales subroutine), provide sales report
  GetSales()
  DaySales = CupsSold * CupPrice / 100.0
  TotalSales = TotalSales + DaySales
  TextWindow.WriteLine("")
```

```
  TextWindow.WriteLine(CupsSold + " cups of lemonade were sold,
earning $" + DaySales + ".")
  If (dayNumber > 1) Then
    TextWindow.WriteLine("Total sales after " + DayNumber + " days
are $" + TotalSales + ".")
  EndIf
  ' go to next day
  DayNumber = DayNumber + 1
EndWhile
TextWindow.WriteLine("")
TextWindow.WriteLine("The lemonade stand is now closed.")

Sub GetSales
  '
  '  GetSales subroutine
  '  input temperature Temperature and price CupPrice
  '  output number of cups sold - CupsSold
  '
  '  find best price
  BestPrice = (Temperature - 60) * (46 - Math.GetRandomNumber(20))
/ 40 + 20
  ' find maximum sales
  MaxSales = (Temperature - 60) * (231 -
Math.GetRandomNumber(100)) / 40 + 20
  ' find sales adjustment
  Adjustment = 1.0 - Math.Abs((CupPrice - BestPrice) / BestPrice)
  If (Adjustment < 0.0) Then
    Adjustment = 0.0
  EndIf
  ' compute adjusted sales
  CupsSold = Math.Floor(Adjustment * MaxSales)
EndSub
```

Run the Program

Run the program. Eliminate any syntax, run-time or logic errors you may encounter. You may have to recheck your typing, especially in the subroutine. You should now see something like this in the text window:

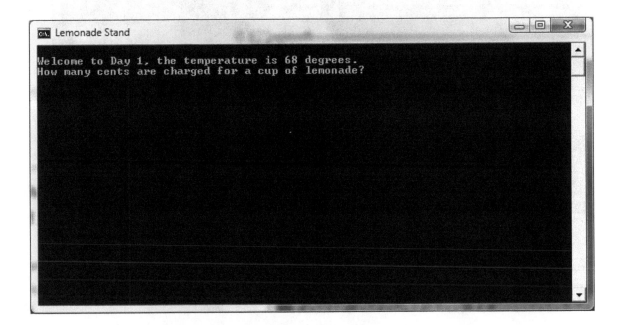

Enter a value for cup price (in cents) and you should see something like:

Continue playing until the lemonade stand has run for five days. Here's my try at five days:

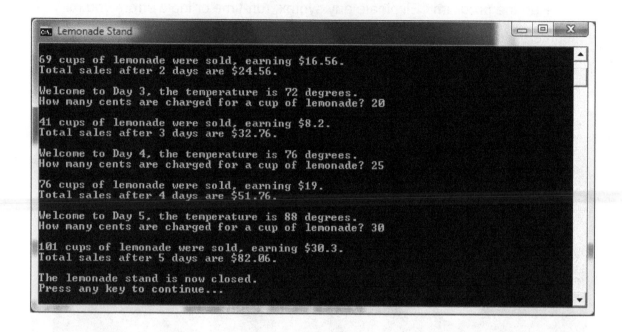

Try several runs to see if you can improve your playing skills. Save your program if you needed to make any changes.

Other Things to Try

You have the beginnings of a fun computer simulation. Can you think of changes you would like to make? Add more days, change the rules in **GetSales**? Why not add another loop so you can play it over and over again without having to rerun the application each time? We have some ideas.

To make lemonade, you need products: cups, lemons, sugar. These cost money and cut into your profit. A great modification would be to add the need for shopping into the simulation. You would need to figure out how much of each product is needed to make a cup of lemonade. Research at a grocery store would tell you the cost to make a cup of lemonade. Then, you can determine how much profit is made on sales. This gives the program more of a "real-world" flavor.

Add more randomness into the program. Maybe consider both temperature and weather conditions. Add a chance of precipitation into the computations. You wouldn't sell as much lemonade on a hot rainy day as you would on a hot clear day. Try these and any other ideas you have.

In this class, with the added capabilities of looping and subroutines, we greatly expanded our Small Basic programming skills. Being able to repeat blocks of code lets us build far more useful programs. We used this capability to allow multiple guesses in our Guess the Number game and the Lemonade Stand program was seen to be a fun computer simulation. In the next class, we'll study another looping method that gives us even more programming power.

7

More Small Basic Looping Arrays

Review and Preview

In the last class, we introduced the idea of looping – repeating code blocks. In this class' Small Basic lesson, we look at another way to loop (the Small Basic **For** loop) and at a new way to refer to variables. And, as a program, we build a version of the card game War. We'll learn how to get the computer how to shuffle a deck of cards!

Small Basic - The Fifth Lesson

In this Small Basic lesson, we look at a technique for counting (another looping method) and ways to store large numbers of variables.

Small Basic For Loops

In an earlier class, we looked at two types of loops – the **While** loop and the **Goto** loop. In each of these, we loop (repeat code) until some particular condition is met, perhaps not knowing how many times the loop would be repeated. If we know how many times we want to loop, we call that counting. Small Basic offers a convenient way to do counting: the **For** loop.

A **For** loop has this structure:

```
For LoopCounter = StartValue To EndValue Step Increment
  ' Small Basic code to execute goes here]
EndFor
```

The **For** statement creates a loop (place where code is repeated) in which the variable **LoopCounter** (called the **loop index**) is initialized at **StartValue** and is then incremented (changed) by **Increment** each time the program executes the loop. The words "Step Increment" are optional. If they are omitted, an increment (Step) of one is assumed. The end of the loop is marked by the **EndFor** statement. The loop is repeated until LoopCounter reaches or exceeds **EndValue**. When the loop is completed, program execution continues after the EndFor statement. Each **For** statement in your Small Basic program must have a matching **EndFor** statement. The code between the For and EndFor should be indented. For loops can be nested (one loop in another), but that's beyond this class.

Let's look at a few For examples to see how they work. This loop will repeat 10 times:

```
For LoopCounter = 1 To 10
  TextWindow.WriteLine(LoopCounter)
EndFor
```

LoopCounter has a value of 1 the first time through loop, 2 the second time through, and repeats until LoopCounter has a value of 10 the final time through. Run this in Small Basic and you'll see:

How about a rocket launch countdown? This loop will do the job:

```
For LoopCounter = 10 To 0 Step -1
  TextWindow.WriteLine(LoopCounter)
EndFor
```

Here LoopCounter starts at 10 and goes <u>down</u> by 1 (Step -1) each time the loop is repeated. Yes, you can have negative Step values. Running this in Small Basic shows:

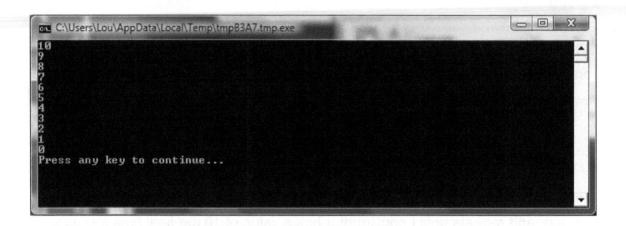

And, you can have increments that are not 1. This loop counts from 0 to 200 by 5's:

```
For LoopCounter = 0 To 200 Step 5
  TextWindow.WriteLine(LoopCounter)
EndFor
```

Run this in Small Basic and you get:

```
C:\Users\Lou\AppData\Local\Temp\tmpD346.tmp.exe
90
95
100
105
110
115
120
125
130
135
140
145
150
155
160
165
170
175
180
185
190
195
200
Press any key to continue...
```

Study each of these examples so you have an idea of how the For loops work. Use them when you need to count. A very useful application of these loops is when working with a new type of variable – the array. We look at that now.

Variable Arrays

The local school principal has recognized your great Small Basic programming skills and has come for your help. Everyone (300 students) in the school has just taken a basic skills test. The principal wants you to write a program that stores each student's name and score. The program should rank (put in order) the scores and compute the average score. The code to do this is not that hard. The problem we want to discuss here is how do we define all the variables we need? To write this test score program, you need 300 variables to store student names and 300 variables to store student scores. We are required to create and set a value for every variable we use. We could use variables like this:

```
Student1
Student2
Student3
    .

    .
Student300

Score1
Score2
Score3
    .

    .
Score300
```

And, to get this information input, we could type code like this:

```
TextWindow.Write("Enter Student 1 Name - ")
Student1 = TextWindow.Read()
TextWindow.Write("Enter Student 1 Score - ")
Score1 = TextWindow.Read()
TextWindow.Write("Enter Student 2 Name - ")
Student2 = TextWindow.Read()
TextWindow.Write("Enter Student 2 Score - ")
Score2 = TextWindow.Read()
TextWindow.Write("Enter Student 3 Name - ")
Student3 = TextWindow.Read()
TextWindow.Write("Enter Student 3 Score - ")
Score3 = TextWindow.Read()
   .
   .
   .
TextWindow.Write("Enter Student 300 Name - ")
Student300 = TextWindow.Read()
TextWindow.Write("Enter Student 300 Score - ")
Score300 = TextWindow.Read()
```

This would work, but I don't think you want to type all this code. Let's look at another way.

Small Basic provides a way to store a large number of variables under the same name - **variable arrays**. Each variable in an array, called an **element**, must have the same data type, and they are distinguished from each other by an array index. For the student example, we could use two arrays:

```
Student[1]
Student[2]
Student[3]
   .
   .
Student[300]
```

```
Score[1]
Score[2]
Score[3]
   .
   .
Score[300]
```

We now have the student names stored in the **Student** array and the scores in the **Score** array. The numbers in brackets are the array **indices**.

We now have 300 **Student** variables and 300 **Score** variables available for our use. Each variable in an array is referred to by its name and index. For example, to assign the 150th student's information, we write two lines of code like this:

```
Student[150] = "Billy Gates"
Score[150] = 100
```

With these new definitions of student names and scores, the process of getting each name and score can be placed in a For loop:

```
For StudentNumber =1 to 300
   TextWindow.Write("Enter Student " + StudentNumber + " Name - ")
   Student[StudentNumber] = TextWindow.Read()
   TextWindow.Write("Enter Student " + StudentNumber + " Score - ")
   Score[StudentNumber] = TextWindow.Read()
EndFor
```

Study this code to convince yourself that it is the same as that long code we showed earlier. I think you agree this is much simpler (and easy to modify if there are more or fewer students).

Array variables can be used anywhere regular variables are used. They can be used on the left side of assignment statements or in expressions. To add up the first three test scores, you would write:

```
Sum = Score[1] + Score[2] + Score[3]
```

Or this For loop averages all 300 scores:

```
ScoreSum = 0
For StudentNumber = 1 to 300
  ScoreSum = ScoreSum + Score[StudentNumber]
EndFor
Average = ScoreSum / 300
```

To find an average of a group of numbers, you add up all the numbers then divide by the number of numbers you have. In this code, ScoreSum represents the sum of all the numbers. We set this to zero to start. Then, each time through the loop, we add the next score to that "running" sum. The loop adds up all 300 scores making use of the Score array. The first time through it adds in Score[1], then Score[2], then Score[3], and so on, until it finishes by adding in Score[300]. Once done, the Average is computed by dividing ScoreSum by 300.

Do you see how the For loop greatly simplifies the task of adding up 300 numbers? This is a nice shortcut method we can use when working with arrays. We will start to use arrays in our Small Basic programs. You will learn very quickly how nice they are when working with lots of variables.

"Shuffle" Method

Let's use our new knowledge of arrays and for loops to write a very useful subroutine. A common task in any computer program is to randomly sort a list of consecutive integer values. Why would you want to do this? Say you have four answers in a multiple choice quiz. Randomly sort the integers 1, 2, 3, and 4, so the answers are presented in random order. Or, you have a quiz with 30 questions. Randomly sort the questions for printing out as a worksheet. Or, the classic application is shuffling a deck of standard playing cards (there are 52 cards in such a deck). In that case, you can randomly sort the integers from 1 to 52 to "simulate" the shuffling process. Let's build a "shuffle" routine. We call it a shuffle routine, recognizing it can do more than shuffle a card deck. Our routine will sort any number of consecutive integers.

Usually when we need a computer version of something we can do without a computer, it is fairly easy to write down the steps taken and duplicate them in Small Basic code. We've done that with the programs built so far in this course. Other times, the computer version of a process is easy to do on a computer, but hard or tedious to do off the computer. When we shuffle a deck of cards, we separate the deck in two parts, then interleaf the cards as we fan each part. I don't know how you could write Small Basic code to do this. There is a way, however, to write Small Basic code to do a shuffle in a more tedious way (tedious to a human, easy for a computer).

We will perform what could be called a "one card shuffle." In a one card shuffle, you pull a single card (at random) out of the deck and lay it aside on a pile. Repeat this 52 times and the cards are shuffled. Try it! I think you see this idea is simple, but doing a one card shuffle with a real deck of cards would be awfully time-consuming. We'll use the idea of a one card shuffle here, with a slight twist. Rather than lay the selected card on a pile, we will swap it with the bottom card in the stack of cards remaining to be shuffled. This takes the selected card out of the deck and replaces it with the remaining bottom card. The result is the same as if we lay it aside.

Here's how the shuffle works with N numbers:

* Start with a list of N consecutive integers.
* Randomly pick one item from the list. Swap that item with the last item. You now have one fewer items in the list to be sorted (called the remaining list), or N is now N - 1.
* Randomly pick one item from the remaining list. Swap it with the item on the bottom of the remaining list. Again, your remaining list now has one fewer items.
* Repeatedly remove one item from the remaining list and swap it with the item on the bottom of the remaining list until you have run out of items. When done, the list will have been replaced with the original list in random order.

Confusing? Let's show a simple example with N = 5 (a very small deck of cards).

The starting list is (with 5 remaining items):

1   2   3   4   5

Remaining List

We want to pick one item, at random, from this list. Using the Small Basic random number generator, we would choose a random number from 1 to 5. Say it was 3. We take the third item in the list (the 3) and swap it with the last item in the list (the 5). We now have:

1   2   5   4   3

Remaining List

There are 4 items in the remaining list. Pick a random number from 1 to 4 - say it's 4. The fourth item in the remaining list is 4. Swap it with the last item in the remaining list. Wait a minute! The last item in the remaining list is the 4. In this case, we swap it with itself, or it stays put. If the random number was something other than 4, there really would have been a swap here. We now have:

1   2   5   4   3

Remaining List

There are 3 items in the remaining list. Pick a random number from 1 to 3 - say it's 1. The first item in the list is 1. Swap the 1 with the last item in the remaining list (the 5), giving us:

5   2   1   4   3

Remaining List

There are 2 items in the remaining list. Pick a random number from 1 to 2 - say it's 1. The first item in the list is 5. Swap the 5 with the last item in the remaining list (the 2), giving us the final result, the numbers 1 to 5 randomly sorted:

2   5   1   4   3

Pretty neat how this works, huh?

We want to describe the one card shuffle with Small Basic code. Most of the code is straightforward. The only question is how to do the swap involved in each step. This swap is easy on paper. How do we do a swap in Small Basic? Actually, this is a common Small Basic task and is relatively simple. At first thought, to swap variable A with variable B, you might write:

```
A = B
B = A
```

The problem with this code is that when you replace A with B in the first statement, you have destroyed the original value of A. The second statement just puts the newly assigned A value (B) back in B. Both A and B now have the original B value! Actually, swapping two variables is a three step process. First, put A in a temporary storage variable. Then, replace A by B. Then, replace B by the temporary variable (which holds the original A value). If T is the temporary variable, a swap of A and B is done using:

```
T = A
A = B
B = T
```

You use swaps like this in all kinds of Small Basic applications.

Now, we'll see the Small Basic code (a subroutine) that uses a one card shuffle to randomly sort N consecutive integer values. The subroutine is named **NIntegers** and has a single input value **NumberOfIntegers**, the number of integers to shuffle. When done the random list of integers is in the array **NumberList**. Other variables used in the subroutine are:

TempValue - temporary variable used for swapping
LoopCounter - loop counter variable
ItemPicked - variable giving item picked in remaining list
Remaining - loop variable giving number of items in remaining list

The code is:

```
Sub NIntegers
  'One card shuffle code
  'Initialize NumberList
  For LoopCounter = 1 to NumberOfIntegers
    NumberList[LoopCounter] = LoopCounter
  EndFor
  'Work through Remaining values
  'Start at NumberOfItems and swap one value
  'at each For loop step
  'After each step, Remaining is decreased by 1
  For Remaining = NumberOfIntegers to 2 Step -1
    'Pick item at random
    ItemPicked = Math.GetRandomNumber(Remaining)
    'Swap picked item with bottom item
    TempValue = NumberList[Remaining]
    NumberList[Remaining] = NumberList[ItemPicked]
    NumberList[ItemPicked] = TempValue
  EndFor
EndSub
```

Study this code and see how it implements the procedure followed in the simple five number example. It's not that hard to see. Understanding how such code works is a first step to becoming a good Small Basic programmer. Notice this bit of code uses both things we talked about in this class' Small Basic lesson: For loops and arrays.

Let's build a quick example using **Small Basic** to try all these new concepts and see how the shuffle routine works using 10 integers. Start Small Basic and add this code to the editor:

```
NumberOfIntegers = 10
NIntegers()
For I = 1 To 10
  TextWindow.WriteLine("Integer " + I + " is " + NumberList[i])
EndFor
```

This code computes an array **NumberList** of length 10 (**NumberOfIntegers** = 10). This array is filled with the random integers 1 to 10 by calling the **NIntegers** subroutine. The results are printed using 10 calls to **WriteLine** in the **For** loop.

Now, type in the **NIntegers** subroutine as shown earlier. Make sure this code goes after the main code above. The finished code looks like this:

```
NumberOfIntegers = 10
NIntegers()
For I = 1 To 10
  TextWindow.WriteLine("Integer " + I + " is " + NumberList[i])
EndFor

Sub NIntegers
  'One card shuffle code
  'Initialize NumberList
  For LoopCounter = 1 to NumberOfIntegers
    NumberList[LoopCounter] = LoopCounter
  EndFor
  'Work through Remaining values
  'Start at NumberOfItems and swap one value
  'at each For loop step
  'After each step, Remaining is decreased by 1
  For Remaining = NumberOfIntegers to 2 Step -1
    'Pick item at random
    ItemPicked = Math.GetRandomNumber(Remaining)
    'Swap picked item with bottom item
    TempValue = NumberList[Remaining]
    NumberList[Remaining] = NumberList[ItemPicked]
    NumberList[ItemPicked] = TempValue
  EndFor
EndSub
```

Once this code is in, run the program. Correct any errors that might occur. Double-check you have entered the NIntegers subroutine correctly. When I run this little example, I get (you will get different numbers – remember they're random!):

```
C:\Users\Lou\AppData\Local\Temp\tmpC937.tmp.exe
Integer 1 is 9
Integer 2 is 2
Integer 3 is 7
Integer 4 is 6
Integer 5 is 4
Integer 6 is 8
Integer 7 is 5
Integer 8 is 3
Integer 9 is 10
Integer 10 is 1
Press any key to continue...
```

Notice how the array (**MyIntegers**) contains a random listing of the integers from 1 to 10, as desired. If I run it again, I get:

```
C:\Users\Lou\AppData\Local\Temp\tmp646D.tmp.exe
Integer 1 is 2
Integer 2 is 9
Integer 3 is 3
Integer 4 is 4
Integer 5 is 7
Integer 6 is 1
Integer 7 is 8
Integer 8 is 10
Integer 9 is 6
Integer 10 is 5
Press any key to continue...
```

Obviously, the list is now different. For your reference, this program has been saved in the **Shuffle** folder in the course programs folder (**\BeginSB\BSB Code**).

Program – Card Wars

In this program, we create a simplified version of the kid's card game - War. You play against the computer. You each get half a deck of cards (26 cards). Each player turns over one card at a time. The  one with the higher card wins the other player's card. The one with the most cards at the end wins. Obviously, the shuffle routine will come in handy here. We call this program Card Wars! This program is saved in the **CardWars** folder in the programs folder **(\BeginSB\BSB Code)**.

Program Design

The game is conceptually simple. The steps to follow are:

1. Shuffle a deck of cards.
2. Computer gives itself a card and player a card.
3. Computer compares cards, the player with the higher card wins both cards.
4. Scores are computed and displayed.
5. Process continues until all cards have been dealt from the deck.

We can use our shuffle routine to shuffle the deck of cards (compute 52 random integers from 1 to 52). Describing the handed-out cards requires converting the integer card value to an actual card in the deck (value and suit). We will create a Small Basic method to do this. Comparing the cards is relatively easy (we'll add the capability to our card display method), as is updating and displaying the scores (we will use our old friend, the **WriteLine** method). No input is ever needed from the user (besides pressing a key on the keyboard to see the cards) – he/she merely watches the results go by.

Program Development

Before building the program, let's do a little "up front" work. In the **Program Design**, we see a need for a method that, given a card number (1 to 52), (1) determines and displays which card (suit, value) in a deck it represents, and (2) determines its corresponding **numerical** value to allow comparisons. We will create this method now.

Displaying a card consists of answering two questions: what is the card suit and what is the card value? The four suits are hearts, diamonds, clubs, and spades. The thirteen card values, from lowest to highest, are: 2, 3, 4, 5, 6, 7, 8, 9, 10, Jack (J), Queen (Q), King (K), Ace (A). We've seen in our shuffle routine that a card number will range from 1 to 52. How do we translate that card number to a card suit and value? (Notice the distinction between card **number** and card **value** - card number ranges from 1 to 52, card value can only range from 2 to Ace.) We need to develop some type of translation rule. This is done all the time in Small Basic. If the number you compute with or work with does not directly translate to information you need, you need to make up rules to do the translation. For example, the numbers 1 to 12 are used to represent the months of the year. But, these numbers tell us nothing about the names of the month. We need a rule to translate each number to a month name.

We know we need 13 of each card suit. Hence, an easy rule to decide suit is: cards numbered 1 - 13 are hearts, cards numbered 14 - 26 are diamonds, cards numbered 27 - 39 are clubs, and cards numbered 40 - 52 are spades. Suit is represented on the displayed card by the two picture boxes: picPlayer (your card) and picComputer (computer's card). For card values, lower numbers should represent lower cards. A rule that does this for each number in each card suit is:

Card Numbers

Hearts	Diamonds	Clubs	Spades	Card Value
1	14	27	40	2
2	15	28	41	3
3	16	29	42	4
4	17	30	43	5
5	18	31	44	6
6	19	32	45	7
7	20	33	46	8
8	21	34	47	9
9	22	35	48	10
10	23	36	49	J
11	24	37	50	Q
12	25	38	51	K
13	26	39	52	A

As examples, notice card 23 is a Jack of Diamonds. Card 31 is a 6 of Clubs. We now can describe cards. How do we compare them?

Card comparisons must be based on a numerical value, not displayed card value - it's difficult to check if K is greater than 7, though it can be done. So, one last rule is needed to relate card value to numerical value. It's a simple one - start with a 2 having a numerical value of 1 (lowest) and go up, with an Ace (A) having a numerical value of 13 (highest). This makes numerical card comparisons easy. Notice hearts card numbers already go from 1 to 13. If we subtract 13 from diamonds numbers, 26 from clubs numbers, and 39 from spades numbers, each of those card numbers will also range from 1 to 13. This gives a common basis for comparing cards. This all may seem complicated, but look at the Small Basic code and you'll see it really isn't.

Here is a Small Basic subroutine (**CardDisplay**) that takes the card number (**CardNumber**) as an input and returns its numeric value (**CardValue**) (1 to 13) to allow comparisons. The method also prints a description (value and suit) of the corresponding card, using the above table for translation .

```
Sub CardDisplay
  ' given CardNumber (1 - 52), prints description
  ' and returns numeric value CardValue
  Value[1] = "Two"
  Value[2] = "Three"
  Value[3] = "Four"
  Value[4] = "Five"
  Value[5] = "Six"
  Value[6] = "Seven"
  Value[7] = "Eight"
  Value[8] = "Nine"
  Value[9] = "Ten"
  Value[10] = "Jack"
  Value[11] = "Queen"
  Value[12] = "King"
  Value[13] = "Ace"
  'determine  card's suit,  numeric value CardValue
  If (CardNumber >= 1 And CardNumber <= 13) Then
    Suit = "Hearts"
    CardValue = CardNumber
  ElseIf (CardNumber >= 14 And CardNumber <= 26) Then
    Suit = "Diamonds"
    CardValue = CardNumber - 13
  ElseIf (CardNumber >= 27 And CardNumber <= 39) Then
    Suit = "Clubs"
    CardValue = CardNumber - 26
  Else
    Suit = "Spades"
    CardValue = CardNumber - 39
  EndIf
  ' print description
  TextWindow.WriteLine(Value[CardValue] + " of " + Suit)
EndSub
```

You should be able to see how this works. With this subroutine built, we can use it to create the complete Card Wars program.

Start **Small Basic**. Click the **New Program** button in the toolbar. A blank editor will appear. Immediately save the program as **CardWars** in a folder of your choice.

First, type the following header information and add a window title:

```
'
'  Card Wars
'  Beginning Small Basic
'

TextWindow.Title = "Card Wars"
```

We will use several variables. The current card number will be **CardIndex**, the two player scores are **ComputerScore** and **YourScore**. The values of the player cards are **ComputerCard** and Your Card. The shuffled 'deck' of cards is in the array **MyCards**. Start with necessary variable initializations:

```
CardIndex = 1
ComputerScore = 0
YourScore = 0
```

Next, shuffle the cards using the shuffle subroutine and setup the playing **While** loop (we keep playing as long as there are cards left):

```
'  shuffle the cards
NumberOfIntegers = 52
NIntegers()
MyCards = NumberList

' while loop starting game
While ((53 - cardIndex) > 0)
EndWhile
```

Now, in the While loop, start with the code that picks and displays the cards:

```
' display computer card, then your card
TextWindow.Write("My card:    ")
CardNumber = MyCards[CardIndex]
CardDisplay()
ComputerCard = CardValue
TextWindow.Write("Your card: ")
CardNumber = MyCards[CardIndex + 1]
CardDisplay()
YourCard = CardValue
```

In this code, we use the Write method, not **WriteLine**. This allows the card description to print on the same line as the "My card:" and "Your card:" headings.

Next, we check to see who wins (or if there is a tie) and compute the scores:

```
' see who won
If (YourCard > ComputerCard) Then
   TextWindow.WriteLine("You win!")
   YourScore = YourScore + 2
ElseIf (ComputerCard > YourCard) Then
   TextWindow.WriteLine("I win!")
   ComputerScore = ComputerScore + 2
Else
   TextWindow.WriteLine("It's a tie.")
   YourScore = YourScore + 1
   ComputerScore = ComputerScore + 1
EndIf
```

Next, we print the results:

```
TextWindow.WriteLine("My Score:    " + ComputerScore)
TextWindow.WriteLine("Your Score: " + YourScore)
CardIndex = CardIndex + 2
TextWindow.Write("There are " + (53 - cardIndex) + " cards
remaining.  Press any key.")
TextWindow.Read()
TextWindow.WriteLine("")
```

Note how we stop the code waiting for some user input to continue. This closes out the While loop. After the WhileEnd statement, a final game over message is printed::

```
TextWindow.WriteLine("Game over.")
```

After typing this code, you still need to add two subroutines: **DisplayCard** and the **NIntegers** shuffle subroutine. You can copy and paste NIntegers from the Shuffle program we built earlier in this class. And, if you want, you can copy and paste DisplayCard from these notes into the editor of Small Basic. That would save you lots of typing. But, go ahead and type the subroutines, if you'd like. In any case, make sure the two subroutines are there, after the main code.

For completeness, here is all the code from the Small Basic editor for the Card Wars program, including all methods (get ready, it's long!):

```
'
'  Card Wars
'  Beginning Small Basic
'
TextWindow.Title = "Card Wars"
CardIndexCardIndex == 1CardIndex = 1
ComputerScore = 0
YourScore = 0
'  shuffle the cards
NumberOfIntegers = 52
NIntegers()
```

```
MyCards = NumberList

' while loop starting game
While ((53 - cardIndex) > 0)
  ' display computer card, then your card
  TextWindow.Write("My card:    ")
  CardNumber = MyCards[CardIndex]
  CardDisplay()
  ComputerCard = CardValue
  TextWindow.Write("Your card: ")
  CardNumber = MyCards[CardIndex + 1]
  CardDisplay()
  YourCard = CardValue
  ' see who won
  If (YourCard > ComputerCard) Then
    TextWindow.WriteLine("You win!")
    YourScore = YourScore + 2
  ElseIf (ComputerCard > YourCard) Then
    TextWindow.WriteLine("I win!")
    ComputerScore = ComputerScore + 2
  Else
    TextWindow.WriteLine("It's a tie.")
    YourScore = YourScore + 1
    ComputerScore = ComputerScore + 1
  EndIf
  TextWindow.WriteLine("My Score:    " + ComputerScore)
  TextWindow.WriteLine("Your Score: " + YourScore)
  CardIndex = CardIndex + 2
  TextWindow.Write("There are " + (53 - cardIndex) + " cards
remaining.  Press any key.")
  TextWindow.Read()
  TextWindow.WriteLine("")
EndWhile
TextWindow.WriteLine("Game over.")


Sub CardDisplay
  ' given CardNumber (1 - 52), prints description
  ' and returns numeric value CardValue
  Value[1] = "Two"
  Value[2] = "Three"
  Value[3] = "Four"
  Value[4] = "Five"
  Value[5] = "Six"
  Value[6] = "Seven"
  Value[7] = "Eight"
```

```smallbasic
    Value[8] = "Nine"
    Value[9] = "Ten"
    Value[10] = "Jack"
    Value[11] = "Queen"
    Value[12] = "King"
    Value[13] = "Ace"
    'determine  card's suit,  numeric value CardValue
    If (CardNumber >= 1 And CardNumber <= 13) Then
      Suit = "Hearts"
      CardValue = CardNumber
    ElseIf (CardNumber >= 14 And CardNumber <= 26) Then
      Suit = "Diamonds"
      CardValue = CardNumber - 13
    ElseIf (CardNumber >= 27 And CardNumber <= 39) Then
      Suit = "Clubs"
      CardValue = CardNumber - 26
    Else
      Suit = "Spades"
      CardValue = CardNumber - 39
    EndIf
    ' print description
    TextWindow.WriteLine(Value[CardValue] + " of " + Suit)
EndSub

Sub NIntegers
  'One card shuffle code
  'Initialize NumberList
  For LoopCounter = 1 to NumberOfIntegers
    NumberList[LoopCounter] = LoopCounter
  EndFor
  'Work through Remaining values
  'Start at NumberOfItems and swap one value
  'at each For loop step
  'After each step, Remaining is decreased by 1
  For Remaining = NumberOfIntegers to 2 Step -1
    'Pick item at random
    ItemPicked = Math.GetRandomNumber(Remaining)
    'Swap picked item with bottom item
    TempValue = NumberList[Remaining]
    NumberList[Remaining] = NumberList[ItemPicked]
    NumberList[ItemPicked] = TempValue
  EndFor
EndSub
```

Run the Program

Run the program. Eliminate any syntax, run-time or logic errors you may encounter. You may have to recheck your typing, especially in the method. You should see something like:

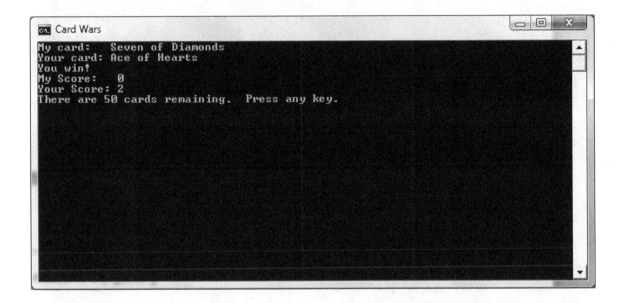

All you do at this point is press any key to see the next set of cards. You continue doing this until the card deck is empty (all 52 cards have been used). Make sure the program works correctly. Play through one game and check each comparison to make sure you get the correct result and score with each new card.

Here's the middle of my game:

```
Card Wars

Your Score: 10
There are 32 cards remaining.  Press any key.

My card:    Three of Clubs
Your card: Three of Diamonds
It's a tie.
My Score:   11
Your Score: 11
There are 30 cards remaining.  Press any key.

My card:    Seven of Clubs
Your card: King of Spades
You win!
My Score:   11
Your Score: 13
There are 28 cards remaining.  Press any key.

My card:    Jack of Diamonds
Your card: Nine of Clubs
I win!
My Score:   13
Your Score: 13
There are 26 cards remaining.  Press any key.
```

And here's the end:

```
Card Wars

Your card: Eight of Clubs
You win!
My Score:   21
Your Score: 27
There are 4 cards remaining.  Press any key.

My card:    Ten of Clubs
Your card: King of Diamonds
You win!
My Score:   21
Your Score: 29
There are 2 cards remaining.  Press any key.

My card:    Four of Hearts
Your card: King of Hearts
You win!
My Score:   21
Your Score: 31
There are 0 cards remaining.  Press any key.

Game over.
Press any key to continue...
```

Go through the usual process of making sure the program works as it should. Once you're convinced everything is okay, have fun playing the game. Share your creation with friends. If you made any changes during the running process, make sure you save the program.

Other Things to Try

Possible changes to the Card Wars program are obvious, but not easy. One change would be to have more than two players. Set up three and four player versions. Perhaps add another loop to allow playing another game (without restarting the application).

In Card Wars, we stop the game after going through the deck one time. In the real card game of War, after the first round, the players pick up the cards they won, shuffle them, and play another round. Every time a player uses all the cards in their "hand," they again pick up their winnings pile, reshuffle and continue playing. This continues until one player has lost all of their cards. Another change to Card Wars would be to write code that plays the game with these rules. As we said, it's not easy. You would need to add code to keep track of which cards each player won, when they ran out of cards to play, how to reshuffle their remaining cards, and new logic to see when a game was over. Such code would use more arrays, more For loops, and more variables. If you want a programming challenge, go for it!

And, while you're tackling challenges, here's another. In the usual War game, when two cards have the same value - War is declared! This means each player takes three cards from their "hand" and lays them face down. Then another card is placed face up. The higher card at that time wins all 10 cards! If it's still a tie, there's another War. Try adding this logic to the game. You'll need to check if a player has enough cards to wage War. Another difficult task, but give it a try if you feel adventurous.

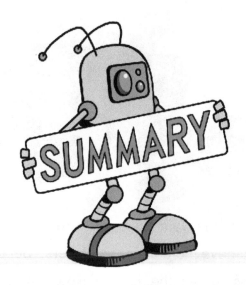

This class presented one of the more challenging programs yet. The code involved in shuffling cards and displaying cards, though straightforward, was quite involved. The use of arrays and For loops made the coding a bit easier. If you completely understood the Card Wars program, you are well on your way to being a good Small Basic programmer. Now, on to the next class, where we introduce an exciting programming area – graphics!

8

Small Basic Graphics, Mouse Methods

Review and Preview

You've seen and learned lots of Small Basic code by now. But, plain text window programs are a bit boring. In this class, we begin looking at a very fun part of Small Basic - adding graphics capabilities to our programs. We will also look at ways for Small Basic to recognize mouse inputs and have some fun with colors. You will build an electronic blackboard program.

Graphic User Interfaces (GUI)

All the Small Basic programs built in this course have been text applications. The computer asks some questions, you answer the questions. Because of the simplicity, using text applications is a good way to learn the Small Basic programming language. But, let's move on. Most programs in use feature what is called a **graphic user interface**. This is abbreviated **GUI** and pronounced "**gooey**." GUI applications are built with **windows** using **controls**, such as menus, toolbars, buttons, text boxes, selection boxes, scroll bars and other devices the user interacts with to operate the program. The primary interaction with these controls is via the computer mouse. If you've used a computer, you have used GUI applications. Examples include video games, spreadsheet programs, word processors, Internet browsers, the Windows operating system itself. The Small Basic environment is a GUI application. In each of these applications, you would be helpless without your mouse!

Running (and building) a GUI application is different than a text application. In a text application, everything runs sequentially – you are asked a series of questions, you provide a series of answers. In a GUI application, the computer sits and waits until the user does something – clicks on a menu item, chooses an option, types somewhere, moves a scroll bar, etc. We say the application is waiting for an **event** to occur. For this reason, GUI applications are called **event-driven**. When a particular event occurs, the application processes a series of statements (Small Basic statements in our applications) associated with that event. That series of statements is called an **event procedure**.

Here's how it works:

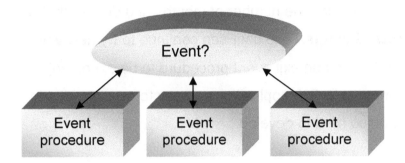

In this "model," the program waits (listens) for an **event** to occur. Once an event is detected, program control transfers to the corresponding **event procedure**. Once that procedure is executed, program control returns to the listener. In Small Basic, these procedures are subroutines. Each procedure is simply a set of Small Basic code with instructions on what to do if the particular event occurs. So, in GUI programming, we spend most of our time writing event procedures.

Let's look at some example of GUI applications and explain their use in the context of event-driven programming. Each of these examples should look very, very familiar. First, how about a **Savings Calculator** program:

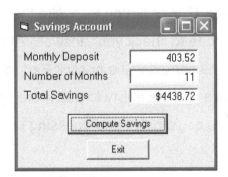

As I said, these examples will look familiar. This is a GUI version of the savings calculator program built in Class 4. This application uses controls called labels to display information and controls called text boxes for input. The user types in information in the boxes and, when done, clicks the button **Compute Savings** to get the desired results. This program has a procedure to process when it "hears"

(listens for) the **click** event on this button. That procedure will do the multiplication of the deposit amount and the number of months and display that result in the text box labeled **Total Savings**. The user can continue to try new values until clicking the **Exit** button (causing an exit event procedure to be executed). You should see some big advantages to GUI applications – easy to use, obvious to use, and they're really not too hard to develop.

How about a GUI **Guess the Number** game (from Class 5):

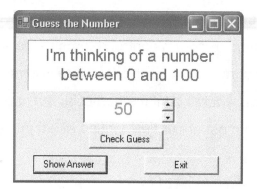

Here the computer tells you about the number it is thinking about. You enter your guess by adjusting the displayed value with the scroll bar control (causing a **scroll** event). You click the **Check Guess** button to invoke the corresponding event procedure where there is code to check your answer. At any time, you can click **Show Answer** to display the correct value or click **Exit** to stop the program. Notice GUI applications give you the ability to add more options. In the text version of this program, you could only keep guessing until you got the right answer.

Next, here's the GUI **Lemonade Stand** from Class 6:

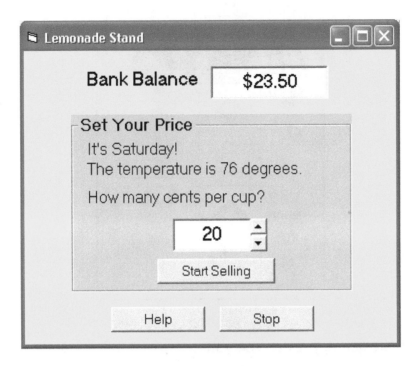

Your bank balance is displayed. You set the selling price (using a scroll bar) and click **Start Selling**. In this button's click event procedure is the code to compute the cups sold and present your sales results. Notice too, you can stop the application (**Stop** button) or even receive some clues (**Help** button). Again, GUI applications are very flexible.

Well, you must have known it was coming – the GUI **Card Wars** game from Class 7:

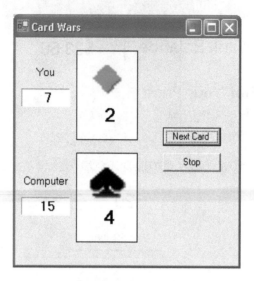

At this point in the game, you can see your score and the computer's score. And, notice rather than see a text description of the cards, a visual picture is shown! Another big advantage of GUI applications – they can show pictures! Clicking **Next Card** will process the code in the procedure to hand out two more cards, see who wins and adjust and display the scores.

You should be convinced by now that GUI applications are the way to go. They offer flexibility, ease of use, familiarity (every user has used a GUI application before), and they're nice to look at. In the rest of this course, we will build GUI (graphical) applications. They won't be as elaborate as the examples just seen. We won't use any controls – Small Basic does not provide controls. The Microsoft **Visual Basic** product does allow building of GUI applications with controls. Kidware Software (our company) produces more advanced courses that teach you the Visual Basic language. If you want to learn more about GUI programs, these courses would be good to take after you finish learning Small Basic. In the remainder of this class, we will gain the skills needed to build a little drawing program. Again, there's a lot to learn and we'll take it step-by-step.

Small Basic Graphics

In this class, we will be looking at Small Basic to do one primary graphics task – drawing with the mouse. There are many steps with many new terms, but I know you are up to the task.

Graphics Window

The basic component of a graphics (GUI) application is the **graphics window**. It is a window with a title bar, a border and an area to build the application. It is the graphic counterpart to the text window we have been using. To display the graphics window, use the **Show** method:

```
GraphicsWindow.Show()
```

Try this and you will see (we've resized the window a bit):

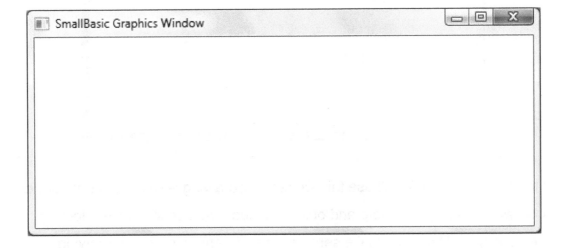

The graphics window has several **properties** we can change. The **Title** property sets the information in the title bar, the **Width** property sets the width of the window, while **Height** sets the height. Try this code:

```
GraphicsWindow.Show()
GraphicsWindow.Title ="Graphics Testing"
GraphicsWindow.Width = 400
GraphicsWindow.Height = 300
```

And you should see this smaller window:

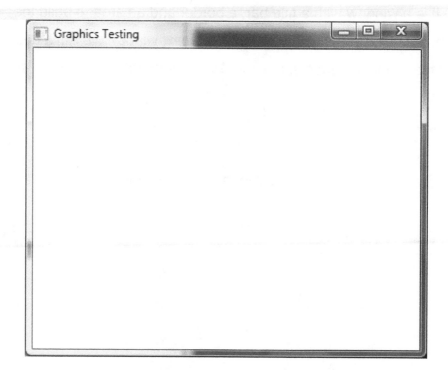

Not too hard, huh?   We will use this window for drawing – save the code for now. Our drawing will require colors and objects called pens, so let's take a look at those concepts. Doesn't it make sense we need pens to do some drawing?

Colors

Colors play a big part in Small Basic graphics applications. Lines, rectangles, ovals can all be drawn and filled in various colors. The background color of the graphics window can be set to a particular color using the **BackgroundColor** property. These colors must be defined in Small Basic code. How do we do this? Small Basic has hundreds of colors we can use all referred to by specific names. The colors are listed in Appendix I to these notes. Some examples are:

Darker colors:

Black	DarkGray
Blue	Gray
Red	

Lighter colors:

White	Green
Cyan	Orange
LightGray	Yellow
Magenta	Pink

There are far more elaborate colors like **BlanchedAlmond**, **Linen**, **NavajoWhite**, **PeachPuff** and **SpringGreen**. As an example, to set the background color of the graphics window to yellow, use:

```
GraphicsWindow.BackgroundColor = "Yellow"
```

If you want, try this with the Graphics Test window we just built.

You can also define variables that take on color values. Say we want to define a variable named **MyRed** to represent the color red. Simply define your color in code using:

```
MyRed = "Red"
```

From this point on, you can use **MyRed** anywhere the red color is desired.

Pen Object

As mentioned, many of the graphics methods (including the method to draw lines) require a **Pen** object. This virtual pen is just like the pen you use to write and draw. You can choose color and width. Lines of code that accomplish this task are:

```
GraphicsWindow.PenColor = Color
GraphicsWindow.PenWidth = Width
```

where **Color** is the color your pen will draw in and **Width** is the integer width (a value of 1 by default) of the line (in pixels) drawn. This pen will draw a solid line.

We're almost ready to draw lines – be patient! Just one more concept and we're on our way.

Graphics Coordinates

We use Small Basic to draw using **graphics methods**. In this class, we will learn to draw lines and rectangles. Before looking at these methods, let's look at how we specify the points used to draw and connect lines. All graphics methods use a default **coordinate system**. This means we have a specific way to refer to individual points in the graphics window. The coordinate system used is:

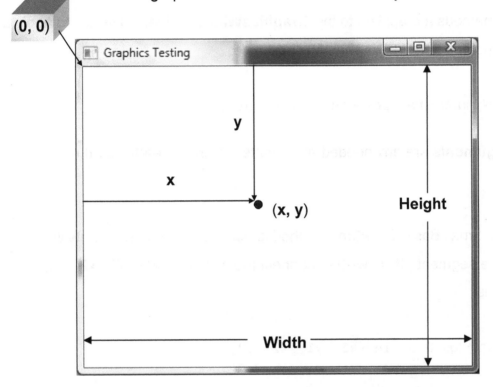

Recall the window is **Width** pixels wide and **Height** pixels high. We use two values (coordinates) to identify a single point in the window. The **x** (horizontal) coordinate increases from left to right, starting at **0**. The **y** (vertical) coordinate increases from top to bottom, also starting at **0**. Points in the region are referred to by the two coordinates enclosed in parentheses, or **(x, y)**. All values shown are in units of **pixels**. A pixel is a single dot in the graphics window. At long last, we're ready to draw some lines.

DrawLine Method

To do graphics (drawing) in Small Basic, we use the built-in **graphics methods**. In this class, we will look at graphics methods that can draw colored lines, rectangles and filled rectangles. As you progress in your programming skills, you are encouraged to study the many other graphics methods that can draw triangles, ellipses, polygons and virtually any shape, in any color. All graphics methods are applied to the **GraphicsWindow** object. Hence, to apply a graphics method named **GraphicsMethod**, use:

```
GraphicsWindow.GraphicsMethod(Arguments)
```

where **Arguments** are any needed arguments, or inputs needed by the graphics method.

The Small Basic **DrawLine** method is used to connect two points with a straight-line segment. If we wish to connect the point (**x1**, **y1**) with (**x2**, **y2**), the statement is:

```
GraphicsWindow.DrawLine(x1, y1, x2, y2)
```

The line will draw in the current pen **Color** and **Width**. To set these values, use (these lines go <u>before</u> the corresponding DrawLine method):

```
GraphicsWindow.PenColor = Color
GraphicsWindow.PenWidth = Width
```

To draw a blue line in our **Graphics Test** example we built earlier, add the three shaded lines to the code:

```
GraphicsWindow.Show()
GraphicsWindow.Title ="Graphics Testing"
GraphicsWindow.Width = 400
GraphicsWindow.Height = 300
GraphicsWindow.PenColor = "Blue"
GraphicsWindow.PenWidth = 1
GraphicsWindowGraphicsWindow.DrawLine(20, 50, 380, 280)
```

Run it in Small Basic. You should see:

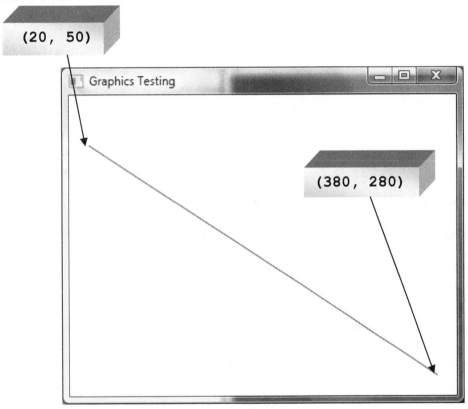

To connect the last point (**380, 280**) to another point (**200, 40**), add this line:

```
GraphicsWindow.DrawLine(380, 280, 200, 40)
```

This produces:

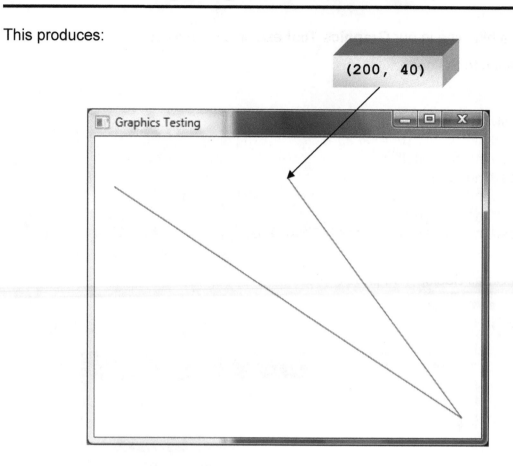

To continue the line (changing the pen color to red and width 5) to point (30, 290), add these lines:

```
GraphicsWindow.PenColor = "Red"
GraphicsWindow.PenWidth = 5
GraphicsWindow.DrawLine(200, 40, 30, 290)
```

You will see:

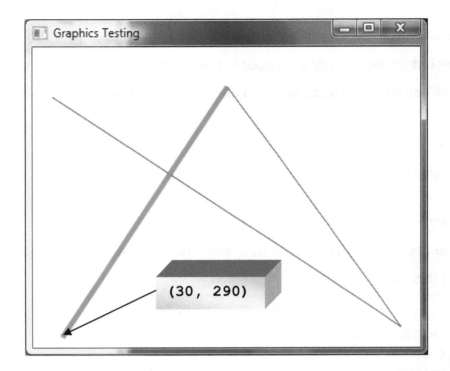

Add more line segments, using other points, colors and pen widths if you like. Note that for every line segment you draw, you need a separate **DrawLine** statement. To connect one line segment with another, you need to save the last point drawn to in the first segment (use two variables, one for x and one for y). This saved point will become the starting point for the next line segment. You can choose to change the color at any time you wish. Using many line segments, with many different colors, you can draw virtually anything you want! We'll do that with the Blackboard program in this class. As mentioned, there are many other graphics methods. Let's look at two more (dealing with rectangles) we will use in the Blackboard program.

DrawRectangle Method

The Small Basic **DrawRectangle** method is used to draw a rectangle. To draw a rectangle, we specify the upper left hand corner's coordinate (**x**, **y**) and the **width** and **height** of the rectangle. To draw such a rectangle in the graphics window:

```
GraphicsWindow.DrawRectangle(x, y, width, height)
```

The rectangle will draw with the current pen. To draw a blue rectangle (pen width 2) with the upper left corner at (20, 50), width 150 and height 100 in our **Graphics Test**, use this code:

```
GraphicsWindow.Show()
GraphicsWindow.Title ="Graphics Testing"
GraphicsWindow.Width = 400
GraphicsWindow.Height = 300
GraphicsWindow.PenColor = "Blue"
GraphicsWindow.PenWidth = 2
GraphicsWindow.DrawRectangle(20, 50, 150, 100)
```

This produces:

(20, 50)

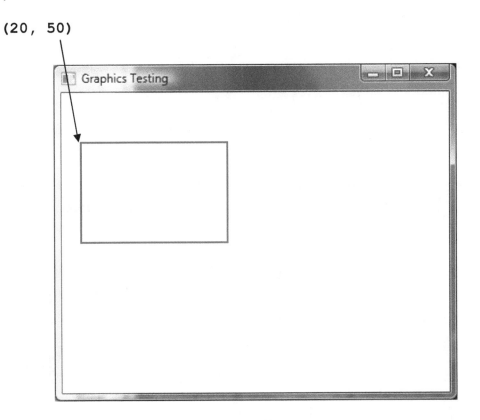

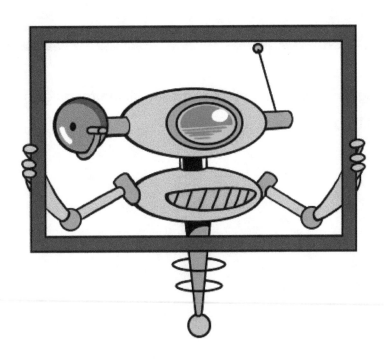

And, to draw a red rectangle of the same size with upper left corner at (140, 130), add these two lines:

```
GraphicsWindow.PenColor = "Red"
GraphicsWindow.DrawRectangle(140, 130, 150, 100)
```

This yields:

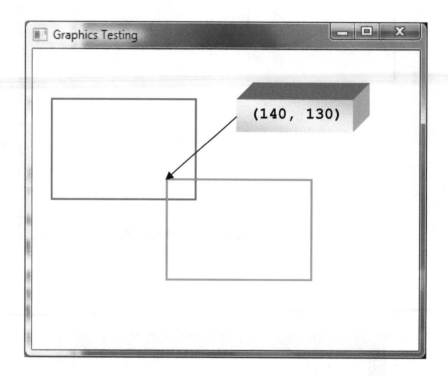

Try more rectangles if you like. Let's see how to fill the rectangles with color. To do this we need to look at the **Brush** object.

Brush Object

A **Brush** object is like a "wide" pen. It is used to fill areas with a color. It has a single property (**Color**). To set the brush color, use:

```
GraphicsWindow.BrushColor = Color
```

A brush is 'solid' – filling areas completely with the specified color.

FillRectangle Method

The Small Basic **FillRectangle** method is used to fill a rectangle with color. To fill a rectangle, we specify the upper left hand corner's coordinate (**x**, **y**) and the **width** and **height** of the rectangle. To draw such a rectangle in the graphics window, the statement is:

```
GraphicsWindow.FillRectangle(x, y, width,height)
```

The rectangle will draw and fill in the current brush object color. To set that color, use:

```
GraphicsWindow.BrushColor = Color
```

To draw and fill a blue rectangle with the upper left corner at (20, 50), width 150 and height 100 in our **Graphics Test**, use this code:

```
GraphicsWindow.Show()
GraphicsWindow.Title ="Graphics Testing"
GraphicsWindow.Width = 400
GraphicsWindow.Height = 300
GraphicsWindow.BrushColor = "Blue"
GraphicsWindow.FillRectangle(20, 50, 150, 100)
```

This produces in the window:

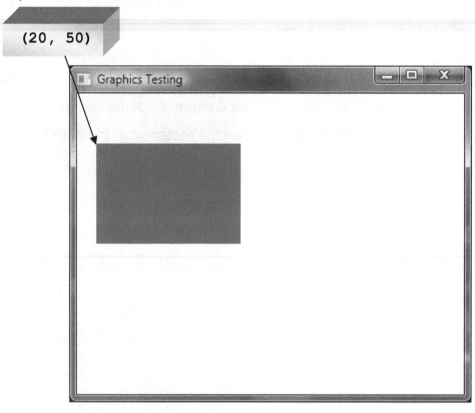

And, to draw a red filled rectangle of the same size with upper left corner at (140, 130), add these two lines of code:

```
GraphicsWindow.BrushColor = "Red"
GraphicsWindow.FillRectangle(140, 130, 150, 100)
```

This yields:

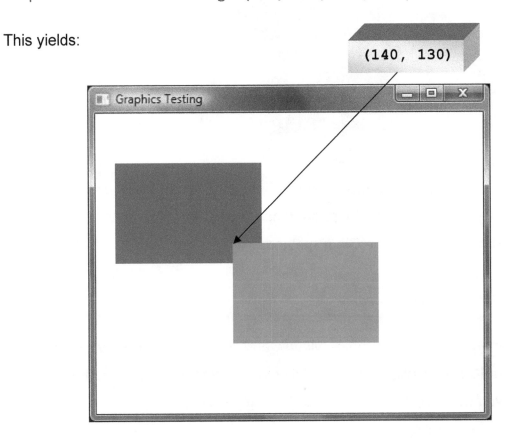

Try more rectangles if you like.

Clear Method

There is one last graphics method to introduce. After all of your hard work drawing in a graphics window, there are times you will want to erase or clear the window. This is done with the **Clear** method:

```
GraphicsWindow.Clear()
```

This statement will clear a graphics window and fill it with the window's specified **BackgroundColor**. Notice if you add this statement to the end of our test example, you will have a blank window. Try it if you like.

Keep playing around with the Graphics Test program. Try drawing more lines and rectangles. Save this program (use the name **GraphicsTest**)– we'll continue working with it. I think you get the idea of drawing. Just pick some points, pick some colors, and draw some lines. But, it's pretty boring to just specify points and see lines being drawn. It would be nice to have some user interaction, where points could be drawn using the mouse. And, that's just what we are going to do. We will use our newly gained knowledge about graphics methods to build a Small Basic drawing program. To do this, though, we need to know how to use the mouse in a program. We do that next.

Small Basic - The Sixth Lesson

In the beginning of this class, we introduced the concept of **events** where the computer responds to something a user does. When an event occurs, program control is transferred to an **event procedure** (Small Basic **subroutine**) where the event code is written. In the Small Basic lesson for this class, we examine how to recognize **mouse events** (clicking mouse buttons, moving the mouse) to help us build a drawing program using a graphics window. The mouse is a primary interface for doing graphics in Small Basic or any GUI application. We are interested in two mouse events: **MouseDown** and **MouseMove**. .

MouseDown Event

The **MouseDown** event is triggered whenever a mouse button is pressed while the mouse cursor is over the graphics window. If the subroutine to be executed in case of such an event is **MouseDownEvent**, we add this event to our program using:

```
GraphicsWindow.MouseDown = MouseDownEvent
```

Note that setting the **MouseDown** subroutine name (**MouseDownEvent**) is similar to setting a property for the **GraphicsWindow** object.

The corresponding subroutine is added to the program in the usual manner and has the form:

```
Sub MouseDownEvent
  ' Small Basic code for MouseDown event
EndSub
```

Every time the user clicks the mouse, a MouseDown event occurs and the subroutine (MouseDownEvent) is called automatically. In drawing applications, the **MouseDown** event is used to initialize a drawing process. The point clicked is used to start drawing a line.

Example

Let's try the **MouseDown** event with the example we've been using. Open that program (**GraphicsTest**) in Small Basic and delete any lines using drawing methods (so we just have a blank window when the program runs). Add this code to test the **MouseDown** event:

```
GraphicsWindow.MouseDown = MouseDownEvent

Sub MouseDownEvent
  GraphicsWindow.BackgroundColor = GraphicsWindow.GetRandomColor()
EndSub
```

With this code, each time the mouse is clicked the graphics window will change background color (a the newly introduced method, **GetRandomColor**, which does just that – sets a color randomly).

The finished code looks like this:

```
GraphicsWindow.Show()
GraphicsWindow.Title ="Graphics Testing"
GraphicsWindow.Width = 400
GraphicsWindow.Height = 300
GraphicsWindow.MouseDown = MouseDownEvent

Sub MouseDownEvent
  GraphicsWindow.BackgroundColor = GraphicsWindow.GetRandomColor()
EndSub
```

Run the program. Each time you click the window, the background color will change. Here's one of my clicks:

You should see it's pretty easy to implement the MouseDown event.

Mouse Properties

When we click the mouse, there is information available to us via **properties** of the Small Basic **Mouse** class. We can determine which button was clicked by examining two properties which return logical values that can be checked in If structures or While loops:

Mouse.IsLeftButtonDown   Returns a true value if left button is pressed.

Mouse.IsRightButtonDown   Returns a true value if right button is pressed.

The coordinates of the mouse cursor when a button is pressed are given by:

Mouse.MouseX   x coordinate of mouse cursor (relative to entire screen) when mouse is pressed

Mouse.MouseY   y coordinate of mouse cursor (relative to entire screen) when mouse is pressed

These coordinates are relative to your entire computer screen – let's see what that means.

Here is a graphics window displayed on your monitor showing **Mouse.MouseX** and **Mouse.MouseY**:

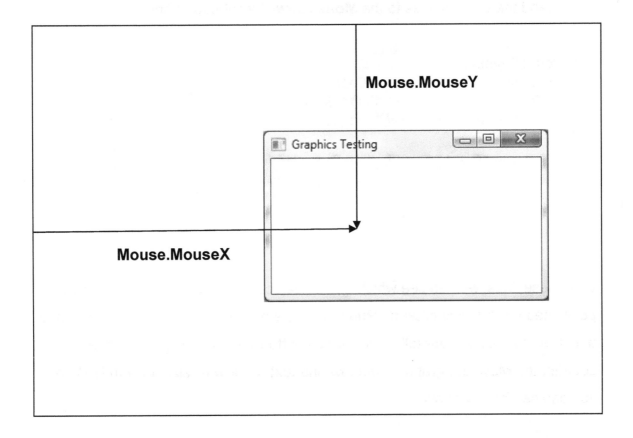

With these coordinates, you would get different results if you move the graphics window on your screen. We want to use our previously defined graphics coordinate system, where the upper left corner of the graphics window is (0, 0). Such coordinates are given by two **GraphicsWindow** properties:

GraphicsWindow.MouseX   x coordinate of mouse cursor in graphics window when mouse is pressed

GraphicsWindow.MouseY   y coordinate of mouse cursor in graphics window when mouse is pressed

Example

Add the shaded lines to the **MouseDownEvent** subroutine:

```
Sub MouseDownEvent
  GraphicsWindow.BackgroundColor = GraphicsWindow.GetRandomColor()
  If (Mouse.IsLeftButtonDown) Then
    TextWindow.WriteLine("You clicked the left mouse button")
  Else
    TextWindow.WriteLine("You clicked the right mouse button")
  EndIf
  TextWindow.WriteLine("At x = " + GraphicsWindow.MouseX + ", y =
" + GraphicsWindow.Mousey)
EndSub
```

With these lines, we can see which button was clicked and where the mouse was positioned when it was clicked. Run the program. Click the graphics window and a text window will appear telling you which button was clicked and the click coordinate. Move the graphics window and text window (resize it if you like) so you can see both windows.

Here's what I got when I clicked the left mouse button:

Click various spots in the window and see how the coordinates change. Try both mouse buttons. Notice you cannot detect mouse clicks in the title bar area. Play with this example until you are comfortable with how the MouseDown event works and what the coordinates mean. Stop and save the program.

MouseMove Event

The **MouseMove** event is continuously triggered whenever the mouse is being moved. If the subroutine to be executed in case of such an event is **MouseMoveEvent**, we add this event to our program using:

```
GraphicsWindow.MouseMove = MouseMoveEvent
```

The corresponding subroutine is added to the program in the usual manner and has the form:

```
Sub MouseMoveEvent
  ' Small Basic code for MouseMove event
EndSub
```

Whenever a user moves the mouse, a MouseMove event occurs and the subroutine (MouseMoveEvent) is called automatically.

In drawing processes, the **MouseMove** event is used to detect the continuation of a previously started line (you also make sure a button is being pressed). If drawing is continuing, the current point is connected to the previous point using the **DrawLine** method.

Example

Modify the graphics example, adding the shaded code:

```
GraphicsWindow.Show()
GraphicsWindow.Title ="Graphics Testing"
GraphicsWindow.Width = 400
GraphicsWindow.Height = 300
GraphicsWindow.MouseDown = MouseDownEvent
GraphicsWindow.MouseMove = MouseMoveEvent

Sub MouseDownEvent
  GraphicsWindow.BackgroundColor = GraphicsWindow.GetRandomColor()
  If (Mouse.IsLeftButtonDown) Then
    TextWindow.WriteLine("You clicked the left mouse button")
  Else
    TextWindow.WriteLine("You clicked the right mouse button")
  EndIf
  TextWindow.WriteLine("At x = " + GraphicsWindow.MouseX + ", y =
" + GraphicsWindow.Mousey)
EndSub

Sub MouseMoveEvent
  TextWindow.WriteLine("Moved to x = " + GraphicsWindow.MouseX +
", y = " + GraphicsWindow.Mousey)
EndSub
```

We establish a **MouseMove** event and in the corresponding subroutine (**MouseMoveEvent**), we use a **WriteLine** statement to specify the x and y coordinate the mouse has been moved to. This last version of the **GraphicsTest** is saved in the course programs folder (**\BeginSB\BSB Code**).

Run the program. Move the cursor into the graphics window and a text window will appear showing you the changing cursor location. Click the graphics window and notice the clicked point is displayed. Move the mouse around the window. Notice the coordinates (x, y) continuously change as the mouse is moving. Here's the text window from one of my runs:

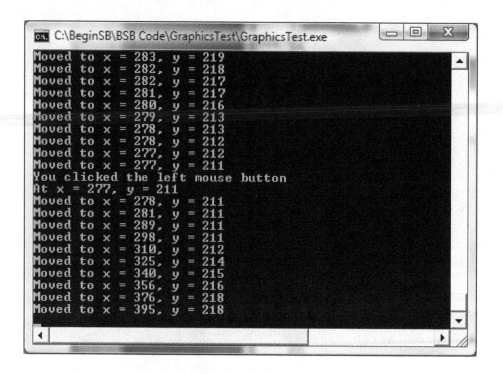

Program – Blackboard Fun

Have you ever drawn on a blackboard with colored chalk? You'll be doing that with the "electronic" blackboard you build in this program. This program is saved in the **Blackboard** folder in the course programs folder (**\BeginSB\BSB Code**).

Program Design

This is a simple program in concept. Using the mouse, you draw colored lines on a computer blackboard. A graphics window will represent the blackboard. We will use rectangles drawn along the edge of the window to choose "chalk" color. Mouse events will control the drawing and color selection process. The basic program steps are very simple:

1. Establish graphics window, add event procedures and setup color choice rectangles.
2. Listen for mouse down, when one is detected, either change the color or initialize drawing process.
3. Listen for mouse moving. If mouse is moving (with button press), continue drawing line in current color.

We will write code that takes care of all the initialization steps and write code for each (MouseDown, MouseMove) event procedures.

Program Development

To help visualize what's going to be in this program, let's look ahead at how we want to layout the window. We will create a window that is 600 pixels wide and 450 pixels high. On the right-edge of the window, we will draw 9 small filled rectangles. These rectangles will be used to select drawing color. The coordinates used for all this are:

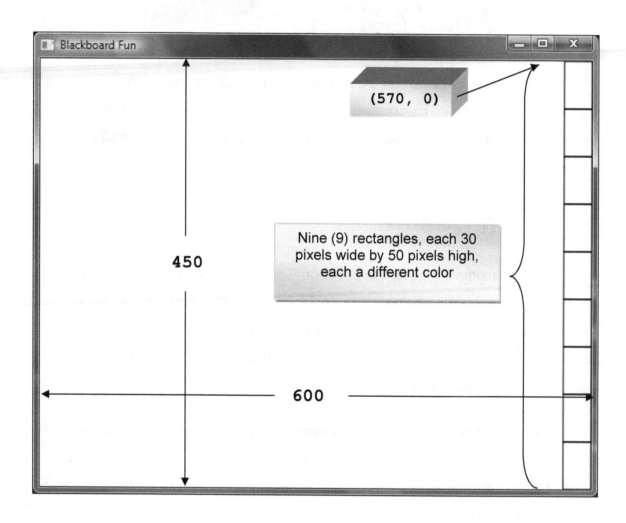

This program will work like any paint type program you may have used. Click on a color in one of the eight rectangles to choose a color to draw with. Then, move to the blackboard area, <u>left</u>-click to start the drawing process. Drag the mouse to draw lines. Release the mouse button to stop drawing. It's that easy. Clicking in the black rectangle under the eight color selection rectangles will clear the blackboard and, as usual, clicking the **X** in the upper right corner of the graphics window will stop the program. Every step, but initializing things and stopping the program, is handled by the mouse events.

     Start **Small Basic**. Click the **New Program** button in the toolbar. A blank editor will appear. Immediately save the program as **Blackboard** in a folder of your choice.

     First, type the following header information, add a window title and establish a graphics window:

```
'
'  Blackboard Fun
'  Beginning Small Basic
'
GraphicsWindow.Title = "Blackboard Fun"
GraphicsWindow.Show()
GraphicsWindow.Width = 600
GraphicsWindow.Height = 450
GraphicsWindow.BackgroundColor = "Black"
```

Save the program.

Run the program to make sure the graphics window appears (it should be black, like a blackboard!):

In long, detailed programs like this, it is good practice to occasionally stop and try your program even if it's not complete. This gives you some confidence things are working okay and you can move on.

As a variable, **DrawingColor** will hold the current drawing color. And, we need two variables (**PreviousX** and **PreviousY**) that save the last point drawn in a line (we will always connect the "current" point to the "last" point).

We need to establish some initial values. First, draw the nine rectangles we will use for color selection. Add these lines:

```
' setup color choice rectangles
GraphicsWindow.BrushColor = "White"
GraphicsWindow.FillRectangle(570, 0, 30, 50)
GraphicsWindow.BrushColor = "LightGray"
GraphicsWindow.FillRectangle(570, 50, 30, 50)
GraphicsWindow.BrushColor = "RoyalBlue"
GraphicsWindow.FillRectangle(570, 100, 30, 50)
GraphicsWindow.BrushColor = "Cyan"
GraphicsWindow.FillRectangle(570, 150, 30, 50)
GraphicsWindow.BrushColor = "Green"
GraphicsWindow.FillRectangle(570, 200, 30, 50)
GraphicsWindow.BrushColor = "Magenta"
GraphicsWindow.FillRectangle(570, 250, 30, 50)
GraphicsWindow.BrushColor = "Yellow"
GraphicsWindow.FillRectangle(570, 300, 30, 50)
GraphicsWindow.BrushColor = "Red"
GraphicsWindow.FillRectangle(570, 350, 30, 50)
GraphicsWindow.BrushColor = "Black"
GraphicsWindow.FillRectangle(570, 400, 30, 50)
```

You should see that this code just draws and fills eight rectangles along the side of the window. The eight colors were selected to look good on a black background. A last step is to initialize the DrawingColor:

```
' initialize drawing color
DrawingColor = "White"
GraphicsWindow.PenColor = DrawingColor
GraphicsWindow.PenWidth = 1
```

You'll see that this is pretty cool in how it works. Save and run the program to test it out. The color choice rectangles should appear:

Now, we are ready to code the drawing process. There are two events we look for:

- Mouse button press (**MouseDown**) – picks color <u>or</u> starts drawing (if left mouse button)
- Mouse moving (**MouseMove**) - continues drawing (if left mouse button is pressed)

Each of these is a separate mouse event. Add these lines to establish subroutines for these events:

```
' setup event subroutines
GraphicsWindow.MouseDown = MouseDownEvent
GraphicsWindow.MouseMove = MouseMoveEvent

Sub MouseDownEvent
EndSub

Sub MouseMoveEvent
EndSub
```

The **MouseDown** event is executed when a mouse button is clicked. We will only look for **left** button clicks. When that happens, we check the x coordinate (GraphicsWindow.MouseX) to see if it exceeds 570 (the boundary of the color selection rectangles). If so, we determine which rectangle has been clicked (by checking the value of GraphicsWindow.MouseY) and change the **DrawingColor** variable. If the lowest rectangle (the black area) is selected, the graphics window is cleared. If the x coordinate is less than 570, we are starting to draw a line. In this case, we initialize the "last point" variables, **PreviousX** and **PreviousY**.

The event procedure is (it's kind of long):

```
Sub MouseDownEvent
   ' drawing begins or color is changed with left button click
   If (Mouse.IsLeftButtonDown) Then
      If (GraphicsWindow.MouseX > 570) Then
         ' new color
         If (GraphicsWindow.MouseY > 400) Then
            ' clear drawing area
            GraphicsWindow.BrushColor = "Black"
            GraphicsWindow.FillRectangle(0, 0, 570, 450)
         ElseIf (GraphicsWindow.MouseY > 350) Then
            DrawingColor = "Red"
         ElseIf (GraphicsWindow.MouseY > 300) Then
            DrawingColor = "Yellow"
         ElseIf (GraphicsWindow.MouseY > 250) Then
            DrawingColor = "Magenta"
         ElseIf (GraphicsWindow.MouseY > 200) Then
            DrawingColor = "Green"
         ElseIf (GraphicsWindow.MouseY > 150) Then
            DrawingColor = "Cyan"
         ElseIf (GraphicsWindow.MouseY > 100) Then
            DrawingColor = "RoyalBlue"
         ElseIf (GraphicsWindow.MouseY > 50) Then
            DrawingColor = "LightGray"
         Else
            DrawingColor = "White"
         EndIf
      else
      '  drawing begins, save point
         PreviousX = GraphicsWindow.MouseX
         PreviousY = GraphicsWindow.MouseY
      EndIf
   EndIf
EndSub
```

You might wonder why we don't use the **Clear** method to erase the window. Doing this would clear the entire window including the color selection windows. In this code, we use the **FillRectangle** method to 'black out' everything but those rectangles. Save and run to make sure the code is correct. You can't draw yet but you can eliminate any errors.

The **MouseMove** event is executed when the mouse is being moved over the graphics window. In this event, (if the left button is still down) we connect the last point (**PreviousX, PreviousY**) to the current point (**GraphicsWindow.MouseX, GraphicsWindow.MouseY**) using the **DrawLine** method. Once done drawing, the "last point" becomes the "current point." This event subroutine is:

```
Sub MouseMoveEvent
  If (Mouse.IsLeftButtonDown) Then
    '  drawing continues
    GraphicsWindow.PenColor = DrawingColor
    GraphicsWindow.DrawLine(PreviousX, PreviousY,
GraphicsWindow.MouseX, GraphicsWindow.MouseY)
    PreviousX = GraphicsWindow.MouseX
    PreviousY = GraphicsWindow.MouseY
  EndIf
EndSub
```

That's all the code. Make sure both mouse event procedures are typed correctly in the proper location. Save the program by clicking the **Save** button in the Small Basic toolbar.

Here is the complete Blackboard Fun Small Basic code listing (from the editor) – it's your biggest program yet:

```
'
'  Blackboard Fun
'  Beginning Small Basic
'
GraphicsWindow.Title = "Blackboard Fun"
GraphicsWindow.Show()
GraphicsWindow.Width = 600
GraphicsWindow.Height = 450
GraphicsWindow.BackgroundColor = "Black"
' setup color choice rectangles
GraphicsWindow.BrushColor = "White"
GraphicsWindow.FillRectangle(570, 0, 30, 50)
GraphicsWindow.BrushColor = "LightGray"
GraphicsWindow.FillRectangle(570, 50, 30, 50)
GraphicsWindow.BrushColor = "RoyalBlue"
GraphicsWindow.FillRectangle(570, 100, 30, 50)
GraphicsWindow.BrushColor = "Cyan"
GraphicsWindow.FillRectangle(570, 150, 30, 50)
GraphicsWindow.BrushColor = "Green"
GraphicsWindow.FillRectangle(570, 200, 30, 50)
GraphicsWindow.BrushColor = "Magenta"
GraphicsWindow.FillRectangle(570, 250, 30, 50)
GraphicsWindow.BrushColor = "Yellow"
GraphicsWindow.FillRectangle(570, 300, 30, 50)
GraphicsWindow.BrushColor = "Red"
GraphicsWindow.FillRectangle(570, 350, 30, 50)
GraphicsWindow.BrushColor = "Black"
GraphicsWindow.FillRectangle(570, 400, 30, 50)
' initialize drawing color
DrawingColor = "White"
GraphicsWindow.PenColor = DrawingColor
GraphicsWindow.PenWidth = 1

' setup event subroutines
GraphicsWindow.MouseDown = MouseDownEvent
GraphicsWindow.MouseMove = MouseMoveEvent

Sub MouseDownEvent
   '  drawing begins or color is changed with left button click
   If (Mouse.IsLeftButtonDown) Then
     If (GraphicsWindow.MouseX > 570) Then
```

```
        ' new color
        If (GraphicsWindow.MouseY > 400) Then
          ' clear drawing area
          GraphicsWindow.BrushColor = "Black"
          GraphicsWindow.FillRectangle(0, 0, 570, 450)
        ElseIf (GraphicsWindow.MouseY > 350) Then
          DrawingColor = "Red"
        ElseIf (GraphicsWindow.MouseY > 300) Then
          DrawingColor = "Yellow"
        ElseIf (GraphicsWindow.MouseY > 250) Then
          DrawingColor = "Magenta"
        ElseIf (GraphicsWindow.MouseY > 200) Then
          DrawingColor = "Green"
        ElseIf (GraphicsWindow.MouseY > 150) Then
          DrawingColor = "Cyan"
        ElseIf (GraphicsWindow.MouseY > 100) Then
          DrawingColor = "RoyalBlue"
        ElseIf (GraphicsWindow.MouseY > 50) Then
          DrawingColor = "LightGray"
        Else
          DrawingColor = "White"
        EndIf
      else
      ' drawing begins, save point
        PreviousX = GraphicsWindow.MouseX
        PreviousY = GraphicsWindow.MouseY
      EndIf
    EndIf
EndSub

Sub MouseMoveEvent
  If (Mouse.IsLeftButtonDown) Then
    ' drawing continues
    GraphicsWindow.PenColor = DrawingColor
    GraphicsWindow.DrawLine(PreviousX, PreviousY,
GraphicsWindow.MouseX, GraphicsWindow.MouseY)
    PreviousX = GraphicsWindow.MouseX
    PreviousY = GraphicsWindow.MouseY
  EndIf
EndSub
```

Run the Program

Run the program. By building and testing in stages, any errors seen now (if any) should be minimal. The finished running product should look like this:

Choose a color by clicking one of the eight displayed rectangles. Draw a line in the window. Try other colors. Draw something.

Here's my attempt at art:

I've had students draw perfect pictures of Fred Flintstone and Homer Simpson using this program. Make sure each color works. Make sure the clear function (click below the last colored rectangle) works. As always, thoroughly test your program. Save it if you had to make any changes while running it.

Do you see how simple the drawing part of this program is? Most of the code is used just to set and select colors. The actual drawing portion of the code (MouseDown, MouseMove events) is only a few lines of Small Basic! This shows two things: (1) those drawing programs you use are really not that hard to build and (2) there is a lot of power in the Small Basic graphics methods.

Other Things to Try

The Blackboard Fun program offers lots of opportunity for improvement with added options. Add the ability to change the background color of the blackboard. Determine and build logic that allows drawing different colored lines depending on whether you press the left or right mouse button. For this, I'd suggest creating a left pen and a right pen. You will also need some way for the user to choose colors for each pen. Then, apply the appropriate pen in the various mouse events depending on what button is pressed.

As written, you can draw lines in the color selection area. Correct this problem. Notice, too, if you click a color and move the mouse before releasing the mouse button, unintended lines are drawn. See if you can correct this problem.

Have a adjustable pen width. Here's a little picture I drew with a pen 20 pixels wide:

Here's another possibility to try. Delete (or 'comment out') these lines in the **MouseMove** event:

```
PreviousX = GraphicsWindow.MouseX
PreviousY = GraphicsWindow.MouseY
```

By doing this, the first point clicked (in the Mousedown event) is always the last point and all line drawing originates from this original point. Now, run the program again. Notice the "fanning" effect. Pretty, huh?

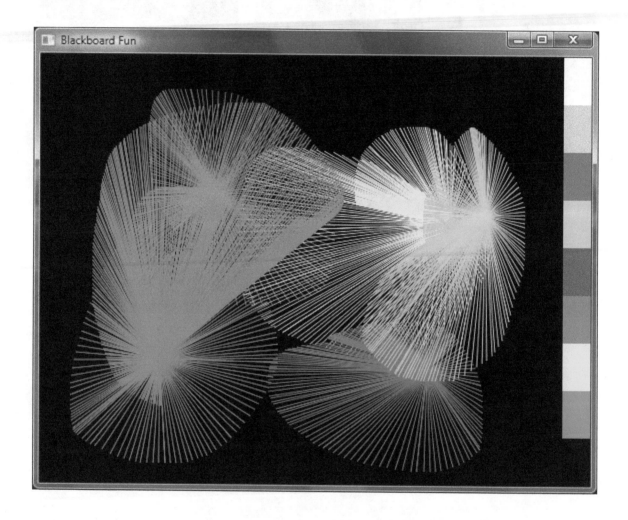

Play around and see what other effects (change colors randomly, draw little filled rectangles). Have fun!

You've now had your first experience with graphics programming in Small Basic using the DrawLine, DrawRectangle and FillRectangle methods. You learned about two important events to help in drawing: MouseDown and MouseMove. And, you learned about colors. In the next class, we'll continue looking at using graphics in programs. And, we'll look at some ways to design simple computer games.

9

Timers, Animation, Keyboard Methods

Review and Preview

By now, you should have some confidence in your abilities as a Small Basic programmer. In this class, we'll look at another item that's a lot of fun - the Timer object. It's a key object for adding animation (motion) to graphics in programs using the Shapes object. We study some animation techniques. We will also examine how to recognize user inputs from the keyboard via keyboard events. You'll build another program - your first video game! And, we'll see how you can share your programs with others over the Internet.

Timer Object

In the Class 8, we saw that event procedures (subroutines) were executed in a GUI application when the user caused some event to happen (usually with the mouse). The Small Basic **Timer object** has an interesting feature. It can generate events (called **Tick** events) without any input from the user. Timer objects work in your program's background, generating events at time intervals you specify. This event generation feature comes in handy for graphics animation where screen displays need to be updated at regular intervals.

Using a timer object is fairly simple:

- Assign the timer's **Tick** event to an event procedure (subroutine) that contains code to be executed with each event.
- Decide how often you want to generate Tick events; this is the timer's **Interval** property. The interval is measured in milliseconds. There are 1000 milliseconds in one second.

These steps are straightforward. Here is code to assign the **Tick** event to a subroutine named **TimerTickEvent** and set the **Interval** property to 1000 milliseconds.

```
Timer.Tick = TimerTickEvent
Timer.Interval = 1000
```

The **TimerTickEvent** would be in a subroutine of the form:

```
Sub TimerTickEvent
  ' code to execute with each Tick event
EndSub
```

There are two timer object methods we need to monitor status. To start a timer and begin event processing, use:

```
Timer.Resume()
```

To stop the timer and stop event processing, use:

```
Timer.Pause()
```

Note: By default, the timer is "turned on" meaning event processing will immediately begin when starting a program with a timer object.

Examples

A few examples should clarify how the timer object works. It's very simple and very powerful. To review, here's what happens. When a timer is running, every **Interval** milliseconds, Small Basic will generate an event and execute the corresponding **Tick** event subroutine. No user interaction is needed.

The Interval property is important. This property is set to the number of milliseconds between timer events. A millisecond is 1/1000th of a second, or there are 1,000 milliseconds in a second. If you want to generate N events per second, set the delay to 1000 / N. For example, if you want a timer event to occur 4 times per second, use a delay of 250. About the lowest practical value for delay is 50 and values that differ by 5, 10, or even 20 are likely to produce similar results. It all depends on your particular computer. Now, let's try some examples.

Start Small Basic, start a new program and save it as **Timer**. Add this code:

```
GraphicsWindow.Show()
GraphicsWindow.Width = 400
GraphicsWindow.Height = 300
GraphicsWindow.Title = "Timer Example"
Timer.Tick = TimerTickEvent
Timer.Interval = 1000

Sub TimerTickEvent
  Sound.PlayBellRing()
EndSub
```

In this listing, the first four lines of the code should be familiar and understood by you – it just creates and sizes a graphics window.

The remaining code states the **TimerTickEvent** will be the subroutine holding code for the timer's **Tick** event and that the timer's **Interval** is 1000 milliseconds (1 second). The TimerTickEvent subroutine has a single line of code:

```
Sub TimerTickEvent
  Sound.PlayBellRing()
EndSub
```

This line makes your computer play a bell ringing sound, or is that obvious? The code uses the Small Basic **Sound** object which has some built-in sounds.

Save and run the program. A blank graphics window will appear. Recall the timer is on by default, so your computer will play a bell sound every second (the Tick event is generated every 1000 milliseconds, the Interval value) until you stop the program. Notice it does this no matter what else is going on. It requires no input (once the timer is on) from you, the user. Stop the program when you get tired of the ringing.

Let's modify the program so you can control starting and stopping of the ringing. When the user clicks the graphics window, we want the timer (and associated ringing) to start. When it is clicked again, we want it to stop. Add the shaded lines to the 'main' code in the program:

```
GraphicsWindow.Show()
GraphicsWindow.Width = 400
GraphicsWindow.Height = 300
GraphicsWindow.Title = "Timer Example"
Timer.Tick = TimerTickEvent
Timer.Interval = 1000
Timer.Pause()
TimerOn = "false"
GraphicsWindow.MouseDown = MouseDownEvent
```

Here, we make sure the timer object is initially off (paused). We establish a variable **TimerOn** to keep track of timer status (initially set to "false"). And we point the **MouseDown** event to the **MouseDownEvent** subroutine, where we will turn the timer on and off.

Add the **MouseDownEvent** subroutine:

```
Sub MouseDownEvent
  If (TimerOn = "true") Then
    TimerOn = "false"
    Timer.Pause()
  Else
    TimerOn = "true"
    Timer.Resume()
  EndIf
EndSub
```

This code is executed whenever the graphics window is clicked by the mouse. What does this code do? If the timer is on (TimerOn is "true"), it stops (Pause method) the timer and vice versa. We say this code "toggles" the timer.

Save and run the program. A blank graphics window will appear. There should be no ringing since the timer is off. Click the window. The timer will start and your computer will play a bell sound every second (the Tick event is generated every 1000 milliseconds, the Interval value) until you click the window again. Once again, stop the program when you get tired of the ringing.

Add the shaded line to the timer's **TimerTickEvent** subroutine, so it reads:

```
Sub TimerTickEvent
  Sound.PlayBellRing()
  GraphicsWindow.BackgroundColor = GraphicsWindow.GetRandomColor()
EndSub
```

Can you see that this code changes the graphics window background color using random values? Run the program. Click the window. Now, every second, the computer rings and the window changes color. Stop the timer. Stop the program.

Let's use the timer to do some flashier stuff. Change the timer **Interval** property to **50**. Replace the **TimerTickEvent** subroutine with this code:

```
Sub TimerTickEvent
  GraphicsWindow.PenColor = GraphicsWindow.GetRandomColor()
  GraphicsWindow.DrawEllipse(Delta, Delta, 400 - 2 * Delta, 300 -
2 * Delta)
  Delta = Delta + 1
  If (Delta > 150) Then
    Delta = 0
    GraphicsWindow.Clear()
  EndIf
EndSub
```

You should recognize most of what's here. We've speeded up the timer object. In the event subroutine, a random color is selected and used to draw an ellipse. This (**DrawEllipse**) is a graphics method we haven't seen before. You should be able to understand it and you'll see it gives a really neat effect in this example.

The **DrawEllipse** method has the form:

```
GraphicsWindow.DrawEllipse(x, y, width, height)
```

This statement draws an ellipse, with a width **width** and height **height**, in the graphics window starting at the point (**x**, **y**). A picture shows the result:

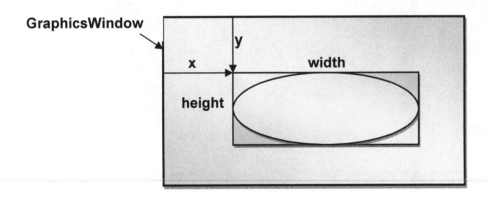

In your work with Small Basic, you will often see code you don't recognize. Use the usual reference facilities, such as the on-line help offered by Small Basic, other programmers, text books or the old reliable Microsoft website in these cases. Try it with **DrawEllipse**. Also look at **FillEllipse** – it has an identical form as DrawOval, the difference being an oval filled with the current brush color will be drawn.

Back to the code, you should see the **DrawEllipse** method draws the first ellipse around the border of the window (**x = 0** initially). The surrounding rectangle moves "in" an amount **Delta** (in each direction) with each "tick" of the timer, resulting in a smaller rectangle (the width and height are decreased by both **2 * Delta**). Once Delta (incremented by one in each step) exceeds half of the window height (150 in this case), it is reset to 0, the window is cleared and the process starts all over. Run the program. Click the window. Are you hypnotized? Here's one of my runs:

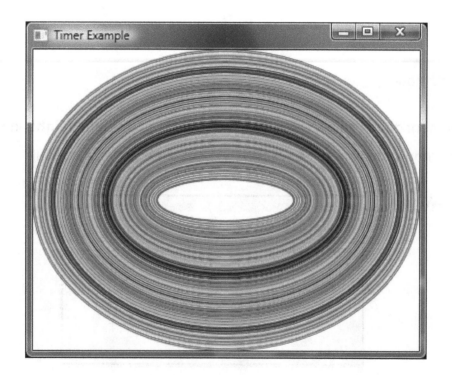

Can you think of other things you could draw using other graphics methods? Look at **DrawRectangle** for example. Try your ideas.

In this last example, the periodic (every 0.050 seconds) changing of the display in the graphics object, imparted by the timer object, gives the appearance of motion – the ovals seem to be moving inward. This is the basic concept behind a very powerful graphics technique - **animation**. In animation, we have a sequence of pictures, each a little different from the previous one. With the ellipse example, in each picture, we add a new ellipse. By displaying this sequence over time, we can trick the viewer into thinking things are moving. It all has to do with how fast the human eye and brain can process information. That's how cartoons work - 24 different pictures are displayed every second - it makes things look like they are moving, or animated. Obviously, the timer object is a key element to animation, as well as for other Small Basic timing tasks. In the Small Basic lesson for this class, we will look at how to do simple animations and some other things.

For your reference, this last version of the program is saved in the **Timer** folder in the course programs folder (**BeginSB\BSB Code**).

Small Basic - The Final Lesson

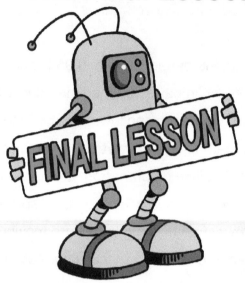

In this last Small Basic lesson, we look at how to add text to a graphics application, study some simple animation techniques using shapes, look at math needed with animations, and learn how to detect keyboard events.

DrawText Method

We would like some capability to add text information to a window. We'll use this in the program we build at the end of this class. You will find it useful for adding labeling information to graphics applications. The method that does such a task is the **DrawText** graphics method – yes, text is "drawn" to the window. The **DrawText** method is:

```
GraphicsWindow.DrawText(x, y, text)
```

In this statement, **text** represents the string to print in the window and the point (**x, y**) is where the string will be located. The string will draw in the graphics window using the current brush color using the default font. Note this method uses the brush color, not the pen color – text is truly drawn like other graphics objects.

Let's try a quick example. Start Small Basic, start a new program. Use this code:

```
GraphicsWindow.Show()
Graphicswindow.Width = 400
GraphicsWindow.Height = 300
GraphicsWindow.DrawText(40, 100, "Isn't Beginning Small Basic
fun?")
```

This code simply creates a graphics window and displays the text information "Isn't Beginning Small Basic fun?" Run the program. You should see:

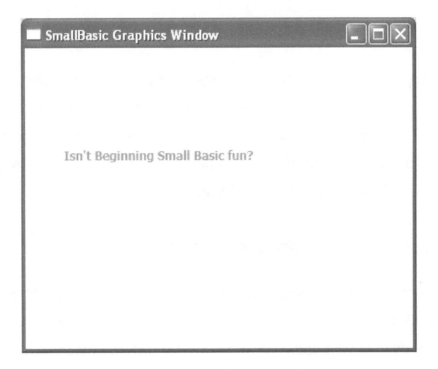

By setting the (x, y) point, you can left or right justify the text, or center it horizontally and/or vertically by knowing the window dimensions. It is possible to change the font (type, size, style) using Small Basic code, but that is beyond our discussion in this class. Perhaps, you can do some research on your own to figure out how to do this. It involves something called a **Font** object – what else?

Animation

In an earlier example (the one with the hypnotic ellipses), we saw that by using a timer to periodically change the display in a window, a sense of motion, or animation, is obtained. We will use that idea here to do a specific kind of animation - moving objects around. This is the basis for nearly every video game ever made. The objects we move will be rectangular regions like rectangles and ellipses. As you advance in your Small Basic programming, you will find that all graphics objects (including pictures) are rectangular, so the information here will apply when you learn how to add pictures to a program. The objects we move are Small Basic **Shapes** objects.

A **Shapes** object is a rectangular region we can add, move and remove within the graphics window. Such an object makes animation (moving objects) very simple. For now, we will use two types of **Shapes** objects – a rectangle and an ellipse. To create a rectangular shape (**MyRectangle**) that is **RectW** pixels wide and **RectH** pixels high, use the **AddRectangle** method:

```
MyRectangle = Shapes.AddRectangle(RectW, RectH)
```

This will create a 'bordered' rectangle. The current pen color establishes the rectangle's border color, while the current brush color establishes the fill color. By default, it will be put in the upper left corner of the graphics window.

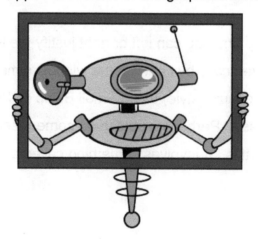

Start Small Basic and type these lines of code in the editor:

```
GraphicsWindow.Show()
GraphicsWindow.PenColor = "Blue"
GraphicsWindow.BrushColor = "Red"
MyRectangle = Shapes.AddRectangle(100, 50)
```

Run the program to see the resulting rectangle (100 pixels wide, 50 pixels high, blue border, red fill) in the upper left corner of the window:

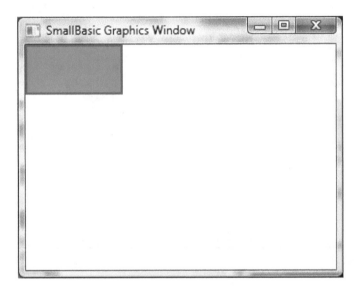

Analogously, to create an elliptical shape (**MyEllipse**) that is **EllW** pixels wide and **EllH** pixels high, use the **AddEllipse** method:

```
MyEllipse = Shapes.AddEllipse(EllW, EllH)
```

This will create a 'bordered' ellipse. The current pen color establishes the ellipse border color, while the current brush color establishes the fill color. By default, it will be put in the upper left corner of the graphics window.

Replace the code in the Small Basic editor with this code:

```
GraphicsWindow.Show()
GraphicsWindow.PenColor = "Red"
GraphicsWindow.BrushColor = "Yellow"
MyEllipse = Shapes.AddRectangle(50, 100)
```

When run this, you will see an ellipse 50 pixels wide by 100 pixels high with a red border and yellow fill:

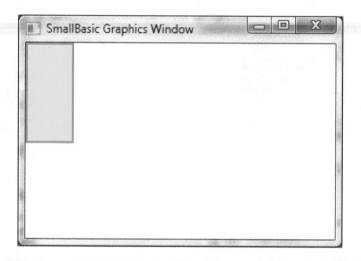

Moving shape objects in a graphics window is easy to do. It is a simple two step process: use some rule to determine a new position, then redraw it in this new position using the Shapes object **Move** method. If you have a shape object named **MyShape** and you want to move it to (**NewX**, **NewY**), the code is:

```
Shapes.Move(MyShape, NewX, NewY)
```

This code will 'erase' **MyShape** at its current position, then 'redraw' it at the newly specified position. Successive transfers (or moves) gives the impression of motion, or animation. Modify the ellipse example by adding the one line of code using the **Move** method:

```
Shapes.Move(MyEllipse, 100, 50)
```

Rerun and you will see the ellipse has disappeared from the upper left corner](0, 0)] of the window and moved to the new position at (100, 50).

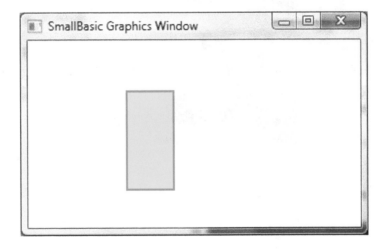

Where do we put the statements implementing this erase-then-draw process? Each object to be moved must have an associated timer object. The "drawing" statement is placed in the timer object's Tick event. Whenever a timer event is triggered, a new shape position is computed and the corresponding graphics method to move the shape is executed. This periodic movement is animation. Let's look at an example to see how simple animation with shapes really is.

Example

Return to Small Basic and start a new program. Name it **Animate**. We resize the graphics window to make it taller than it is wide. We add a timer object (100 millisecond **Interval**) and an empty **Tick** event subroutine (**TimerTickEvent**). We make sure the timer is off initially (using **TimerOn** to monitor status). We also add a **MouseDown** event subroutine (**MouseDownEvent**) to toggle the timer. You can copy much of this code from the **Timer** example we tried earlier. The code is:

```
GraphicsWindow.Show()
GraphicsWindow.Width = 200
GraphicsWindow.Height = 400
GraphicsWindow.Title = "Animation"
Timer.Tick = TimerTickEvent
Timer.Interval = 100
Timer.Pause()
TimerOn = "false"
GraphicsWindow.MouseDown = MouseDownEvent

Sub TimerTickEvent
EndSub

Sub MouseDownEvent
  If (TimerOn = "true") Then
    TimerOn = "false"
    Timer.Pause()
  Else
    TimerOn = "true"
    Timer.Resume()
  EndIf
EndSub
```

We will use this example a lot.

Save and run to make sure things look okay – the graphics window should appear as:

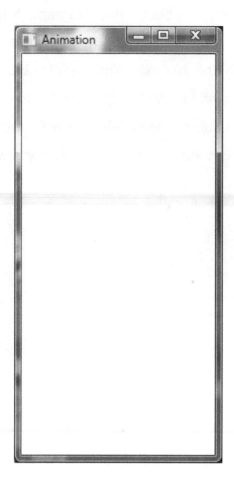

Now, let's add the code to try some animation.

We will see if we can make a ball (represented by an ellipse) drop down the window. Add this code to the 'main' code region to define a shape object (**Ball**):

```
BallX = 75
BallY = 0
BallW = 50
BallH = 50
BallDir = 1
GraphicsWindow.PenColor = "Black"
GraphicsWindow.BrushColor = "Red"
Ball = Shapes.AddEllipse(BallW, BallH)
Shapes.Move(Ball, BallX, BallY)
```

The ball is 50 pixels wide (**BallW**) and 50 pixels high (**BallH**) (which technically makes it a circle, not an ellipse) and is colored red, with a black border. We use a variable (**BallY**) to keep track of the vertical position. We initially move the ball to horizontally center it (using **BallX** = 75) at the top of the window. Now, use this code in the timer's **TimerTickEvent** subroutine to move the ball:

```
Sub TimerTickEvent
  BallY = BallY + 10
  Shapes.Move(Ball, BallX, BallY)
EndSub
```

In this routine, the vertical position of the ball (**BallY**) is increased by 10 pixels each time the event is executed (every 0.1 seconds). The ball is moving down. It should take 40 executions of this routine, or about 4 seconds, for the ball to reach the bottom of the window. Let's try it.

Run the example program. Click the window to start the timer. Watch the ball drop. Here's what it should look like:

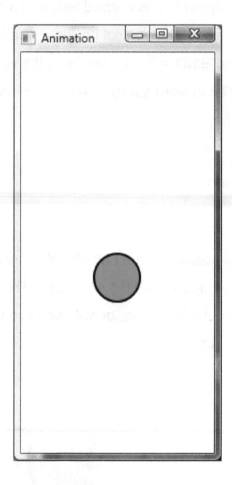

Pretty easy, wasn't it? How long does it take the ball to reach the bottom? What happens when it reaches the bottom? It just keeps on going down through the window and out through the bottom of your computer monitor to who knows where! We need to be able to detect this disappearance and do something about it. We'll look at two ways to handle this. First, we'll make the ball reappear at the top of the window, or scroll. Then, we'll make it bounce. Stop the program. Save it too. We'll be using it again.

Object Disappearance

When shape objects are moving in a window, we need to know when they move out of the window across a border. Such information is often needed in video type games. We just saw this need with the falling ball example. When an **object disappearance** happens, we can either ignore that object or perhaps make it "scroll" around to other side of the window. How do we decide if an object has disappeared? It's basically a case of comparing various positions and dimensions.

We need to detect whether an object has completely moved across one of four window borders (top, bottom, left, right). Each of these detections can be developed using this diagram of a rectangular object within a graphics window (**GraphicsWindow**):

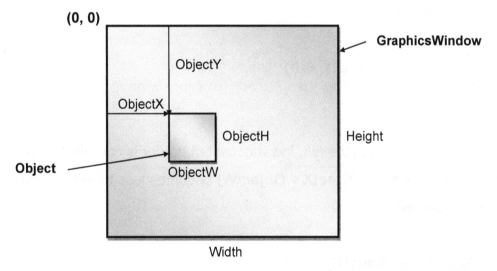

Notice the object is located at (**ObjectX**, **ObjectY**) and is **ObjectW** pixels wide and **ObjectH** pixels high.

The graphics window is **Width** pixels wide and **Height** pixels high. You usually know these values from the statement that originally created the window. To obtain these values in code, you can use (this makes your code more general):

```
Width = GraphicsWindow.Width
Height = GraphicsWindow.Height
```

If the object is moving down, it completely crosses the window bottom border when its top (**ObjectY**) is lower than the bottom border. The bottom of the window is **GraphicsWindow.Height**. Small Basic code for a bottom border disappearance is:

```
If (ObjectY > GraphicsWindow.Height) Then
  'Small Basic code for bottom border disappearance
EndIf
```

If the object is moving up, the window top border is completely crossed when the bottom of the object (**ObjectY + ObjectH**) becomes less than 0. In Small Basic, this is detected with:

```
If ((ObjectY + ObjectH) < 0) Then
  'Small Basic code for top border disappearance
EndIf
```

If the object is moving to the left, the window left border is completely crossed when object right side (**ObjectX + ObjectW**) becomes less than 0. In Small Basic, this is detected with:

```
If ((ObjectX + ObjectW) < 0) Then
  'Small Basic code for left border disappearance
EndIf
```

If the object is moving to the right, it completely crosses the window right border when its left side (**ObjectX**) passes the border. The right side of the window is **GraphicsWindow.Width**. Small Basic code for a right border disappearance is:

```
If (ObjectX > GraphicsWindow.Width) Then
  'Small Basic code for right border disappearance
EndIf
```

Let's add disappearance detection to our "falling ball" example. Return to that program. Say, instead of having the ball disappear when it reaches the bottom, we have it magically reappear at the top of the window - the object is scrolling. Modify the **TimerTickEvent** subroutine to this (new lines are shaded):

```
Sub TimerTickEvent
  BallY = BallY + 10
  If (BallY > GraphicsWindow.Height) Then
    BallY = -BallH
  EndIf
  Shapes.Move(Ball, BallX, BallY)
EndSub
```

We added the bottom border disappearance logic. When the ball disappears, we reset its BallY value so it is repositioned just off the top of the window. Run the program. Watch the ball scroll. Pretty easy, wasn't it? Stop and save the program.

Border Crossing

What if, in the falling ball example, instead of scrolling, we want the ball to bounce back up when it reaches the bottom border? This is another common animation task - detecting the initiation of **border crossings**. Such crossings are used to change the direction of moving objects, that is, make them bounce. How do we detect border crossings?

The same diagram used for image disappearances can be used here. Checking to see if an image has crossed a window border is like checking for object disappearance, except the object has not moved quite as far. For top and bottom checks, the object movement is less by an amount equal to its height (ObjectH). For left and right checks, the movement is less by an amount equal to its width (ObjectW). Look back at that diagram and you should see these code segments accomplish the respective border crossing directions:

```
If (ObjectY < 0) Then
  'Small Basic code for top border crossing
EndIf


If ((ObjectY + ObjectH) > GraphicsWindow.Height) Then
  'Small Basic code for bottom border crossing
EndIf


If (ObjectX < 0) Then
  'Small Basic code for left border crossing
EndIf


If ((ObjectX + ObjectW) > GraphicsWindow.Width) Then
  'Small Basic code for right border crossing
EndIf
```

Let's modify the falling ball example to have it bounce when it reaches the bottom of the window. Define a new variable **BallDir.** BallDir is used to indicate which way the object (ball) is moving. When BallDir is 1, the ball is moving down (BallY is increasing). When BallDir is -1, the ball is moving up (BallY is decreasing). Initialize the variable to 1 in the main code:

```
BallDir = 1
```

Change the **TimerTickEvent** subroutine to this (again, changed and/or new lines are shaded):

```
Sub TimerTickEvent
  BallY = BallY + BallDir * 10
  If ((BallY + BallH) > GraphicsWindow.Height) Then
    BallY = GraphicsWindow.Height - BallH
    BallDir = -1
  EndIf
  Shapes.Move(Ball, BallX, BallY)
EndSub
```

We modified the calculation of BallY to account for the BallDir variable. Notice how it is used to impart the proper direction to the ball motion (down when BallDir is 1, up when BallDir is –1). We have also added the If structure for a bottom border crossing. Notice when a crossing is detected, the ball is repositioned (by resetting BallY) at the bottom of the window (**GraphicsWindow.Height - BallH**) and BallDir is set to -1 (direction is changed so the ball will start moving up). Run the program. Now when the ball reaches the bottom of the window, it reverses direction and heads back up. We've made the ball bounce! But, once it reaches the top, it's gone again!

Add top border crossing detection, so the timer **TimerTickEvent** subroutine is now (changes are shaded):

```
Sub TimerTickEvent
  BallY = BallY + BallDir * 10
  If ((BallY + BallH) > GraphicsWindow.Height) Then
    BallY = GraphicsWindow.Height - BallH
    BallDir = -1
    Sound.PlayBellRing()
  ElseIf (BallY < 0) Then
    BallY = 0
    BallDir = 1
    Sound.PlayBellRing()
  EndIf
  Shapes.Move(Ball, BallX, BallY)
EndSub
```

In the top crossing code (the ElseIf portion), we reset BallY to 0 (the top of the window) and change BallDir to 1. We've also added a couple of "bell ring" statements so there is some audible feedback when either bounce occurs. Run the program again. Your ball will now bounce up and down, ringing with each bounce, until you stop it. Stop and save the program.

The code we've developed here for checking and resetting object positions is a common task in Small Basic. As you develop your programming skills, you should make sure you are comfortable with what all these locations and dimensions mean and how they interact. As an example, can you see why a horizontal position of 75 centers the ball in the window? The equation used was:

```
BallX = 0.5 * (GraphicsWindow.Width - BallW)
```

Plug in the window width of 200 and ball width of 50 and the calculation gives you the resulting 75.

You've now seen how to do lots of things with animations. You can make objects move, make them disappear and reappear, and make them bounce. Do you have some ideas of simple video games you would like to build? You still need two more skills – object erasure and collision detection - which are discussed next.

Object Erasure

The **Shapes** method **Move** erases a shape in its previous location before moving it to a new location. This erasure is automatic. What if you need to do this in a program – that is, you need to remove a shape from the graphics window? Perhaps in a video game, your spaceship shoots down an alien ship and you need to erase that ship. The **Shapes** method that does this is **Remove**. If we want to completely erase a previously defined shape object (**MyShape**) from the graphics window, use:

```
Shapes.Remove(MyShape)
```

This does not delete the shape object from the program. It is still available for animation use. Subsequent Move methods can be used to place the shape back in the window.

Collision Detection

Another requirement in animation is to determine if two objects have collided. This is needed in games to see if a ball hits a paddle, if an alien rocket hits its target, or if a cute little character grabs some reward. Each object is described by a rectangular area, so the **collision detection** problem is to see if two rectangles collide, or overlap. This check is done using each object's position and dimensions.

Here are two objects (**Object1** and **Object2**) in a window:

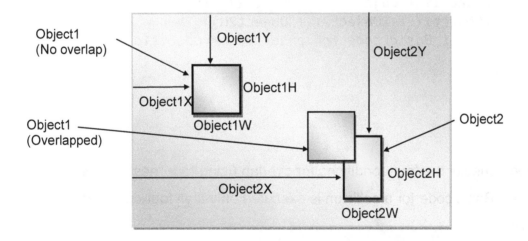

Object1 is positioned at (**Object1X**, **Object1Y**), is **Object1W** wide and **Object1H** high. Similarly, **Object2** is positioned at (**Object2X**, **Object2Y**), is **Object2W** wide and **Object2H** high.

Looking at this diagram, you should see there are four requirements for the two rectangles to overlap:

1. The right side of Object1 (**Object1X + Object1H**) must be "farther right" than the left side of Object2 (**Object2X**)

2. The left side of Object1 (**Object1X**) must be "farther left" than the right side of Object2 (**Object2X + Object2W**)

3. The bottom of Object1 (**Object1Y + Object1H**) must be "farther down" than the top of Object2 (**Object2Y**)

4. The top of Object1 (**Object1Y**) must be "farther up" than the bottom of Object2 (**Object2Y + Object2H**)

All four of these requirements must be met for a collision.

The Small Basic code to check if these rectangles overlap is:

```
If ((Object1X + Object1W) > Object2X) Then
  If (Object1X < (Object2X + Object2W)) Then
    If ((Object1Y + Object1H) > Object2Y) Then
      If (Object1Y < (Object2Y + Object2H)) Then
        ' Small Basic code for overlap, or collision
      EndIf
    EndIf
  EndIf
EndIf
```

This code checks the four conditions for overlap using four "nested" If structures. The Small Basic code for a collision is executed only if all four conditions are found to be true.

Let's try some collision detection with the bouncing ball example. We will draw a small paddle (a rectangle) near the bottom of the window and see if the ball collides with the paddle. Add these variables to establish the paddle object (**Paddle**) (I placed these lines at the end of my main code):

```
PaddleX = 100
PaddleY = 380
PaddleW= 20
PaddleH = 20
GraphicsWindow.PenColor = "Black"
GraphicsWindow.BrushColor = "Blue"
Paddle = Shapes.AddRectangle(PaddleW, PaddleH)
Shapes.Move(Paddle, PaddleX, PaddleY)
```

Modify the timer **TimerTickEvent** subroutine code to (added code is shaded):

```
Sub TimerTickEvent
  BallY = BallY + BallDir * 10
  Collision = "false"
  If ((BallX + BallW) > PaddleX) Then
    If (BallX < (PaddleX + PaddleW)) Then
      If ((BallY + BallH) > PaddleY) Then
        If (BallY < (PaddleY + PaddleH)) Then
          Collision = "true"
        EndIf
      EndIf
    EndIf
  EndIf
  If (Collision = "true") Then
    BallY = PaddleY - BallH
    BallDir = -1
    Sound.PlayBellRing()
  ElseIf (BallY < 0) Then
    BallY = 0
    BallDir = 1
    Sound.PlayBellRing()
  EndIf
  Shapes.Move(Ball, BallX, BallY)
EndSub
```

We use a variable **Collision** to indicate an overlap (true for overlap, false for no overlap). The overlap code (using the paddle object variables PaddleX, PaddleY, PaddleW, PaddleH) precedes the Move method. If a collision is detected, the object (ball) is repositioned so it just touches the top of the rectangle, its direction is reversed and a ring is played. The code for bouncing off the top of the window is unchanged.

Run the program. You should see:

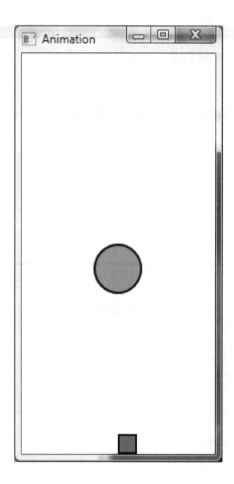

Notice the ball now bounces off the paddle. Stop the program. Move the paddle out of the way (set PaddleX to 0) so the ball won't collide with it. The ball should just drop off the screen. See how close the ball can pass by the paddle without colliding to make sure the overlap routine works properly. Stop and save the program.

Now that you know how to detect collisions, you're well on your way to knowing how to build a simple video game. Next, we'll learn how to detect keyboard events from the user. One possible use for these events, among many, is to allow a user to move the little paddle to "hit" the dropping ball. The collision technique we just learned will come in handy for such a task.

Keyboard Methods

In Class 8, we looked at ways for a user to interact with a Small Basic program using the mouse for input. We studied two mouse events and associated methods: **MouseDown** and **MouseMove**. Another input device available for use is the computer keyboard. Here we look at **keyboard events** which give our programs the ability to detect user input from the keyboard. Just one keyboard event is studied: the **KeyDown** event.

KeyDown Event

The **KeyDown** event has the ability to detect the pressing of a key on the computer keyboard. Among others, it can detect:

- Letter and number keys
- Numeric keypad keys (it can distinguish these numbers from those on the top row of the keyboard)
- Cursor control keys

The **KeyDown** event is triggered whenever a key is pressed. If the subroutine to be executed in case of such an event is **KeyDownEvent**, we add this event to our program using:

```
GraphicsWindow.KeyDown = KeyDownEvent
```

The corresponding subroutine is added to the program in the usual manner and has the form:

```
Sub KeyDownEvent
  ' Small Basic code for KeyDown event
EndSub
```

To determine which key was pressed, use the **LastKey** method of the graphics window:

```
KeyPressed = GraphicsWindow.LastKey
```

KeyPressed returns a string representation of the pressed key. Here are returned values for some of the keys on a standard keyboard.

Letter and Number Keys

Key	Value	Key	Value	Key	Value	Key	Value
A	"A"	J	"J"	S	"S"	1	"D1"
B	"B"	K	"K"	T	"T"	2	"D2"
C	"C"	L	"L"	U	"U"	3	"D3"
D	"D"	M	"M"	V	"V"	4	"D4"
E	"E"	N	"N"	W	"W"	5	"D5"
F	"F"	O	"O"	X	"X"	6	"D6"
G	"G"	P	"P"	Y	"Y"	7	"D7"
H	"H"	Q	"Q"	Z	"Z"	8	"D8"
I	"I"	R	"R"	0	"D0"	9	"D9"

Numeric Keypad Keys

Key	Value	Key	Value
0	"NumPad0"	8	"NumPad8"
1	"NumPad1"	9	"NumPad9"
2	"NumPad2"	/	"Divide"
3	"NumPad3"	*	"Multiply"
4	"NumPad4"	-	"Subtract"
5	"NumPad5"	+	"Add"
6	"NumPad6"	Enter	"Return"
7	"NumPad7"	.	"Decimal"

Cursor Control Keys

Key	Value	Key	Value
Left arrow	"Left"	Delete	"Delete"
Right arrow	"Right"	Home	"Home"
Up arrow	"Up"	End	"End"
Down arrow	"Down"	Page Up	"PageUp"
Insert	"Insert"	Page Down	"Next"

Using the **KeyDown** event is not easy. There is a lot of work involved in interpreting the information provided in the KeyDown event and **LastKey** method. For example, the KeyDown event cannot distinguish between an upper and lower case letter and many symbols (!, @, #, …) cannot be easily recognized (it is possible to make such distinctions but beyond the scope of this tutorial).   You usually use an If structure to determine which key was pressed. For example, to see if the letter Q is pressed, we would write code like this:

```
If (GraphicsWindow.LastKey = "Q") Then
   ' code to execute if Q is pressed
EndIf
```

Notice you must enclose the desired key value in quotes since it is a string value. Let's see how to use KeyDown to recognize some keys.

Start Small Basic and start a new program. Add this code:

```
GraphicsWindow.KeyDown = KeyDownEvent

Sub KeyDownEvent
  TextWindow.WriteLine("You pressed " + GraphicsWindow.LastKey)
EndSubEndSub
```

Here we assign the **KeyDown** event to the **KeyDownEvent** subroutine. In this subroutine, we have a single line that writes out the pressed key value (using the **LastKey** method) in the text window.

Run this little program. An empty graphics window will appear. Press a key – a text window will appear with a message indicating which key you pressed. Move the graphics and text windows so you can see them both. At this point, click in the graphics window to make it the active window and able to accept further key presses. Type a letter. The letter's corresponding **LastKey** value (without quotes) is shown. Press the same letter while holding down the <Shift> key. The same value will appear – there is no distinction between upper and lower case. Press each of the four arrow keys to see their different values. Type numbers using the top row of the keyboard and the numeric keypad. Notice the keypad numbers have different key code values than the "keyboard numbers." This lets us distinguish the keypad from the keyboard. Try various keys on the keyboard to see which keys have a key code (all of them). Notice it works with function keys, cursor control keys, letters, numbers, everything! Stop the program.

Now, let's modify the animation example we've been working on to use the left and right cursor control keys to move the little rectangle. Open your saved copy of the animation program (**Animate**). Add this line of code (in the main code area) to set up the **KeyDown** event:

```
GraphicsWindow.KeyDown = KeyDownEvent
```

Add the **KeyDownEvent** subroutine:

```
Sub KeyDownEvent
  '  compute new location of paddle
  If (GraphicsWindow.LastKey = "Left") Then
    PaddleX = PaddleX -1
  ElseIf (GraphicsWindow.LastKey = "Right") Then
    PaddleX = PaddleX + 1
  EndIf
  ' move paddle
  Shapes.Move(Paddle, PaddleX, PaddleY)
EndSub
```

In this code, if either the left or right cursor key is pressed, the paddle's x coordinate is updated. The paddle is moved. Save and run the program.

Notice how the cursor control keys move the rectangle. We have that "paddle" we've been looking for. This last version is saved in the **Animate** folder in the course program folder (**\BeginSB\BSB Code**).

Program – Balloons

In this class program, we will build a little video game. Colorful balloons are dropping from the sky. You maneuver a popping device under them to make them pop and get a point. You try to pop as many balloons as you can in one minute. This program is saved in the **Balloons** folder in the programs folder (**\BeginSB\BSB Code**).

Program Design

All of the game action will go on in a graphics window. There will be five possible balloons, all ellipse shape objects. An arrow (a triangle shape object) will be the "popping arrow." This arrow will be moved using cursor keys on the keyboard. Clicking the graphics window will control starting and stopping the game. The current score (number of balloons popped) will be displayed in the window. The steps of the program we will follow:

1. Initialize score and balloon locations.
2. When graphics window is clicked, start the timer dropping the balloons.
3. Monitor KeyDown event for arrow movement.
4. Monitor timer's Tick event for collisions and misses – update score.

When writing the code, we will look at each of these steps in more detail.

Program Development

The Balloons game is simple, in concept. To play, click the window. The five balloons will drop down the window, each at a different speed. Use the left and right arrow keys to move the arrow. If the arrow is under a balloon when a collision occurs, the balloon pops and you get a point. Balloons reappear at the top after popping or after reaching the bottom of the screen without being popped. You pop as many balloons as you can in 60 seconds. At that point, the game ends.

There are a few events to write code for: clicking the window to start and checking for arrow key presses. And, we will also need a timer (and its Tick event) to control the balloon animation, updating the window 10 times a second (Interval will be 100). There is a substantial amount of Small Basic code to write here, even though you will see there is a lot of repetition. We suggest writing the event subroutines in stages. Write one subroutine or a part of a subroutine. Save and run the program. Make sure the code you wrote works. Add more code. Run the program again. Make sure the added code works. Continue adding code until complete. Building a program this way minimizes the potential for error and makes the debugging process much easier. Let's go.

Start Small Basic and start a new program. Save it as **Balloons**. Add this initial code:

```
'
'  Balloons
'  Beginning Small Basic
'
GraphicsWindow.Show()
GraphicsWindow.Title = "Balloons"
GraphicsWindow.Width = 400
GraphicsWindow.Height = 400
' start message
GraphicsWindow.BrushColor = "Black"
GraphicsWindow.DrawText(100, 200 "Click Window To Start")
```

This just sets up the graphics window and prints a starting message. Save and run the program to insure you have a good starting point. Note the window is 400 x 400 pixels in size. This lets us space five balloons (50 pixels wide) across the window (with 10 pixels between each balloon). We also leave some room on the right side of the window to print the score.

Here's what I see when I run this little program:

Clicking the window with the mouse will initialize the game, setting up the balloons and popping arrow. The **MouseDown** method does the work. Add this line after the code printing the message:

```
GraphicsWindow.MouseDown = MouseDownEvent
```

And add the empty subroutine:

```
Sub MouseDownEvent
EndSub
```

The balloons will be represented by an array of shape objects (**Balloon**). Each balloon will be a different color and occupy a square region, 50 pixels (**BalloonSize**) wide by 50 pixels high. We will also use arrays to keep track of each balloon's location (**BalloonX**, **BalloonY**) and dropping speed (**BalloonSpeed**). The arrow will be a shape object (**Arrow**). Its width (**ArrowSize**) will be half the width of a balloon and its position will be given by **ArrowX**. When the program first starts, we need to follow these steps:

- Create each balloon object and initialize the positions
- Create the arrow object and initialize its position
- Initialize the score

Let's add code to the editor to perform each of these steps. First, set up the balloon objects with this code in the **MouseDownEvent** subroutine:

```
Sub MouseDownEvent
  GraphicsWindow.Clear()
  Score = 0
  UpdateScore()
  BalloonSize = 50
  GraphicsWindow.PenColor = "Black"
  GraphicsWindow.BrushColor = "Red"
  Balloon[1] = Shapes.AddEllipse(BalloonSize, BalloonSize)
  GraphicsWindow.BrushColor = "Blue"
  Balloon[2] = Shapes.AddEllipse(BalloonSize, BalloonSize)
  GraphicsWindow.BrushColor = "Green"
  Balloon[3] = Shapes.AddEllipse(BalloonSize, BalloonSize)
  GraphicsWindow.BrushColor = "Magenta"
  Balloon[4] = Shapes.AddEllipse(BalloonSize, BalloonSize)
  GraphicsWindow.BrushColor = "Cyan"
  Balloon[5] = Shapes.AddEllipse(BalloonSize, BalloonSize)
  ' put 10 pixels between each balloon
  For i = 1 To 5
    BalloonX[i] = 10 + (i - 1) * (BalloonSize + 10)
    BalloonY[i] = 0
    BalloonSpeed[i] = Math.GetRandomNumber(4) + 2
    Shapes.Move(Balloon[i], BalloonX[i], BalloonY[i])
  EndFor
EndSub
```

First, it clears the message screen, initializes the score (**Score**) and calls a yet unwritten subroutine (**UpdateScore**) to display this score. Next, it sets up the balloons. A little about how we determined balloon speeds. The array **BalloonSpeed** holds the five speeds, representing the number of pixels a balloon will drop with each update of the viewing window. We want each balloon to drop at a different rate. In code, each speed is computed using:

```
Math.GetRandomNumber(4) + 2
```

Or, it will be a random value between 3 and 6. A new speed will be computed each time a balloon starts its trip down the window. How do we know this will be a good speed, providing reasonable dropping rates? We didn't before the program began. This expression was arrived at by 'trial and error.' We built the game and tried different speeds until we found values that worked. You do this a lot in developing games. You may not know values for some numbers before you start. So, you go ahead and build the game and try all kinds of values until you find ones that work. Then, you build these numbers into your code.

As mentioned, for this code to work, we need one additional subroutine. The subroutine (**UpdateScore**) to update the score is:

```
Sub UpdateScore
  ' draw the score
  GraphicsWindow.BrushColor = GraphicsWindow.BackgroundColor
  GraphicsWindow.FillRectangle(340, 80, 400, 120)
  GraphicsWindow.BrushColor = "Black"
  GraphicsWindow.DrawText(320, 60, "Your Score:")
  GraphicsWindow.DrawText(350, 90, Score)
EndSub
```

Here, we clear any previous score, then redraw it in the graphics window. Add this subroutine.

Save and run the program. Click the window and this is what you should see:

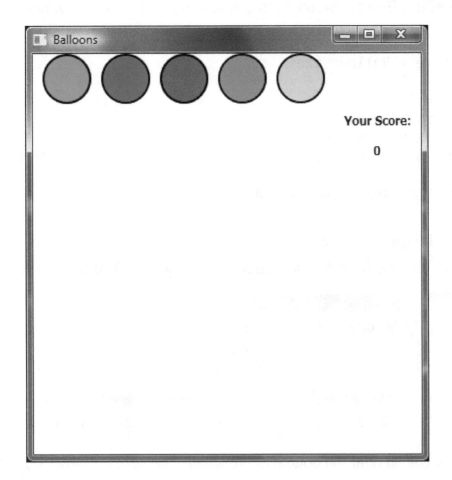

The five created balloon objects are at the top of the graphics window. The initial score is show to the right.

Let's add the arrow. Add this code (after the code setting up the balloons in the MouseDownEvent subroutine) to create and position the arrow object:

```
ArrowSize = BalloonSize / 2
ArrowX = 150
ArrowY = 370
GraphicsWindow.PenColor = "Black"
GraphicsWindow.BrushColor = "Yellow"
Arrow = Shapes.AddTriangle(0, 20, ArrowSize / 2, 0, ArrowSize, 20)
Shapes.Move(Arrow, ArrowX, ArrowY)
```

The **AddTriangle** method draws a triangle connecting the three points given. You should see that this code draws a black outlined, yellow filled triangle connecting these points:

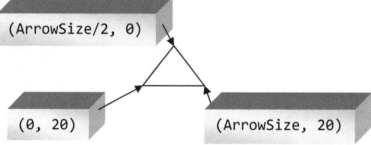

It is initially placed near the bottom approximately centered horizontally in the window.

Run to make sure you have no errors. Click and now you should see the score, the balloons and the popping arrow:

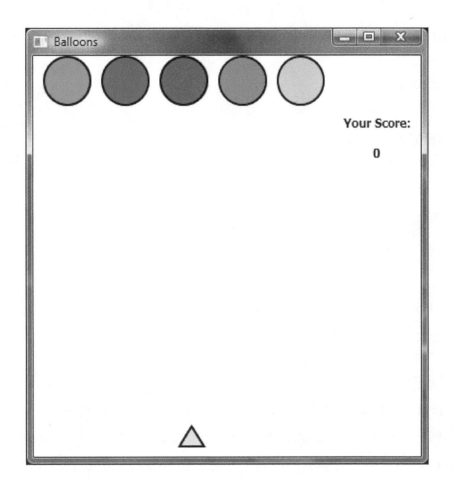

To move the arrow, we need a **KeyDown** event subroutine   Pick a key that will move the arrow to the left and a key that will move it to the right. I chose **F** for **left** movement and **J** for **right** movement. Why? The keys are in the middle of the keyboard, with F to the left of J, and are easy to reach with a natural typing position. You could pick others. The arrow keys are one possibility. I hardly ever use these because they are always at some odd location on a keyboard and just not "naturally" reached. Also, the arrow keys are often used (in more elaborate GUI programs) to move among controls in the window and this can get confusing.

In the main code region, add this line to establish the subroutine (**KeyDownEvent**):

```
GraphicsWindow.KeyDown = KeyDownEvent
```

And the subroutine is:

```
Sub KeyDownEvent
  ' Check for F key (left) and J key (right) and compute arrow
position
  If (GraphicsWindow.LastKey = "F") Then
    ArrowX = ArrowX - 5
  ElseIf (GraphicsWindow.LastKey = "J") Then
    ArrowX = ArrowX + 5
  EndIf
  ' Position arrow
  Shapes.Move(Arrow, ArrowX, ArrowY)
EndSub
```

Notice if the F key is pressed, the arrow is moved to the left by 5 pixels. The arrow is moved right by 5 pixels if the J key is pressed. Again, the 5 pixels value was found by 'trial and error' - it seems to provide smooth motion. After typing in this subroutine, save the program, then run it. Click the window to start things. Make sure the arrow moves as expected. It should start near the middle of the window. Notice there is no code that keeps the arrow from moving out of the window - you could add it if you like. You would need to detect a left or right border crossing. Stop the program.

Let's add capability to use a timer object to control the balloon's dropping. Add these lines to assign the subroutine **TimerTickEvent** to the **Tick** event and establish the **Interval** property:

```
Timer.Tick = TimerTickEvent
Timer.Interval = 100
Timer.Pause()
```

Notice we also make sure the timer is initially paused. Add these two lines at the end of the **MouseDownEvent** subroutine to turn on the timer and initialize a variable **TickCount**:

```
Timer.Resume()
TickCount = 0
```

TickCount is used to determine when to stop the game. It counts how many time's the timer's Tick event occurs. Once it reaches a particular value, we stop the game. We choose to let a game last for 60 seconds. Since the Tick event Interval is 100 or 0.1 seconds, we will stop the game once **TickCount** reaches **600**.

Now, what goes on in the timer event subroutine (**TimerTickEvent**)? Let's do the easy part first – stopping the game after 60 seconds. Recall we will use the **TickCount** variable to stop the game – once **TickCount** exceeds 600, we stop the game and setup for another game, if desired. The code that does this is:

```
Sub TimerTickEvent
  ' increment TickCount
  TickCount = TickCount + 1
  If (TickCount > 600) Then
    ' game over
    Timer.Pause()
    GraphicsWindow.Clear()
    GraphicsWindow.BrushColor = "Black"
    GraphicsWindow.DrawText(50, 200, "Game is over. Final score is
" + Score + " points.")
    GraphicsWindow.DrawText(50, 250, "Click window to play
again.")
  EndIf
EndSub
```

Save the program and run it. Play with the arrow again. After about 60 seconds, you should see the 'Game Over' notice pop up in the window. If this happens, the game stopping code is working. If it doesn't happen, you need to fix something.

Now, to the heart of the Balloons game. We haven't seen any dropping balloons yet. Here's where we do that, and more. Additional code in the **TimerTickEvent** subroutine handles the animation sequence. It drops the balloons down the screen, checks for popping, and checks for balloons reaching the bottom of the window. It gets new balloons started. There's a lot going on. The procedure steps are identical for each balloon. They are:

- Move the balloon.
- Check to see if balloon has popped. If so, sound a noise, make the balloon disappear, increment score and make balloon reappear at the top with a new speed.
- Check to see if balloon has reached the bottom without being popped. If so, start a new balloon with a new speed.

The steps are easy to write, just a little harder to code. Moving a balloon simply involves using the shape object **Move** method to position it at its new location (determined by the **BalloonY** value). To check if the balloon has reached the bottom, we use the border crossing logic discussed earlier. The trickiest step is checking if a balloon has popped. One way to check for a balloon pop is to check to see if the balloon rectangle overlaps the arrow rectangle using the collision detection logic developed earlier. This would work, but a balloon would pop if the arrow barely touched the balloon. In our code, we modify the collision logic such that we will not consider a balloon to be popped unless the entire width of the arrow is within the width of the balloon.

Here's the modified **TimerTickEvent** subroutine implementing these steps. The new code is shaded and placed before the code used to check if the game should stop. The balloons are handled individually within the structure of a For loop:

```
Sub TimerTickEvent
  For i = 1 To 5
    ' move balloon
    BalloonY[i] = BalloonY[i] + BalloonSpeed[i]
    ' check if balloon has popped
    If ((BalloonY[i] + BalloonSize) > ArrowY) Then
      If (BalloonX[i] < ArrowX) Then
        If ((BalloonX[i] + BalloonSize) > (ArrowX + ArrowSize)) Then
          ' Balloon has popped
          ' Increase score - move back to top
          Sound.PlayChime()
          Score = Score + 1
          UpdateScore()
          BalloonY[i] = - BalloonSize
          BalloonSpeed[i] = Math.GetRandomNumber(4) + 2
        EndIf
      EndIf
    EndIf
    ' check for moving off bottom
    If ((BalloonY[i] + BalloonSize) > GraphicsWindow.Height) Then
      ' Balloon reaches bottom without popping
      ' Move back to top with new speed
      BalloonY[i] = -BalloonSize
      BalloonSpeed[i] = Math.GetRandomNumber(4) + 2
    EndIf
    ' redraw balloon at new location, redraw arrow too
    Shapes.Move(Balloon[i], BalloonX[i], BalloonY[i])
  EndFor
  ' increment TickCount
  TickCount = TickCount + 1
  If (TickCount > 600) Then
    ' game over
    Timer.Pause()
    GraphicsWindow.Clear()
    GraphicsWindow.BrushColor = "Black"
    GraphicsWindow.DrawText(50, 200, "Game is over. Final score is
" + Score + " points.")
```

```
      GraphicsWindow.DrawText(50, 250, "Click window to play
again.")
  EndIf
EndSub
```

Do you see how all the steps are implemented? We added a sounding chime statement for some audio feedback when a balloon pops.

      The code is complete. Make sure you have saved the files. The **Balloons** listing from the Small Basic editor is:


```
'
'  Balloons
'  Beginning Small Basic
'
GraphicsWindow.Show()
GraphicsWindow.Title = "Balloons"
GraphicsWindow.Width = 400
GraphicsWindow.Height = 400
' start message
GraphicsWindow.BrushColor = "Black"
GraphicsWindow.DrawText(100, 200 "Click Window To Start")
GraphicsWindow.MouseDown = MouseDownEvent
GraphicsWindow.KeyDown = KeyDownEvent
Timer.Tick = TimerTickEvent
Timer.Interval = 100
Timer.Pause()


Sub MouseDownEvent
  GraphicsWindow.Clear()
  Score = 0
  UpdateScore()
  BalloonSize = 50
  GraphicsWindow.PenColor = "Black"
  GraphicsWindow.BrushColor = "Red"
  Balloon[1] = Shapes.AddEllipse(BalloonSize, BalloonSize)
  GraphicsWindow.BrushColor = "Blue"
  Balloon[2] = Shapes.AddEllipse(BalloonSize, BalloonSize)
  GraphicsWindow.BrushColor = "Green"
  Balloon[3] = Shapes.AddEllipse(BalloonSize, BalloonSize)
  GraphicsWindow.BrushColor = "Magenta"
```

```
Balloon[4] = Shapes.AddEllipse(BalloonSize, BalloonSize)
GraphicsWindow.BrushColor = "Cyan"
Balloon[5] = Shapes.AddEllipse(BalloonSize, BalloonSize)
' put 10 pixels between each balloon
For i = 1 To 5
  BalloonX[i] = 10 + (i - 1) * (BalloonSize + 10)
  BalloonY[i] = 0
  BalloonSpeed[i] = Math.GetRandomNumber(4) + 2
  Shapes.Move(Balloon[i], BalloonX[i], BalloonY[i])
EndFor
ArrowSize = BalloonSize / 2
ArrowX = 150
ArrowY = 370
GraphicsWindow.PenColor = "Black"
GraphicsWindow.BrushColor = "Yellow"
Arrow = Shapes.AddTriangle(0, 20, ArrowSize / 2, 0, ArrowSize,
20)
  Shapes.Move(Arrow, ArrowX, ArrowY)
  Timer.Resume()
  TickCount = 0
EndSub

Sub UpdateScore
  ' draw the score
  GraphicsWindow.BrushColor = GraphicsWindow.BackgroundColor
  GraphicsWindow.FillRectangle(340, 80, 400, 120)
  GraphicsWindow.BrushColor = "Black"
  GraphicsWindow.DrawText(320, 60, "Your Score:")
  GraphicsWindow.DrawText(350, 90, Score)
EndSub

Sub KeyDownEvent
  ' Check for F key (left) and J key (right) and compute arrow
position
  If (GraphicsWindow.LastKey = "F") Then
    ArrowX = ArrowX - 5
  ElseIf (GraphicsWindow.LastKey = "J") Then
    ArrowX = ArrowX + 5
  EndIf
  ' Position arrow
  Shapes.Move(Arrow, ArrowX, ArrowY)
EndSub

Sub TimerTickEvent
  For i = 1 To 5
    ' move balloon
```

```
      BalloonY[i] = BalloonY[i] + BalloonSpeed[i]
      ' check if balloon has popped
      If ((BalloonY[i] + BalloonSize) > ArrowY) Then
        If (BalloonX[i] < ArrowX) Then
          If ((BalloonX[i] + BalloonSize) > (ArrowX + ArrowSize))
Then
            ' Balloon has popped
            ' Increase score - move back to top
            Sound.PlayChime()
            Score = Score + 1
            UpdateScore()
            BalloonY[i] = - BalloonSize
            BalloonSpeed[i] = Math.GetRandomNumber(4) + 2
          EndIf
        EndIf
      EndIf
      ' check for moving off bottom
      If ((BalloonY[i] + BalloonSize) > GraphicsWindow.Height) Then
        ' Balloon reaches bottom without popping
        ' Move back to top with new speed
        BalloonY[i] = -BalloonSize
        BalloonSpeed[i] = Math.GetRandomNumber(4) + 2
      EndIf
      ' redraw balloon at new location, redraw arrow too
      Shapes.Move(Balloon[i], BalloonX[i], BalloonY[i])
    EndFor
    ' increment TickCount
    TickCount = TickCount + 1
    If (TickCount > 600) Then
      ' game over
      Timer.Pause()
      GraphicsWindow.Clear()
      GraphicsWindow.BrushColor = "Black"
      GraphicsWindow.DrawText(50, 200, "Game is over. Final score is
" + Score + " points.")
      GraphicsWindow.DrawText(50, 250, "Click window to play
again.")
    EndIf
EndSub
```

I know this is lots of code, but by building in stages, using subroutines, the work has not been too difficult, I hope.

Run the Program

Run the program. Click the window to get the balloons dropping. Make sure it works. Make sure each balloon falls. Make sure when a balloon reaches the bottom, a new one is initialized. Make sure you can pop each balloon. And, following a pop, make sure a new balloon appears. Make sure the score changes by one with each pop. Here's my finished version:

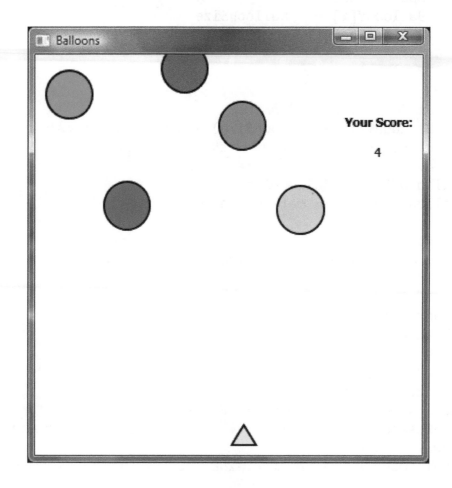

And here's my final screen:

By building and testing the program in stages, you should now have a thoroughly tested, running version of Balloons. So relax and have fun playing it. Show your friends and family your great creation. If you do find any bugs and need to make any changes, make sure you resave your program.

Other Things to Try

I'm sure as you played the Balloons game, you thought of some changes you could make. Go ahead - give it a try! Here are some ideas we have.

When a balloon pops, it just disappears from the screen. Can you think of a more dramatic way to show popping? Maybe flash the window background color. Give the balloons a random color each time a new one appears.

Add selectable difficulty levels to the game. This could be used to make the game easy for little kids and very hard for experts. What can you do to adjust the game difficulty? One thing you could do is adjust the size of the popping arrow. To pop a balloon, the entire arrow width must fit within the width of a balloon. Hence, a smaller (narrower) arrow would make it easier to pop balloons before they reach the bottom of the window. A larger (wider) arrow makes popping harder. The balloon dropping speed also affects game difficulty. Slowly dropping balloons are easy to pop - fast ones are not. Play with the game to see what speeds would work for different difficulty levels.

Make it possible to play longer games and, as the game goes on, make the game more difficult using some of the ideas above (smaller arrow, faster balloons). You've seen this in other games you may have played - games usually get harder as time goes on.

Players like to know how much time they have left in a game. Add this capability to your game. Use **DrawText** to print this on the window. The TickCount variable can be used to compute this value. You should be comfortable making such a change to your program.

Another thing players like to know is the highest score on a game. Add this capability. Define a new variable to keep track of the highest score. After each game is played, compare the current score with the highest score to see if a new high has been reached. Decide how to display the highest score. One problem, though. When you stop the program, the highest score value will be lost. A new high needs to be established each time you run the program. As you become a more advanced Small Basic programmer, you'll learn ways to save the highest score.

Sharing a Small Basic Program

I bet you're ready to show your friends and colleagues some of the programs you have built using Small Basic. Just give them a copy of your code, ask them to install Small Basic and learn how to open and run a program. Then, have them open your program and run it. I think you'll agree this might be asking a lot of your friends, colleagues, and, ultimately, your user base. We need to know how to run a program **without** Small Basic.

To run a program without Small Basic, you need to create an **executable** version of the program. So, how is an executable created? A little secret is that Small Basic builds an executable version of a program every time we run the program! This executable file is in the same folder you save your program in. Open the folder for any program you have built and you'll see a file with your program name of type **Program**. For example, using Windows Explorer to open the program folder for the **Balloons** program we just built:

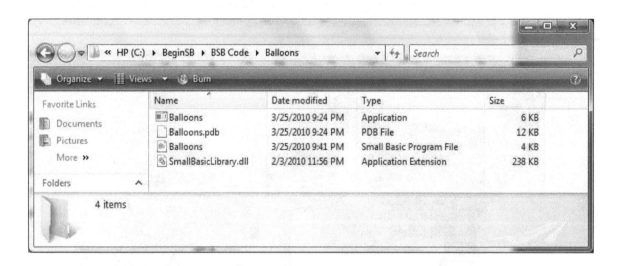

The file named **Balloons** of type **Application** (size 6 KB) is the executable version of the program. If I make sure Small Basic is not running and double-click this file, the following appears:

Voila! The Balloons program is running outside of the Small Basic development environment! Go ahead and play the game if you like.

So distributing a Small Basic program is as simple as giving your user a copy of the executable file (and the **SmallBasic.dll** file in your program folder - this has some support code), having them place the files in a folder on their computer and double-clicking the executable file to run it? Maybe. This worked on my computer (and will work on yours) because I have a very important set of files known as the **.NET Framework** installed (they are installed when Small Basic is installed). Every Small Basic program needs the .NET Framework to be installed on the hosting computer.

The next question is: how do you know if your user has the .NET Framework installed on his or her computer? And, if they don't, how can you get it installed? These are difficult questions. So, in addition to our program's executable file, we also need to give a potential user the Microsoft .NET Framework files and inform them how to install and register these files on their computer. Things are getting complicated. Let's look at an easier and very flashy solution – letting users access and run your programs over the Internet!

Start Small Basic and take a look at the toolbar. There are two buttons there we haven't talked about yet. Between the buttons to open and save files and the ones for editing are buttons marked **Import** and **Publish**:

These are remarkable buttons. Clicking **Import** will take you to a Microsoft website where you can import and open a program stored on the Internet by you or other users. **Publish** allows you to store your programs on the Internet for others to use.

Make sure your computer is connected to the Internet. Go ahead and click **Import**. You should see:

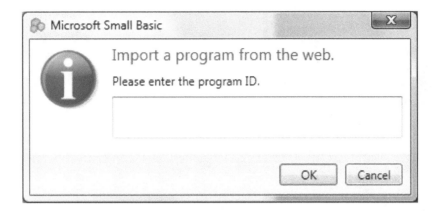

To import a program, you require a **Program ID**. How do you get such an ID? It is assigned when you **Publish** a program, so let's try that. Click the **Cancel** button for now.

Open one of your Small Basic programs. I'll be using the **Balloons** program we just built. Make sure the program runs and is free of errors. Click **Publish**. You will see a message something like this:

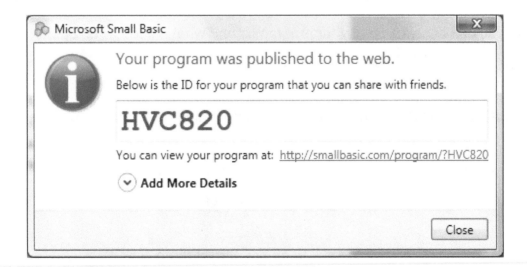

Your program is assigned a Program **ID** (remember we need this to import a program). Click **Add More Details**:

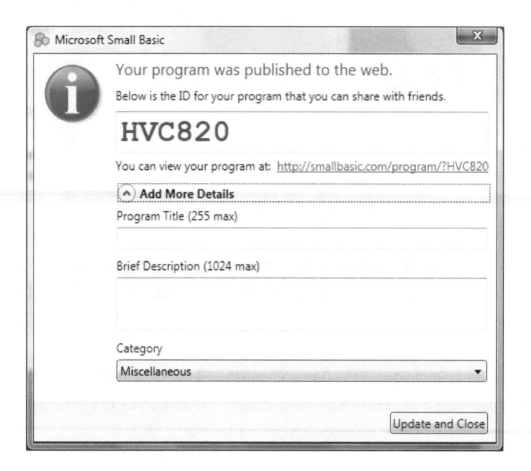

Here, you can describe what your program is and what it does. You can provide a category. This will help users find your program

Also listed in this window is this very interesting piece of information:

You can view your program at:
http://smallbasic.com/program/?HVC820

If you click this link (or give the link to others and let them click it), "magic" occurs.

When I click it, I am taken to this website hosted by Microsoft:

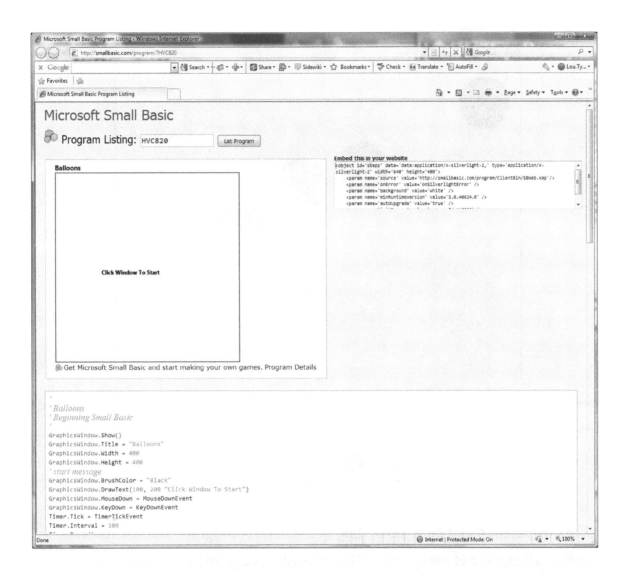

The running **Balloons** program is shown, along with a code listing.

If I click the **Balloons** program window, I can play the game on-line!

Balloons

Your Score:

4

Looks like there might be a "color" bug in the current program, but it is running. I think you'll agree this pretty neat. To share your programs with other users, **Publish** them, then give them the program link given to you. If they click the link, they can run the program. Well, almost. To use this feature, a user's computer must have a Microsoft product called **Silverlight** installed on their computer. It can be downloaded from this website:

http://www.silverlight.net/

If a user attempts to access your Small Basic program via a provided link and they do not have the required Silverlight product, they will be taken through the installation steps.

Return to the website with your running program. In the upper right corner is a box marked **Embed this in your website**. In this box is some code that allows you to put your running application on your own website, if you have one. The steps to do this are beyond this discussion, but I wanted you to know such a step was possible.

Before leaving, lets return to the **Import** button in Small Basic. Click it again and enter the program ID for your program (I used **HVC820**):

Click **OK**. The imported code will appear in your editor:

```
hvc820 - Imported *                                    ⌃ Details    ✕
  1  '
  2  ' Balloons
  3  ' Beginning Small Basic
  4  '
  5  GraphicsWindow.Show()
  6  GraphicsWindow.Title = "Balloons"
  7  GraphicsWindow.Width = 400
  8  GraphicsWindow.Height = 400
  9  'start message
 10  GraphicsWindow.BrushColor = "Black"
 11  GraphicsWindow.DrawText(100, 200 "Click Window To Start")
 12  GraphicsWindow.MouseDown = MouseDownEvent
 13  GraphicsWindow.KeyDown = KeyDownEvent
 14  Timer.Tick = TimerTickEvent
 15  Timer.Interval = 100
 16  Timer.Pause()
 17
 18
 19  Sub MouseDownEvent
 20     GraphicsWindow.Clear()
 21     Score = 0
                                                            1,1
```

So, you have access to any code published to the Microsoft Small Basic library. I'm guessing this library will be growing very quickly.

In this class, we found that the timer object is a key element in computer animation. By periodically changing the display in a window, the sensation of motion was obtained. We studied "animation math" - how to detect if an object disappeared from a window, how to detect if an object crosses the border of a window, and how to detect if two objects (rectangles) collide. We learned how to detect keyboard events. You built your first video game. And, you learned how to share your work with others and look at programs others have written using Small Basic.

The **Beginning Small Basic** class is over. Before you leave, though, try the bonus programs in Class 10. You've come a long way. Remember back in the first class when you first learned about coding? You're a coding expert by now. But, that doesn't mean you know everything there is to know about programming. Computer programming is a never-ending educational process. There are always new things to learn - ways to improve your skills.

What is your next step for improvement? You could move on to writing more advanced games and simulations using our **Programming Games with Microsoft Small Basic** tutorial. In that advanced Small Basic tutorial you will build some fun 2D games and simulations similar to Frogger and Lunar Lander. Another thing to consider is moving up to a more advanced programming environment like Microsoft Visual Basic, Visual C#, or Java. You can build professional looking programs complete with GUI controls using these products. And, Microsoft offers Visual Basic Express and Visual C# Express for free (after product registration).

Our company, Kidware Software, offers tutorials that cover Visual Basic and Visual C# for both beginners and more advanced programmers. These tutorials are self-paced, study guides that provide an overview of Visual Basic and Visual C# for building advanced GUI applications. What would you gain from our computer programming tutorials? Here are a few new things you would learn:

- How to build detailed GUI applications that use Visual Basic & C# controls
- How to distribute your programs to other users
- How to read and write files to disk (this could be used to save high scores in games)
- How to do more detailed animations
- How to play elaborate sounds (the chime and ring are pretty boring)
- How to use your printer
- How to create your own on-line help system

We also publish Java programming tutorials as well. Please contact us if you want more information visit our website at the address on the title page for this course.

10

More Programs

Preview

By now, you should feel pretty comfortable with the steps involved in building a Small Basic program. In this last chapter, we give you more programs you can build and try. We'll present the steps involved in building each program - **Program Design**, **Program Development**, **Run the Program**, and **Other Things to Try**. But, we won't give you detailed discussion of what's going on in the code. We will just give you the code listing and point out any new ideas. You should be able to figure that out by now (with the help of the code comments). Actually, a very valuable programming skill to have is the ability to read and understand someone else's code.

The programs included are: Computer Stopwatch, Loan Calculator, Unit Conversions, Times Tables, State Capitals, Dice Rolling, Memory Game, Tic-Tac-Toe, and Decode. The first five programs will be text applications. Dice Rolling, Memory Game, Tic-Tac-Toe and Decode will use the graphics window.

Program 1 - Computer Stopwatch

Program Design

In this program, we build a computer stopwatch that measures elapsed time in seconds (to three decimal places). When <Enter> is pressed, the stopwatch will start. When <Enter> is pressed again, the stopwatch will stop and display elapsed time. The program is saved in the **Stopwatch** folder in the program folder (**\BeginSB\BSB Code**).

Program Development

Start Small Basic. Start a new program and save it as **Stopwatch**. Type in (or copy and paste from these notes) the complete **Stopwatch** Small Basic code:

```
'
'  Stopwatch Program
'  Beginning Small Basic
'
TextWindow.Title = "Stopwatch"
Start:
TextWindow.WriteLine("")
TextWindow.Write("Press <Enter> to start stopwatch (enter a 0 to
stop the program). ")
Stop = TextWindow.Read()
If Stop <> "0" Then
  TextWindow.WriteLine("Stopwatch is running ...")
  GetSeconds()
  StartTime = Seconds
  TextWindow.Write("Press <Enter> to stop stopwatch. ")
  StopIt = TextWindow.Read()
```

```
  GetSeconds()
  EndTime = Seconds
  TextWindow.WriteLine("Elapsed time is " + (EndTime - StartTime)
+ " seconds.")
  Goto Start
EndIf
Sub GetSeconds
  Seconds = Clock.Hour * 3600 + Clock.Minute * 60 + Clock.Second +
Clock.Millisecond / 1000
EndSub
```

Let's discuss this code.

We have three variables: **StartTime** (starting time in seconds), **EndTime** (ending time in seconds) and **Stop**, used to see if we should stop the program. Ask the user to press <Enter> to start and stop the stopwatch and display the results. To stop the program, the user is asked to enter a 0 (zero) when starting the stopwatch. The timing code repeats as long as the **Stop** string is "not equal" to 0. The code logic is very straightforward. The only part of this code that might be difficult to understand is computing the times. This is done in the subroutine **GetSeconds**:

```
Sub GetSeconds
  Seconds = Clock.Hour * 3600 + Clock.Minute * 60 + Clock.Second +
Clock.Millisecond / 1000
EndSub
```

This routine uses the Small Basic **Clock** object which holds the current time in different parts (Hour, Minute, Second, and Millisecond). This routine converts each to seconds and adds them up.

Run the Program

Save your work. Run the program. Press <**Enter**> to start the stopwatch. Press <**Enter**> to stop the stopwatch. Make sure you understand how the elapsed time is computed and displayed. Here's a few of my example runs:

```
Stopwatch                                                    _ □ X
Press <Enter> to start stopwatch (enter a 0 to stop the program).
Stopwatch is running ...
Press <Enter> to stop stopwatch.
Elapsed time is 4.278 seconds.

Press <Enter> to start stopwatch (enter a 0 to stop the program).
Stopwatch is running ...
Press <Enter> to stop stopwatch.
Elapsed time is 5.831 seconds.

Press <Enter> to start stopwatch (enter a 0 to stop the program).
Stopwatch is running ...
Press <Enter> to stop stopwatch.
Elapsed time is 7.083 seconds.

Press <Enter> to start stopwatch (enter a 0 to stop the program). 0
Press any key to continue...
```

Stop the program when you get bored (enter a 0, instead of pressing <Enter> when asked to start the stopwatch).

Other Things to Try

Many stopwatches allow you to continue timing after you've stopped one or more times. That is, you can measure total elapsed time in different segments. You'll need a variable to keep track of total elapsed time and a way to tell the stopwatch you are done timing (use some other **Stop** value). Add a "lap timing" feature by displaying the time measured in each segment (a segment being defined as the time between each Start and Stop press of <Enter>).

Program 2 - Loan Calculator

Program Design

Do you want to know how much that new car will cost each month or how long it will take to pay off a credit card? This program will do the job. You enter a loan amount, a yearly interest, and a number of months, and the program computes your monthly payment. The program is saved in the **Loan** folder in the program folder (**\BeginSB\BSB Code**).

Program Development

Start Small Basic, create a new program and save it as **Loan**. Type in (or copy and paste from these notes) the complete **Loan** Small Basic code:

```
'
'  Loan Program
'  Beginning Small Basic
'
TextWindow.Title = "Loan Calculator"
GetInputs:
TextWindow.Write("Enter loan amount (enter 0 to stop): ")
Loan = TextWindow.ReadNumber()
If (Loan <> 0) Then
  TextWindow.Write("Enter yearly interest rate:  ")
  Interest = TextWindow.ReadNumber()
  TextWindow.Write("Enter number of months to pay back loan: ")
  Months = TextWindow.ReadNumber()
  ' Compute interest multiplier
  Multiplier = Math.Power((1 + Interest / 1200), Months)
  ' Compute payment
  Payment = Loan * Interest * Multiplier / (1200 * (Multiplier -
1))
  TextWindow.WriteLine("Your monthly payment is $" + Payment)
  TextWindow.WriteLine("")
  Goto GetInputs
EndIf
```

The code is pretty straightforward. The user is asked for loan amount, yearly interest and number of months. The values are input and the payment is computed (using a standard financial formula) and displayed.

Run the Program

Save your work. Run the program. Provide a loan amount, an interest, and a number of months. Press <Enter> to determine and display the monthly payment. Try a loan amount of $5,000 (don't type in the comma), an interest rate of 18%, and 24 months. Your payment should be $249.62:

```
Loan Calculator

Enter loan amount (enter 0 to stop): 5000
Enter yearly interest rate:  18
Enter number of months to pay back loan: 24
Your monthly payment is $249.62050984754568682306739554

Enter loan amount (enter 0 to stop):
```

What can you do with this? Well, you can find monthly payments like we just did. Or, try this. Say you have a credit card balance of $2,000. The interest rate is 15% and you can make $100 payments each month. Use 2000 as the loan amount box, and 15 as the interest. Then, try different numbers of months until the computed payment is close to $100. This will tell you how many months it will take you to pay off the credit card. I got 23 months with payments of $100.59 each month.

Other Things to Try

This program is pretty complete. One thing to fix though - what if the interest rate is zero (a very nice bank!)? The program won't work (try it). You'll need a way to compute payments with zero interest. Also can you figure out how to display the payment amounts with exactly two numbers after the decimal point?

Program 3 – Units Conversion

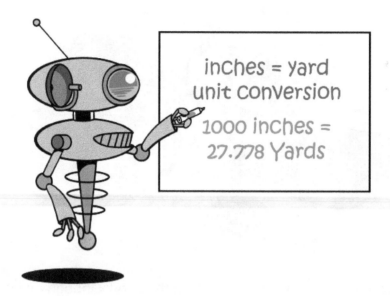

Program Design

In this program, we will build a program that converts length from one unit of measure (inch, foot, yard, mile, centimeter, meter, kilometer) to another. The program is saved in the **Convert** folder in the program folder (**\BeginSB\BSB Code**).

Program Development

Start Small Basic, start a new program and save it as **Convert**. Type in (or copy and paste from these notes) the complete **Convert** Small Basic code:

```
'
'  Convert Program
'  Beginning Small Basic
'
TextWindow.Title = "Units Conversions"
' Establish conversion factors - stored in two dimensional array
' or table - the first number is the table row, the second number
' the table column
Conversions[1][1] = 1.0 ' in to in
```

```
Conversions[1][2] = 1.0 / 12.0 ' in to ft
Conversions[1][3] = 1.0 / 36.0 ' in to yd
Conversions[1][4] = (1.0 / 12.0) / 5280.0 ' in to mi
Conversions[1][5] = 2.54 ' in to cm
Conversions[1][6] = 2.54 / 100 ' in to m
Conversions[1][7] = 2.54 / 100000 ' in to km
For i = 1 To 7
  Conversions[2][i] = 12.0 * Conversions[1][i]
  Conversions[3][i] = 36.0 * Conversions[1][i]
  Conversions[4][i] = 5280.0 * (12.0 * Conversions[1][i])
  Conversions[5][i] = Conversions[1][i] / 2.54
  Conversions[6][i] = 100.0 * Conversions[1][i] / 2.54
  Conversions[7][i] = 100000.0 * (Conversions[1][i] / 2.54)
EndFor

' Initialize variables
Units[1] = "inches (in)"
Units[2] = "feet (ft)"
Units[3] = "yards (yd)"
Units[4] = "miles (mi)"
Units[5] = "centimeters (cm)"
Units[6] = "meters (m)"
Units[7] = "kilometers (km)"

StartLoop:
TextWindow.Write("Enter a value to convert (enter 0 stop): ")
FromValue = TextWindow.ReadNumber()
If (FromValue <> 0) Then
  For i = 1 To 7
    TextWindow.WriteLine(i + " - " + Units[i])
  EndFor
  GetFromUnits:
  TextWindow.Write("What units is the value in? ")
  FromUnits = TextWindow.ReadNumber()
  If (FromUnits < 1 Or FromUnits > 7) Then
    Goto GetFromUnits
  EndIf
  ' Do unit conversion
  TextWindow.WriteLine("")
  TextWindow.WriteLine(FromValue + " " + Units[FromUnits] + "
is:")
  For i = 1 To 7
    TextWindow.WriteLine(FromValue * Conversions[FromUnits][i] + "
" + Units[i])
  EndFor
  TextWindow.WriteLine("")
```

```
    Goto StartLoop
EndIf
```

The idea of the program is simple. Type a value and choose its units. Display that value converted to several other units. Note how the conversion factors are stored in a two-dimensional array (table).

Run the Program

Save your work. Run the program. Type in a value, select its units. Make sure all the options work as designed. Here's what I got for 5280 feet:

```
Units Conversions
Enter a value to convert (enter 0 stop): 5280
1 - inches (in)
2 - feet (ft)
3 - yards (yd)
4 - miles (mi)
5 - centimeters (cm)
6 - meters (m)
7 - kilometers (km)
What units is the value in? 2

5280 feet (ft) is:
63360 inches (in)
5279.9999999999999999999979 feet (ft)
1760.0000000000000000000014 yards (yd)
0.99999999999999999999982080 miles (mi)
160934.40 centimeters (cm)
1609.3440 meters (m)
1.6093440 kilometers (km)

Enter a value to convert (enter 0 stop): _
```

Other Things to Try

The most obvious change to this program is to include other units of measure. You could build a general purpose units conversion program that converts not only length, but weight, volume, density, area, temperature and many others. Such a program would be invaluable.

Program 4 – Times Tables

	1	2	3	4	5	6	7	8	9	10	11	12
1	1	2	3	4	5	6	7	8	9	10	11	12
2	2	4	6	8	10	12	14	16	18	20	22	24
3	3	6	9	12	15	18	21	24	27	30	33	36
4	4	8	12	16	20	24	28	32	36	40	44	48
5	5	10	15	20	25	30	35	40	45	50	55	60
6	6	12	18	24	30	36	42	48	54	60	66	72
7	7	14	21	28	35	42	49	56	63	70	77	84
8	8	16	24	32	40	48	56	64	72	80	88	96
9	9	18	27	36	45	54	63	72	81	90	99	108
10	10	20	30	40	50	60	70	80	90	100	110	120
11	11	22	33	44	55	66	77	88	99	110	121	132
12	12	24	36	48	60	72	84	96	108	120	132	144

Program Design

In this program, you can give a child practice with the times tables using the numbers from 0 to 9. The computer generates a random problem. The child answers and the computer evaluates the performance. The child is given 10 problems to try. The program is saved in the **TimesTables** folder in the program folder (**\BeginSB\BSB Code**).

Program Development

Start Small Basic, start a new program and save it as **TimesTables**. Type in (or copy and paste from these notes) the complete **TimesTables** Small Basic code:

```
'
'  Times Tables Program
'  Beginning Small Basic
'
```

```
TextWindow.Title = "Times Tables"
NumProb = 0
NumRight = 0
' display the problem
For i = 1 To 10
  NumProb = NumProb + 1
  ' Generate random numbers for factors
  Number1 = Math.GetRandomNumber(10) - 1
  Number2 = Math.GetRandomNumber(10) - 1
  ' Find product
  Product = Number1 * Number2
  TextWindow.WriteLine("")
  TextWindow.WriteLine("Problem " + NumProb + ":")
  TextWindow.Write("What is " + Number1 + " x " + Number2 + " = ")
  YourAnswer = TextWindow.ReadNumber()
  ' Check answer and update score
  If (YourAnswer = Product) Then
    NumRight = NumRight + 1
    TextWindow.WriteLine("That's correct!")
  else
    TextWindow.WriteLine("Answer is " + Product)
  EndIf
  TextWindow.WriteLine("Score: " + 100.0 * NumRight / NumProb +
"%")
EndFor
```

The computer generates and displays a multiplication problem. The user types an answer and presses **<Enter>.** If correct, you are told so. If incorrect, the correct answer is given. In either case, the score is updated. Continue answering until 10 problems (a For loop is used) have been answered.

Run the Program

Save your work. Run the program. A multiplication problem will be displayed. Type an answer and press <Enter>. If correct, that's great. If not, you will be shown the correct answer. Continue for 10 problems. Try for a high score. Here's what I got for one round of problems:

```
Times Tables
What is 1 x 5 = 5
That's correct!
Score: 83.33333333333333333333333333%

Problem 7:
What is 7 x 5 = 35
That's correct!
Score: 85.71428571428571428571428571%

Problem 8:
What is 0 x 1 = 0
That's correct!
Score: 87.5%

Problem 9:
What is 2 x 4 = 8
That's correct!
Score: 88.88888888888888888888888889%

Problem 10:
What is 6 x 7 = 42
That's correct!
Score: 90%
Press any key to continue...
```

Other Things to Try

Some suggested changes to make this a more useful program are: (1) make the range of factors an option (small numbers for little kids, large numbers for older kids), (2) allow practice with a specific factor only, (3) give the user more chances at the correct answer with a decreasing score for each try, (4) set up a timer so the faster the user answers, the higher the score, (5) remove the 10 problem limit – allow the user to answer until they decide to quite and (6) expand the program to include other operations such as addition, subtraction and division.

Program 5 – State Capitals

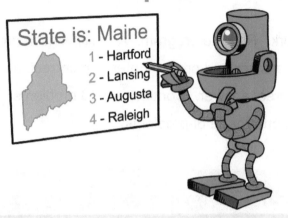

Program Design

In this program, we build a fun game for home and school. You will be given the name of a state in the United States and four possible choices for its capital city. You enter the guess of your choice to see if you are right. (We apologize to our foreign readers – perhaps you can modify this program to build a similar multiple choice type game). The program is saved in the **StateCapitals** folder in the program folder (**\BeginSB\BSB Code**).

Program Development

Start Small Basic, start a new program and save it as **StateCapitals**. Type in (or copy and paste from these notes, especially for the state and capital names) the complete **StateCapitals** Small Basic code:

```
'
'  State Capitals Program
' Beginning Small Basic
'
TextWindow.Title = "State Capitals"
' initialize arrays
State[1] = "Alabama"
Capital[1] = "Montgomery"
State[2] = "Alaska"
Capital[2] = "Juneau"
```

```
State[3] = "Arizona"
Capital[3] = "Phoenix"
State[4] = "Arkansas"
Capital[4] = "Little Rock"
State[5] = "California"
Capital[5] = "Sacramento"
State[6] = "Colorado"
Capital[6] = "Denver"
State[7] = "Connecticut"
Capital[7] = "Hartford"
State[8] = "Delaware"
Capital[8] = "Dover"
State[9] = "Florida"
Capital[9] = "Tallahassee"
State[10] = "Georgia"
Capital[10] = "Atlanta"
State[11] = "Hawaii"
Capital[11] = "Honolulu"
State[12] = "Idaho"
Capital[12] = "Boise"
State[13] = "Illinois"
Capital[13] = "Springfield"
State[14] = "Indiana"
Capital[14] = "Indianapolis"
State[15] = "Iowa"
Capital[15] = "Des Moines"
State[16] = "Kansas"
Capital[16] = "Topeka"
State[17] = "Kentucky"
Capital[17] = "Frankfort"
State[18] = "Louisiana"
Capital[18] = "Baton Rouge"
State[19] = "Maine"
Capital[19] = "Augusta"
State[20] = "Maryland"
Capital[20] = "Annapolis"
State[21] = "Massachusetts"
Capital[21] = "Boston"
State[22] = "Michigan"
Capital[22] = "Lansing"
State[23] = "Minnesota"
Capital[23] = "Saint Paul"
State[24] = "Mississippi"
Capital[24] = "Jackson"
State[25] = "Missouri"
Capital[25] = "Jefferson City"
```

```
State[26] = "Montana"
Capital[26] = "Helena"
State[27] = "Nebraska"
Capital[27] = "Lincoln"
State[28] = "Nevada"
Capital[28] = "Carson City"
State[29] = "New Hampshire"
Capital[29] = "Concord"
State[30] = "New Jersey"
Capital[30] = "Trenton"
State[31] = "New Mexico"
Capital[31] = "Santa Fe"
State[32] = "New York"
Capital[32] = "Albany"
State[33] = "North Carolina"
Capital[33] = "Raleigh"
State[34] = "North Dakota"
Capital[34] = "Bismarck"
State[35] = "Ohio"
Capital[35] = "Columbus"
State[36] = "Oklahoma"
Capital[36] = "Oklahoma City"
State[37] = "Oregon"
Capital[37] = "Salem"
State[38] = "Pennsylvania"
Capital[38] = "Harrisburg"
State[39] = "Rhode Island"
Capital[39] = "Providence"
State[40] = "South Carolina"
Capital[40] = "Columbia"
State[41] = "South Dakota"
Capital[41] = "Pierre"
State[42] = "Tennessee"
Capital[42] = "Nashville"
State[43] = "Texas"
Capital[43] = "Austin"
State[44] = "Utah"
Capital[44] = "Salt Lake City"
State[45] = "Vermont"
Capital[45] = "Montpelier"
State[46] = "Virginia"
Capital[46] = "Richmond"
State[47] = "Washington"
Capital[47] = "Olympia"
State[48] = "West Virginia"
Capital[48] = "Charleston"
```

```
State[49] = "Wisconsin"
Capital[49] = "Madison"
State[50] = "Wyoming"
Capital[50] = "Cheyenne"

' begin questioning loop
BeginLoop:
' Generate the next question at random
Answer = Math.GetRandomNumber(50)
' Display selected state
TextWindow.WriteLine("")
TextWindow.WriteLine("State is: " + State[Answer])
TextWindow.WriteLine("")
' CapitalUsed array is used to see which state Capitals have
'been selected as possible answers
For i = 1 To 50
  CapitalUsed[i] = 0
EndFor
' Pick four different state indices (j) at random
' These are used to set up multiple choice answers
' Stored in the ListedCapital array
For i = 1 To 4
  'Find value not used yet and not the answer
  GetJ:
  j = Math.GetRandomNumber(50)
  If (CapitalUsed[j] <> 0 Or j = Answer) Then
    Goto GetJ
  EndIf
  CapitalUsed[j] = 1
  ListedCapital[i] = j
EndFor
' Now replace one item (at random) with correct answer
ListedCapital[Math.GetRandomNumber(4)] = Answer
' Display multiple choice answers
For i = 1 To 4
  TextWindow.WriteLine(i + " - " + Capital[ListedCapital[i]])
EndFor
TextWindow.WriteLine("")
TextWindow.Write("What is the Capital? (Enter 0 to Stop) ")
CapitalSelected = TextWindow.ReadNumber()
' check answer
If (CapitalSelected <> 0) Then
  If (ListedCapital[CapitalSelected] = Answer) Then
    TextWindow.WriteLine("That's it ... good job!")
  Else
```

```
    TextWindow.WriteLine("Sorry, the answer is " + Capital[Answer]
+".")
  EndIf
  Goto BeginLoop
EndIf
```

A state (**Answer**) is picked at random, then four distinct capital cities for the multiple choice answers (no repeated values). Check the loop that picks these answers. Next, the questioning loop is completed with code to check the user answer (only one try is given):

Run the Program

Save your work. Run the program. A state name and four possible capital cities will be displayed. (Study the code used to choose and sort the possible answers – this kind of code is very useful.) Choose an answer. If correct, an encouraging message is printed and another state is displayed. If incorrect, you will be told the correct answer. Keep playing – enter a 0 as your answer to stop the program. One of my runs looks like this:

Other Things to Try

This would be a fun program to modify. How about changing it to display a capital city with four states as the multiple choices? Or, allow the user to type in the answer instead of picking from a list. Typing the answer brings up a host of programming problems – if not capitalized correctly, is the answer wrong? If slightly misspelled, is the answer wrong? Add some kind of scoring system. Allow more than one chance at the answer. Notice when selecting a multiple choice answer, if you pick something other than 0 through 4, an error will occur. Can you think of a way to fix this?

This program could also be used to build general multiple choice tests from any two lists. You could do language translations (given a word in English, choose the corresponding word in Spanish), given a book, choose the author, or given an invention, name the inventor. Use your imagination.

Program 6 – Dice Rolling

Program Design

It happens all the time. You get your favorite game out and the dice are missing! This program comes to the rescue – it uses the Small Basic random number generator to roll and display two dice for you. The program

is saved in the **Dice** folder in the program folder (**\BeginSB\BSB Code**). This starts the building of graphics programs in this class.

Program Development

Start Small Basic, start a new program and save it as **Dice**. Type in (or copy and paste from these notes) the complete **StateCapitals** Small Basic code:

```
'
'  Dice Rolling Program
'  Beginning Small Basic
'
GraphicsWindow.Show()
GraphicsWindow.Title = "Dice Rolling - Click to Roll"
GraphicsWindow.Width = 380
GraphicsWindow.Height = 230
GraphicsWindow.MouseDown = MouseDownEvent

Sub MouseDownEvent
  GraphicsWindow.Clear()
  Die1 = Math.GetRandomNumber(6)
  DieX = 20
  DieY = 20
  Die = Die1
  DrawDie()
  Die2 = Math.GetRandomNumber(6)
```

```
  DieX = 200
  DieY = 20
  Die = Die2
  DrawDie()
  GraphicsWindow.BrushColor = "Black"
  GraphicsWindow.FontSize = 18
  GraphicsWindow.DrawText(20, 190, "Total is " + (Die1 + Die2))
EndSub

Sub DrawDie
  ' draw a die
  ' upper corner at DieX, DieY - width and height are 160
  GraphicsWindow.PenColor = "Black"
  GraphicsWindow.DrawRectangle(DieX, DieY, 160, 160)
  'draw dots
  GraphicsWindow.BrushColor = "Black"
  DotSize = 20
  If (Die = 4 Or Die = 5 Or Die = 6) Then
    GraphicsWindow.FillEllipse(DieX + 40 - DotSize / 2, DieY + 40
- DotSize / 2, DotSize, DotSize)
  EndIf
  If (Die = 6) Then
    GraphicsWindow.FillEllipse(DieX + 40 - DotSize / 2, DieY + 80
- DotSize / 2, DotSize, DotSize)
  EndIf
  If (Die = 2 Or Die = 3 Or Die = 4 Or Die = 5 Or Die = 6) Then
    GraphicsWindow.FillEllipse(DieX + 40 - DotSize / 2, DieY + 120
- DotSize / 2, DotSize, DotSize)
  EndIf
  If (Die = 1 Or Die = 3 Or Die = 5) Then
    GraphicsWindow.FillEllipse(DieX + 80 - DotSize / 2, DieY + 80
- DotSize / 2, DotSize, DotSize)
  EndIf
  If (Die = 2 Or Die = 3 Or Die = 4 Or Die = 5 Or Die = 6) Then
    GraphicsWindow.FillEllipse(DieX + 120 - DotSize / 2, DieY + 40
- DotSize / 2, DotSize, DotSize)
  EndIf
  If (Die = 6) Then
    GraphicsWindow.FillEllipse(DieX + 120 - DotSize / 2, DieY + 80
- DotSize / 2, DotSize, DotSize)
  EndIf
  If (Die = 4 Or Die = 5 Or Die = 6) Then
    GraphicsWindow.FillEllipse(DieX + 120 - DotSize / 2, DieY +
120 - DotSize / 2, DotSize, DotSize)
  EndIf
EndSub
```

When the graphics window is clicked (**MouseDown** event), two dice are rolled (random numbers generated), the dice are displayed and the total is printed. The code uses a subroutine (**DrawDie**) to draw a die after it rolls. In this routine, I noted there are seven possible places to draw a dot on a die. I then determine which dot to draw depending on the die value (**Die**). A piece of graph paper comes in handy in laying out the dots on the die.

Run the Program

Save your work. Run the program. Click the window to see the dice roll. Look at the code to see how a random number (1 through 6) is generated and how the dice are drawn. Here's one of my clicks:

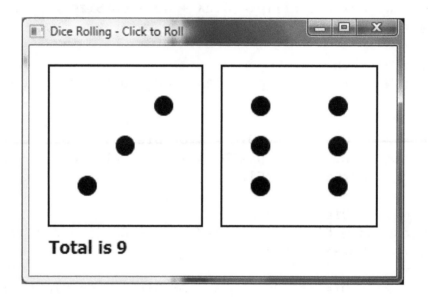

Other Things to Try

The game of Yahtzee requires 5 dice. Modify the program to roll and display five dice. Or, let the user decide how many dice to display. A fun change would be to have the die displays delayed by some amount of time to give the appearance of rolling dice. Small Basic offers a neat little way to induce a delay – the **Program.Delay** method. When the window is clicked, delay, then display each "rolled" die. Perhaps add some sounds too.

Program 7 – Memory Game

Program Design

In this Small Basic game for little kids, ten squares are used to hide five different pairs of shapes. The player (using the mouse) chooses two squares on the board and the shapes behind them are revealed. If the shapes match, those squares are removed from the board. If there is no match, the shapes are recovered and the player tries again. The play continues until all five pairs are matched up. The program is saved in the **Memory** folder in the program folder (**\BeginSB\BSB Code**).

Program Development

Start Small Basic, start a new program and save it as **Memory**. Type in (or copy and paste from these notes) the complete **Memory** Small Basic code:

```
'
'  Memory Game
' Beginning Small Basic
'
' create window
GraphicsWindow.Show()
```

```
GraphicsWindow.Title = "Memory"
GraphicsWindow.Width = 410
GraphicsWindow.Height = 220
' randomly sort integers from 1 to 10
NumberOfIntegers = 10
NIntegers()
Behind = NumberList
' initialize available array to true
' any numbers greater than 5, reduce by 5 for matched set
For i = 1 To 10
  Available[i] = "true"
  If (Behind[i] > 5) Then
    Behind[i] = Behind[i] - 5
  EndIf
EndFor
' pick five random colors for the shapes
For i =1 To 5
  MyColor[i] = Graphicswindow.GetRandomColor()
EndFor
' draw boxes
x = 10
y = 50
BoxColor = GraphicsWindow.GetRandomColor()
GraphicsWindow.BrushColor = BoxColor
For i = 1 To 10
  GraphicsWindow.FillRectangle(x, y, 70, 70)
  x = x + 80
  If (x > 330) Then
    x = 10
    y = y + 80
  EndIf
EndFor
' set to first choice - we're ready to go
Choice = 1
GraphicsWindow.MouseDown = MouseDownEvent
Timer.Interval = 1000
Timer.Tick = TimerTickEvent
Timer.Pause()

Sub MouseDownEvent
  Temp = 0
  ' make sure clicked in box area
  ClickX = GraphicsWindow.MouseX
  ClickY = GraphicsWindow.MouseY
  If (ClickX > 10 And ClickX < 400 And ClickY > 50 And ClickY <
200) Then
```

```
    ' figure out which box was clicked
    If (ClickY > 130) Then
      ' second row (6 to 10)
      Temp = Math.Floor(6 + (ClickX - 5) / 80)
    Else
      ' first row (1 to 5)
      Temp = Math.Floor(1 + (ClickX - 5) / 80)
    EndIf
  EndIf
  If (Temp <> 0) Then
    Picked[Choice] = Temp
    ' only execute following code:
    ' if box is  still available
    ' and not picking same box with second choice
    If (Available[Temp] = "true" And (Choice = 1 Or (Choice = 2
And Picked[1] <> Picked[2]))) Then
      ' draw selected shape
      Shape = Behind[Picked[Choice]]
      Box = Picked[Choice]
      DrawShape()
      If (Choice = 1) Then
        ' first choice - just display
        Choice = 2
      Else
        ' turn on timer to check results
        Timer.Resume()
      EndIf
    Endif
  EndIf
EndSub

Sub TimerTickEvent
  ' check for match once timer event occurs
  Timer.Pause()
  If (Behind[Picked[1]] = Behind[Picked[2]]) Then
    ' If match, remove shapes
    Available[Picked[1]] = "false"
    Available[Picked[2]] = "false"
    Shape = -2
    Box = Picked[1]
    DrawShape()
    Box = Picked[2]
    DrawShape()
  Else
    ' If no match, restore boxes
    Shape = -1
```

```
    Box = Picked[1]
    DrawShape()
    Box = Picked[2]
    DrawShape()
  EndIf
  Choice = 1
EndSub

Sub DrawShape
  'Draw Shape in Box
  ' get coordinates of Box
  If (Box > 5) Then
    yBox = 130
    xBox = 10 + (Box - 6) * 80
  Else
    yBox = 50
    xBox = 10 + (Box - 1) * 80
  EndIf
  ' Clear Box
  GraphicsWindow.BrushColor = GraphicsWindow.BackgroundColor
  GraphicsWindow.FillRectangle(xBox, YBox, 70, 70)
  ' draw shape (do nothing if Shape = -2; it just erases box)
  If (Shape = -1) Then
    'Shape = -1, draw covered box
    GraphicsWindow.BrushColor = BoxColor
    GraphicsWindow.FillRectangle(xBox, YBox, 70, 70)
  ElseIf (Shape = 1) Then
    ' circle
    GraphicsWindow.BrushColor = MyColor[1]
    GraphicsWindow.FillEllipse(xBox, yBox, 70, 70)
  ElseIf (Shape = 2) Then
    ' plus sign
    GraphicsWindow.BrushColor = MyColor[2]
    GraphicsWindow.FillRectangle(xBox, yBox + 25, 70, 20)
    GraphicsWindow.FillRectangle(xBox + 25, yBox, 20, 70)
  ElseIf (Shape = 3) Then
    ' open square
    GraphicsWindow.BrushColor = MyColor[3]
    GraphicsWindow.FillRectangle(xBox, YBox, 70, 70)
    GraphicsWindow.BrushColor = GraphicsWindow.BackgroundColor
    GraphicsWindow.FillRectangle(xBox + 20, yBox + 20, 30, 30)
  ElseIf (Shape = 4) Then
    ' rectangle
    GraphicsWindow.BrushColor = MyColor[3]
    GraphicsWindow.FillRectangle(xBox + 20, yBox, 30, 70)
  ElseIf (Shape = 5) Then
```

```
    ' ellipse
    GraphicsWindow.BrushColor = MyColor[5]
    GraphicsWindow.FillEllipse(xBox + 20, yBox, 30, 70)
  EndIf
EndSub

Sub NIntegers
  'One card shuffle code
  'Initialize NumberList
  For LoopCounter = 1 to NumberOfIntegers
    NumberList[LoopCounter] = LoopCounter
  EndFor
  'Work through Remaining values
  'Start at NumberOfItems and swap one value
  'at each For loop step
  'After each step, Remaining is decreased by 1
  For Remaining = NumberOfIntegers to 2 Step -1
    'Pick item at random
    ItemPicked = Math.GetRandomNumber(Remaining)
    'Swap picked item with bottom item
    TempValue = NumberList[Remaining]
    NumberList[Remaining] = NumberList[ItemPicked]
    NumberList[ItemPicked] = TempValue
  EndFor
EndSub
```

This code sets up the graphics window and event subroutines for mouse presses and timer events (used to implement a delay after displaying shapes). Variables are established to keep track of what shape is behind what box, whether a box has been selected and colors. Notice the hidden shapes are specified by an array of random integers. This computation uses the **NIntegers** subroutine developed back in Class 7. The **MouseDown** event method is used to select boxes (each box is 70 pixels by 70 pixels in size) for display of shapes. The **DrawShape** subroutine is used to draw a particular shape at a particular location. Finally, the timer's subroutine is where we check for a match between selected shapes. The timer is used in the program to insert a one second delay (**Interval** of 1000) between the time the last shape selected is displayed and a decision is made about a match. See if you can follow the code that implements all these steps.

Run the Program

Save your work. Run the program. Ten boxes appear. Click on one and view the shape. Click on another. If there is a match, the two shapes are removed (after a delay). If there is no match, the boxes are restored (also after a delay). The game stops when all matching shape pairs have been found. Here's what the window looks like in the middle of a game:

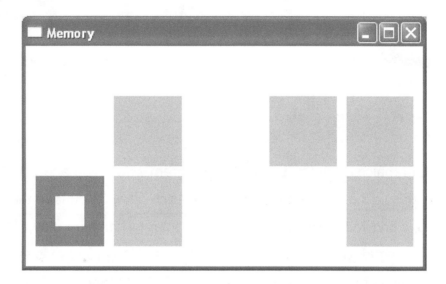

Other Things to Try

Some things to help improve or change this game: add a scoring system to keep track of how many tries you took to find all the matches, make it a two player game where you compete against another player or the computer, or set it up to match other items (colors, upper and lower case letters, numbers and objects, etc.). You might also add logic to let you play again (without rerunning the program), once a game is finished. And, the colors selected are random – what happens if white is selected? See if you can figure out a way to avoid choosing colors that don't look good on a white background.

Program 8 - Tic-Tac-Toe

Program Design

In this graphics program, you build a program where you and someone else can play the classic Tic-Tac-Toe game against each other. You take turns marking a 3 x 3 grid with X's and O's. The computer will monitor play. All selections on the grid will be made using the mouse. The program is saved in the **TicTacToe** folder in the program folder (**\BeginSB\BSB Code**.

Program Development

Start Small Basic, start a new program and save it as **TicTacToe**. Type in (or copy and paste from these notes) the complete **TicTacToe** Small Basic code:

```
'
'  Tic-Tac-Toe Program
'  Beginning Small Basic
'
' create window
GraphicsWindow.Show()
GraphicsWindow.Width = 300
GraphicsWindow.Height = 300
GraphicsWindow.Title = "Tic-Tac-Toe - X's Turn"
```

```
' draw and initialize grid
GraphicsWindow.PenColor = "Black:
For i = 1 To 9
  GridMark[i] = 0
  GraphicsWindow.DrawLine(110, 40, 110, 280)
  GraphicsWindow.DrawLine(190, 40, 190, 280)
  GraphicsWindow.DrawLine(30, 120, 270, 120)
  GraphicsWindow.DrawLine(30, 200, 270, 200)
EndFor
NumberClicks = 0
xTurn = "true"
GraphicsWindow.MouseDown = MouseDownEvent

Sub MouseDownEvent
  x = GraphicsWindow.MouseX
  y = GraphicsWindow.MouseY
  ' If we haven't clicked 9 times, can still click
  If (NumberClicks < 9  And x > 30 And x < 270 And y > 40 And y <
280) Then
    ' determine which grid location was clicked
    ' each square is 80 pixels x 80 pixels
    ' offset by 30 on right and 40 on top
    ' number system:
    '  1 | 2| 3
    ' -----------
    '  4 | 5 | 6
    ' -----------
    '  7 | 8 | 9
    '
    If (y > 200) Then
      ' one of three bottom grids
      GridSelected = Math.Floor(7 + (x - 30) / 80)
      y = 210
    ElseIf (y > 120) Then
      ' one of three middle grids
      GridSelected = Math.Floor(4 + (x - 30) / 80)
      y = 130
    Else
      ' one of three top grids
      GridSelected = Math.Floor(1 + (x - 30) / 80)
      y = 50
    EndIf
    ' If nothing there, can draw new mark
    If (GridMark[GridSelected] = 0) Then
      NumberClicks = NumberClicks + 1
      ' decide where to draw mark
```

```smallbasic
      x = 40 + Math.Remainder(gridSelected - 1, 3) * 80
      If (xTurn = "true") Then
        ' draw X
        GridMark[GridSelected] = 1
        GraphicsWindow.PenColor = "Blue"
        GraphicsWindow.DrawLine(x, y, x + 60, y + 60)
        GraphicsWindow.DrawLine(x, y + 60, x + 60, y)
        xTurn = "false"
        GraphicsWindow.Title = "Tic-Tac-Toe - O's Turn"
      Else
        ' draw O
        GridMark[GridSelected] = 2
        GraphicsWindow.PenColor = "Red"
        GraphicsWindow.DrawEllipse(x, y, 60, 60)
        xTurn = "true"
        GraphicsWindow.Title = "Tic-Tac-Toe - X's Turn"
      EndIf
      If (NumberClicks = 9) Then
        GraphicsWindow.Title = "Tic-Tac-Toe - Game Over"
      EndIf
    EndIf
  EndIf
EndSub
```

In this code, we create a square graphics window and add a subroutine for mouse down events. We use the window title to keep track of whose turn it is. Most of the code is in the **MouseDownEvent** subroutine. In this subroutine, when the window is clicked, if no mark is in the clicked position, one is drawn and it becomes the next player's turn. Try to understand the logic and mathematics of how I determined which grid area was clicked.

Run the Program

Save your work. Run the program. Playing the game is obvious. X goes first and clicks the desired square. Then, it's O's turn. Notice the window title bar tells you whose turn it is. Alternate turns until there is a winner or the grid is full without a winner (a tie). You must restart the program to play another game. Here's a game I played where X is just about to win:

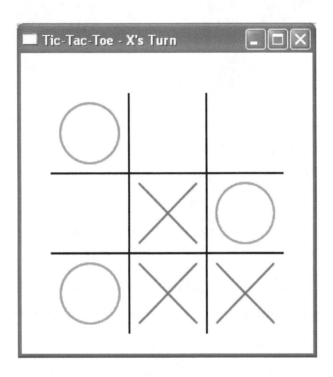

Other Things to Try

Three adaptations to this program jump out. First, can you think of a way to replay a game without rerunning the program? You would need to put all the initialization code and game play code in some kind of loop (similar to what we did for some programs in this course). Second, there is no logic to detect a win. The players must look at the grid and decide if someone has won. See if you can add logic to check if there is a winner after each move. The code would be added at the end of the existing MouseDownEvent subroutine. This code would see if the symbols in the three horizontal directions, three vertical directions or two diagonal directions are the same. If so, a win is declared and the game is stopped. Of use in such code would be elements of the **GridMark** array – that array has values of 0 for an empty space, 1 for an X and 2 for an O.

The last modification (a much tougher one) would be to program the computer to play the game against a human player. You could let the computer have either X's or O's and use some kind of logic (maybe even just random moves for a simple minded computer) for the computer to use in generating moves. You would probably want another a **subroutine** to determine the computer moves. This is one of the first games ever programmed by little Billy Gates!

Program 9 – Decode

Program Design

This program is a classic computer game. The computer generates a four-color code using six possible colors (with no repeating colors). You guess at the code. The computer then tells you how many colors in your guess are correct and how many colors are in the correct location. Based on these clues, you make a new guess. You continue guessing until you have cracked the code. The program is saved in the **Decode** folder in the program folder (**\BeginSB\BSB Code**.

Program Development

Start Small Basic, start a new program and save it as **Decode**. Type in (or copy and paste from these notes) the complete **Decode** Small Basic code:

```
'
'  Decode Program
'  Beginning Small Basic
'
' create frame
GraphicsWindow.Show()
GraphicsWindow.Width = 820
GraphicsWindow.Height = 460
GraphicsWindow.Title = "Decode Colors: R-Red, B-Blue, G-Green, P-Purple, W-White, Y-Yellow"
GraphicsWindow.BackgroundColor = "Gray"
CurrentX = 10
CurrentY = 40
PositionNumber = 1
GameOver = "false"

' put four random digits in array
' use NIntegers method
'we randomize 6 integers, but use first 4, one for each color
NumberOfIntegers = 6
NIntegers()
ComputerCode = NumberList
' drawBlank ovals, give form focus
DrawBlanks()
GraphicsWindow.KeyDown = KeyDownEvent

Sub KeyDownEvent
  If (gameOver = "true") Then
    Goto ExitSub
  EndIf
  If (GraphicsWindow.LastKey = "R") Then
    'red
    EllipseColor = "Red"
    ColorNumber = 1
  ElseIf (GraphicsWindow.LastKey = "B") Then
    'blue
    EllipseColor = "Blue"
    ColorNumber = 2
```

```
ElseIf (GraphicsWindow.LastKey = "G") Then
  'green
  EllipseColor = "Green"
  ColorNumber = 3
ElseIf (GraphicsWindow.LastKey = "P") Then
  'purple
  EllipseColor = "Magenta"
  ColorNumber = 4
ElseIf (GraphicsWindow.LastKey = "W") Then
  'white
  EllipseColor = "White"
  ColorNumber = 5
ElseIf (GraphicsWindow.LastKey = "Y") Then
  'yellow
  EllipseColor = "Yellow"
  ColorNumber = 6
Else
  'some other key
  Goto ExitSub
EndIf
If (PositionNumber > 1) Then
  ' make sure it is a unique choice
  For i = 1 To PositionNumber - 1
    If (YourGuess[i] = ColorNumber) Then
      ' if already used, exit the subroutine
      Goto ExitSub
    EndIf
  EndFor
EndIf
GraphicsWindow.BrushColor = EllipseColor
GraphicsWindow.FillEllipse(CurrentX + (PositionNumber - 1) * 30,
CurrentY, 20, 40)
YourGuess[PositionNumber] = ColorNumber
PositionNumber = PositionNumber + 1
' if 4 colors have been enter - check the guess
If (PositionNumber = 5) Then
  NumberInCode = 0
  NumberInCorrectPosition = 0
  For i = 1 To 4
    For j = 1 To 4
      If (YourGuess[i] = ComputerCode[j]) Then
        NumberInCode = NumberInCode + 1
        If (i = j) Then
          NumberInCorrectPosition = NumberInCorrectPosition + 1
        EndIf
      EndIf
```

```
      EndFor
    EndFor
    ' print score
    GraphicsWindow.BrushColor = "White"
    GraphicsWindow.DrawText(CurrentX + 120, CurrentY + 25,
NumberInCode + "/" + NumberInCorrectPosition)
    If (NumberInCorrectPosition = 4) Then
      ' game over
      GameOver = "true"
      GraphicsWindow.Title = "You got the code ... the game is
over!"
    Else
      ' set up for next guess
      CurrentY = CurrentY + 60
      If (CurrentY > 400) Then
        CurrentY = 40
        CurrentX = CurrentX + 200
      EndIf
      PositionNumber = 1
      DrawBlanks()
    EndIf
  EndIf
ExitSub:
EndSub

Sub DrawBlanks
  ' draw four blank ovals at current position
  GraphicsWindow.PenColor = "White"
  For i = 1 to 4
    GraphicsWindow.DrawEllipse(CurrentX + (i - 1) * 30, CurrentY,
20, 40)
  EndFor
EndSub

Sub NIntegers
  'One card shuffle code
  'Initialize NumberList
  For LoopCounter = 1 to NumberOfIntegers
    NumberList[LoopCounter] = LoopCounter
  EndFor
  'Work through Remaining values
  'Start at NumberOfItems and swap one value
  'at each For loop step
  'After each step, Remaining is decreased by 1
  For Remaining = NumberOfIntegers to 2 Step -1
    'Pick item at random
```

```
    ItemPicked = Math.GetRandomNumber(Remaining)
    'Swap picked item with bottom item
    TempValue = NumberList[Remaining]
    NumberList[Remaining] = NumberList[ItemPicked]
    NumberList[ItemPicked] = TempValue
  EndFor
EndSub
```

Most of the code in this program is involved with generating a four-color computer code and checking the guess you input. Once the window is established, a code is selected (using a variation of the **NIntegers** random integer method we use). You choose colors by typing one of six keys:

R-Red
B-Blue
G-Green
P-Purple (really magenta)
W-White
Y-Yellow

Make sure you understand the code in the **KeyDownEvent** subroutine. See, too, how we make sure the colors selected have not already been used. Once the user selects four colors, their choices are compared to the computer's code. The score is printed out as a text string in the form:

```
NumberInCode/NumberInCorrectPosition
```

Once the code is guessed (NumberInCorrectPosition = 4), the game is over and a message is printed in the window title bar area.

Run the Program

Save your work. Run the program. Type a guess for the four-color code (the title bar lists the color choices). Note the computer will not let you type an illegal guess (non-distinct color). After choosing four colors, the computer will tell you how many colors are correct and how many are in the correct location. The score is displayed as two numbers separated by a slash. The first number is the number of correct colors, the second the number in the correct location. The game stops once you guess the computer's code. Here's a game I played:

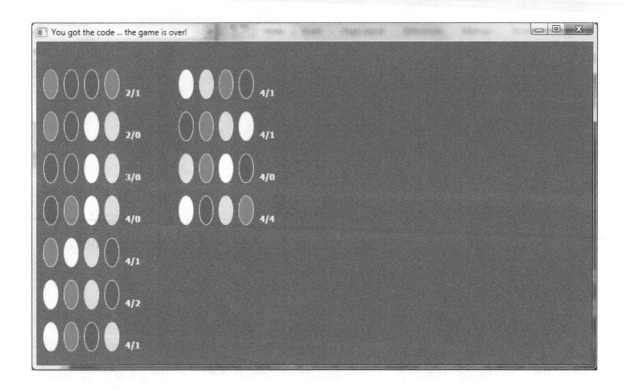

Other Things to Try

You can give this game a variable difficulty by allowing the user to choose how many colors are in the code, how many colors are used to generate the code, and whether colors can repeat. See if you can code up and implement some of these options. You might also implement a "play again" logic or also give the player the option to "give up" and see the correct code.

Lastly, many mathematical papers have been written on developing a computer program that can decode the kinds of codes used here. Do you think you could write a computer program to determine a four color code you make up? The program would work like this: (1) computer makes a guess, (2) you tell computer how many colors are correct and how many are in correct locations, then, (3) computer generates a new guess. The computer would continue guessing until it gave up or guessed your code.

11

Porting Small Basic Computer Games

Using BASIC, Visual Basic, Visual C# and Java

Preview

Back in the early 1980's, there were many computers introduced to the market through such mass retailers as Sears, K Mart, JC Penneys and Radio Shack. Names like Texas Instruments, Atari, Sinclair, Commodore, VIC, Coleco Adam, and TRS-80 appeared everywhere. I personally enjoyed programming each of these computers using the BASIC programming language. The programs below are some of the original BASIC programs I learned to program computers with back in the late 1970s and early 1980s.

This chapter contains two BASIC computer games originally published using BASIC in the classic programming book called "101 Basic Computer Games" originally edited by David H. Ahl and published by DEC. The book was later re-published as "BASIC Computer Games: Microcomputer Edition" by David Ahl in 1973. The original games were simple 'text-only' programs. They had no fancy graphics and no sound. You had to use your

imagination a lot back in those days. Much of the code is structured just like original BASIC programs. The original games were written long before the days of structured programs. However, the games are still fun and invoke a nostalgic feeling in many of us older programmers. Many of us stayed up very late at night typing in all these BASIC games on our computers just so we could learn how to program. BASIC Computer Games made learning the BASIC computer language fun and rewarding.

With special permission of David H. Ahl, this chapter provides you the source code for these original **BASIC COMPUTER GAMES** in four different computer languages: Small Basic, Visual Basic, Visual C#, and Java. This multi-language porting chapter serves several purposes. Atter completing the first ten chapters of this tutorial you should be able to write your own Small Basic programs. This chapter shows you the Small Basic source code to three very simple BASIC Computer Games. We also provide you the source code to these same Computer Games in three other languages so you can see how these games would be programmed in Visual Basic, Visual C# and Java. Kidware Software produces beginning programming tutorials for Visual Basic, Visual C$^#$ and Java so you can study and learn how to program in these popular programming languages yourself. We don't expect you to do that now unless you have already started programming in Visual Basic Express, Visual C# Express or Java.

If you are an experienced Visual Basic, Visual C# or Java developer you can study these classic BASIC Computer Games in your language of choice. Studying the source code in your native programming language will help you transition to programming in Small Basic rather quickly. You also get the added benefit of seeing the source code in other programming languages that you may not have tried yet. Again, we offer several different computer programming tutorials for beginners on our website for each of these languages. The most popular feature of our tutorials is that you develop the exact same games and applications in four different programming languages. This consistent and repetetive multi-language programing technique accelerates the time to learn a new programming langauge.

If you find these classic text based games fun to program in Small Basic, we recently re-published 100 of the original BASIC Computer Games using Microsoft Small Basic. You can find this Special 30th Anniversary Edition of David H. Ahl's **BASIC Computer Games: Small Basic Edition** - on our website.

We also re-published David H. Ahl's classic BASIC COMPUTER ADVENTURES in a new 25th Anniversary Small Basic Editon. These classic text based computer adventure simulation games were fun to program back in the 1980s. The computer adventure simulations you will develop in this tutorial are based on historical personalities like Marco Polo, Amelia Earhart, and on historical events like the Tour de France, The Longest Automobile Race 1908, and the 1847 Oregon Trail. We have also included some fiction adventure simulations like Voyage to Neptune and the Hong Kong Hustle.

SMALL BASIC PROGRAM OPERATION INSTRUCTIONS

The files included with SMALL this tutorial are in a single zipped file. The program files are found in the \SBGames folder. In this folder are four other folders. These folders contain the files needed for each game:

EvenWins - Even Wins files
Mugwump - Mugwump files

To install on your machine, unzip the file to the desired folder. Then, in your Small Basic environment, just open and run the desired SMALL BASIC COMPUTER GAMES program file. The source code requires you to have the Small Basic environment installed on your computer (see our website for details).

VISUAL BASIC PROGRAM OPERATION INSTRUCTIONS

The games were built using Visual Basic.NET and then were converted to Visual Basic Express. Visual Basic Express provides this conversion automatically when you attempt to open a Visual Basic .NET application. So, what's the difference between a Visual Basic .NET application and one built in Visual Basic Express? On the surface, nothing. The controls work the same, the event methods are coded the same way. The applications can be modified using Visual Basic Express. The only difference you will note is in the application file structure. In Visual Basic .NET, all the code written by the environment to establish the controls on a form are included in the form's .vb file. This code will be seen if you expand the "Windows generated form" code icon in the code window. In Visual Basic Express, this code is maintained in a separate form designer file (a Designer.vb file, a partial Class) to keep it hidden from you. Be aware of this slight difference as you build your own Visual Basic Express programs.

The files included with VISUAL BASIC EXPRESS GAMES are in a single zipped file. The program files are found in the VBEGames folder. In this folder are four other folders. These folders contain the files needed for each game:

Even - Even Wins program files
Mugwump - Mugwump program files

To install on your machine, unzip the file to the desired folder. Then, in the Visual Basic Express environment, just load and run the desired VISUAL BASIC EXPRESS GAMES program file.

VISUAL C# PROGRAM OPERATION INSTRUCTIONS

The files included with VISUAL C# EXPRESS GAMES are in a single zipped file. The program files are found in the \VCSEGames folder. In this folder are four other folders. These folders contain the files needed for each game:

Even - Even Wins program files
Mugwump - Mugwump program files

To install on your machine, unzip the file to the desired folder. Then, in the Visual C# Express environment, just load and run the desired VISUAL C# EXPRESS GAMES program file. Running instructions for the four games follow. The programs were originally developed using Visual C# 2005 Express. If you are using a newer version of Visual Studio Express, they will be converted to the newer environment.

JAVA PROGRAM OPERATION INSTRUCTIONS

The files included with JAVA GAMES are in a single zipped file. The program project files are found in the JavaGames folder. In this folder are four other folders. These folders contain the files needed for each game:

EvenProject - Even Wins project files
MugwumpProject - Mugwump project files

To install on your machine, unzip the file to the desired folder. Then, in your Java environment, just load, compile and run the desired JAVA GAMES program file (you also need to compile the Keyin java file in each project folder). I use Xinox JCreator (see http://www.jcreator.com) for my IDE. The download has the corresponding JCreator workspace and project files, if you need them. The source code requires you to have the Java Software Development Kit installed on your computer (see our website for details). Running instructions for the four games follows.

Now on to programming these classic games. EVEN WINS is one of those 'remove the markers' games and MUGWUMP asks you to find the hidden monsters in a grid. Have fun programming these games in Small Basic!

EVEN WINS (Original Author: Eric Peters of Digital Equipment Corporation)
BASIC COMPUTER GAMES, Edited by David H. Ahl, Published in 1978

EVEN WINS is a game between you and the computer. To play, an odd number of markers are displayed on the screen. You take turns with the computer removing between one and four markers each turn. The game ends when there are no markers left and the winner is the one with an even number of markers removed.

When the game begins, the markers (asterisks) are displayed and the computer takes the first turn, removing from one to four markers. Then, on your turn, do the same. Remove from one to four markers by entering 1, 2, 3 or 4 key on your keyboard and pressing <Enter>. After each turn, you are shown how many markers you and the computer have. Continue alternating turns until all markers are gone. You win if you are left with an even number of markers. The computer wins if its score is an even number.

This is an interesting version of this game. The computer starts out only knowing the rules of the game and doesn't play very well. Using simple techniques of artificial intelligence, the computer gradually learns to play from its mistakes until it plays a very good game. After 20 games, the computer is a challenge to beat. Variation in your style of play seems to make the computer learn more quickly. I personally don't know how this code works - maybe you can figure it out. I just typed the code from a magazine - a technique used by many programmers (code 'borrowing').

EVEN WINS – SMALL BASIC SOURCE CODE

```
'
' Even Wins
' Original Author: Bill Palmby, Prairie View, Illinois
' BASIC COMPUTER GAMES,  Edited by David H. Ahl, Published in 1978
' Ported with Permission to Small Basic by Philip Conrod
' © Biblebyte Books, 2010
'
TextWindow.Title = "Even Wins"
TextWindow.WriteLine("Take turns with the computer removing
markers (1 to 4).")
TextWindow.WriteLine("You win if you finish with an even number of
markers.")
'  Variables to help teach computer
For i = 0  to 5
  r[1][i] = 4
  r[0][i] = 4
EndFor

'  Start new game loop
GameLoop:
  gameOver = "false"
  '  number of markers, an odd number
  p = (Math.GetRandomNumber(9) + 3) * 2 + 1
  '  a is your score, b is computer score
  a = 0
  b = 0
  '  Start alternating turn loop
  While (gameOver = "false")
    TextWindow.WriteLine("")
    TextWindow.WriteLine("Computer's turn:")
    drawMarkers()
    ' computers choice and check for win
    e1 = e
    l1 = l
    e = (a / 2 - Math.Floor(a / 2)) * 2
    l = Math.Floor((p / 6 - Math.Floor(p / 6)) * 6 + 0.5)
    if (r[e][l] >= p) then
      '  took last one, game over
      gameOver = "true"
      r[e][l] = p
      m = p
      b = b + p
    else
      gameOver = "false"
```

```
      m = r[e][1]
      b = b + m
    EndIf
    TextWindow.WriteLine("I take " + m + " markers.")
    p = p - m
    if (gameOver = "false") then
      TextWindow.WriteLine("")
      TextWindow.WriteLine("Your turn:")
      ' your turn
      drawMarkers()
      if (p > 4) then
        numberToRemove = 4
      Else
        numberToRemove = p
      EndIf
      GetInput:
      TextWindow.Write("How many markers do you want to remove (1
to " + numberToRemove + ")? ")
      m = TextWindow.ReadNumber()
      If (m <= 0 or m > numberToRemove) Then
        Goto GetInput
      EndIf
      a = a + m
      p = p - m
      if (p = 0) then
        gameOver = "true"
      EndIf

    EndIf

  endwhile

  TextWindow.WriteLine("Game is over. I have " + b + " markers.
You have " + a + " markers.")
  ' find winner
  if (b / 2 = Math.Floor(b / 2)) Then
    TextWindow.WriteLine("I won!!!")
  else
    TextWindow.WriteLine("You won!!!")
    ' computer knowledge gained by you winning
    if (r[e][1] = 1) then
      if (r[e1][11] <> 1) then
        r[e1][11] = r[e1][11] - 1
      endif
    else
      r[e][1] = r[e][1] - 1
```

```
    EndIf
  endif




  TextWindow.Write("Play again? (enter a y for yes) ")
  Answer = TextWindow.Read()
  If (Answer = "y") Then
    Goto GameLoop
  EndIf



  sub drawMarkers
    N = p
    TextWindow.WriteLine("There are " + N + " markers
remaining:")
    for i = 1 to N
      TextWindow.Write("* ")
    EndFor
    TextWindow.WriteLine("")
    TextWindow.WriteLine("I have " + b + " markers.")
    TextWindow.WriteLine("You have " + a + " markers.")
  EndSub
```

EVEN WINS – VISUAL BASIC SOURCE CODE

```
Public Class Form1
    Inherits System.Windows.Forms.Form

#Region " Windows Form Designer generated code "

    Public Sub New()
        MyBase.New()

        'This call is required by the Windows Form Designer.
        InitializeComponent()

        'Add any initialization after the InitializeComponent() call

    End Sub

    'Form overrides dispose to clean up the component list.
    Protected Overloads Overrides Sub Dispose(ByVal disposing As Boolean)
        If disposing Then
            If Not (components Is Nothing) Then
                components.Dispose()
            End If
        End If
        MyBase.Dispose(disposing)
    End Sub

    'Required by the Windows Form Designer
    Private components As System.ComponentModel.IContainer

    'NOTE: The following procedure is required by the Windows Form Designer
    'It can be modified using the Windows Form Designer.
    'Do not modify it using the code editor.
    Friend WithEvents pnlBalls As System.Windows.Forms.Panel
    Friend WithEvents picBall As System.Windows.Forms.PictureBox
    Friend WithEvents lblMessage As System.Windows.Forms.Label
    Friend WithEvents btn1 As System.Windows.Forms.Button
    Friend WithEvents btn2 As System.Windows.Forms.Button
    Friend WithEvents btn3 As System.Windows.Forms.Button
    Friend WithEvents btn4 As System.Windows.Forms.Button
    Friend WithEvents grpInfo As System.Windows.Forms.GroupBox
    Friend WithEvents Label1 As System.Windows.Forms.Label
    Friend WithEvents Label2 As System.Windows.Forms.Label
    Friend WithEvents lblComputer As System.Windows.Forms.Label
    Friend WithEvents lblScore As System.Windows.Forms.Label
    Friend WithEvents GroupBox1 As System.Windows.Forms.GroupBox
    Friend WithEvents btnNew As System.Windows.Forms.Button
    Friend WithEvents btnExit As System.Windows.Forms.Button
    Friend WithEvents timRemove As System.Windows.Forms.Timer
    <System.Diagnostics.DebuggerStepThrough()> Private Sub InitializeComponent()
        Me.components = New System.ComponentModel.Container()
        Dim resources As System.Resources.ResourceManager = New
System.Resources.ResourceManager(GetType(Form1))
        Me.pnlBalls = New System.Windows.Forms.Panel()
        Me.picBall = New System.Windows.Forms.PictureBox()
        Me.lblMessage = New System.Windows.Forms.Label()
        Me.btn1 = New System.Windows.Forms.Button()
```

```
    Me.btn2 = New System.Windows.Forms.Button()
    Me.btn3 = New System.Windows.Forms.Button()
    Me.btn4 = New System.Windows.Forms.Button()
    Me.grpInfo = New System.Windows.Forms.GroupBox()
    Me.lblScore = New System.Windows.Forms.Label()
    Me.lblComputer = New System.Windows.Forms.Label()
    Me.Label2 = New System.Windows.Forms.Label()
    Me.Label1 = New System.Windows.Forms.Label()
    Me.GroupBox1 = New System.Windows.Forms.GroupBox()
    Me.btnExit = New System.Windows.Forms.Button()
    Me.btnNew = New System.Windows.Forms.Button()
    Me.timRemove = New System.Windows.Forms.Timer(Me.components)
    Me.grpInfo.SuspendLayout()
    Me.GroupBox1.SuspendLayout()
    Me.SuspendLayout()
    '
    'pnlBalls
    '
    Me.pnlBalls.BackColor = System.Drawing.Color.White
    Me.pnlBalls.BorderStyle = System.Windows.Forms.BorderStyle.Fixed3D
    Me.pnlBalls.Location = New System.Drawing.Point(8, 8)
    Me.pnlBalls.Name = "pnlBalls"
    Me.pnlBalls.Size = New System.Drawing.Size(424, 176)
    Me.pnlBalls.TabIndex = 0
    '
    'picBall
    '
    Me.picBall.Image = CType(resources.GetObject("picBall.Image"),
System.Drawing.Bitmap)
    Me.picBall.Location = New System.Drawing.Point(24, 376)
    Me.picBall.Name = "picBall"
    Me.picBall.Size = New System.Drawing.Size(32, 32)
    Me.picBall.SizeMode = System.Windows.Forms.PictureBoxSizeMode.StretchImage
    Me.picBall.TabIndex = 1
    Me.picBall.TabStop = False
    Me.picBall.Visible = False
    '
    'lblMessage
    '
    Me.lblMessage.BackColor = System.Drawing.Color.White
    Me.lblMessage.BorderStyle = System.Windows.Forms.BorderStyle.Fixed3D
    Me.lblMessage.Font = New System.Drawing.Font("Arial", 14.25!,
System.Drawing.FontStyle.Regular, System.Drawing.GraphicsUnit.Point, CType(0, Byte))
    Me.lblMessage.ForeColor = System.Drawing.Color.Blue
    Me.lblMessage.Location = New System.Drawing.Point(16, 192)
    Me.lblMessage.Name = "lblMessage"
    Me.lblMessage.Size = New System.Drawing.Size(408, 112)
    Me.lblMessage.TabIndex = 2
    Me.lblMessage.TextAlign = System.Drawing.ContentAlignment.TopCenter
    '
    'btn1
    '
    Me.btn1.Font = New System.Drawing.Font("Microsoft Sans Serif", 12.0!,
System.Drawing.FontStyle.Bold, System.Drawing.GraphicsUnit.Point, CType(0, Byte))
    Me.btn1.Location = New System.Drawing.Point(144, 272)
    Me.btn1.Name = "btn1"
    Me.btn1.Size = New System.Drawing.Size(24, 24)
    Me.btn1.TabIndex = 3
```

```
    Me.btn1.Text = "1"
    Me.btn1.Visible = False
    '
    'btn2
    '
    Me.btn2.Font = New System.Drawing.Font("Microsoft Sans Serif", 12.0!,
System.Drawing.FontStyle.Bold, System.Drawing.GraphicsUnit.Point, CType(0, Byte))
    Me.btn2.Location = New System.Drawing.Point(184, 272)
    Me.btn2.Name = "btn2"
    Me.btn2.Size = New System.Drawing.Size(24, 24)
    Me.btn2.TabIndex = 4
    Me.btn2.Text = "2"
    Me.btn2.Visible = False
    '
    'btn3
    '
    Me.btn3.Font = New System.Drawing.Font("Microsoft Sans Serif", 12.0!,
System.Drawing.FontStyle.Bold, System.Drawing.GraphicsUnit.Point, CType(0, Byte))
    Me.btn3.Location = New System.Drawing.Point(224, 272)
    Me.btn3.Name = "btn3"
    Me.btn3.Size = New System.Drawing.Size(24, 24)
    Me.btn3.TabIndex = 5
    Me.btn3.Text = "3"
    Me.btn3.Visible = False
    '
    'btn4
    '
    Me.btn4.Font = New System.Drawing.Font("Microsoft Sans Serif", 12.0!,
System.Drawing.FontStyle.Bold, System.Drawing.GraphicsUnit.Point, CType(0, Byte))
    Me.btn4.Location = New System.Drawing.Point(264, 272)
    Me.btn4.Name = "btn4"
    Me.btn4.Size = New System.Drawing.Size(24, 24)
    Me.btn4.TabIndex = 6
    Me.btn4.Text = "4"
    Me.btn4.Visible = False
    '
    'grpInfo
    '
    Me.grpInfo.BackColor = System.Drawing.Color.Blue
    Me.grpInfo.Controls.AddRange(New System.Windows.Forms.Control() {Me.lblScore,
Me.lblComputer, Me.Label2, Me.Label1})
    Me.grpInfo.Location = New System.Drawing.Point(72, 312)
    Me.grpInfo.Name = "grpInfo"
    Me.grpInfo.Size = New System.Drawing.Size(288, 72)
    Me.grpInfo.TabIndex = 7
    Me.grpInfo.TabStop = False
    '
    'lblScore
    '
    Me.lblScore.BackColor = System.Drawing.Color.White
    Me.lblScore.BorderStyle = System.Windows.Forms.BorderStyle.Fixed3D
    Me.lblScore.Font = New System.Drawing.Font("Arial", 14.25!,
System.Drawing.FontStyle.Bold, System.Drawing.GraphicsUnit.Point, CType(0, Byte))
    Me.lblScore.Location = New System.Drawing.Point(152, 32)
    Me.lblScore.Name = "lblScore"
    Me.lblScore.Size = New System.Drawing.Size(112, 24)
    Me.lblScore.TabIndex = 3
    Me.lblScore.Text = "0"
```

```
    Me.lblScore.TextAlign = System.Drawing.ContentAlignment.MiddleCenter
    '
    'lblComputer
    '
    Me.lblComputer.BackColor = System.Drawing.Color.White
    Me.lblComputer.BorderStyle = System.Windows.Forms.BorderStyle.Fixed3D
    Me.lblComputer.Font = New System.Drawing.Font("Arial", 14.25!,
System.Drawing.FontStyle.Bold, System.Drawing.GraphicsUnit.Point, CType(0, Byte))
    Me.lblComputer.Location = New System.Drawing.Point(24, 32)
    Me.lblComputer.Name = "lblComputer"
    Me.lblComputer.Size = New System.Drawing.Size(112, 24)
    Me.lblComputer.TabIndex = 2
    Me.lblComputer.Text = "0"
    Me.lblComputer.TextAlign = System.Drawing.ContentAlignment.MiddleCenter
    '
    'Label2
    '
    Me.Label2.Font = New System.Drawing.Font("Arial", 12.0!,
System.Drawing.FontStyle.Regular, System.Drawing.GraphicsUnit.Point, CType(0, Byte))
    Me.Label2.ForeColor = System.Drawing.Color.White
    Me.Label2.Location = New System.Drawing.Point(152, 8)
    Me.Label2.Name = "Label2"
    Me.Label2.Size = New System.Drawing.Size(112, 24)
    Me.Label2.TabIndex = 1
    Me.Label2.Text = "Your Score"
    Me.Label2.TextAlign = System.Drawing.ContentAlignment.TopCenter
    '
    'Label1
    '
    Me.Label1.Font = New System.Drawing.Font("Arial", 12.0!,
System.Drawing.FontStyle.Regular, System.Drawing.GraphicsUnit.Point, CType(0, Byte))
    Me.Label1.ForeColor = System.Drawing.Color.White
    Me.Label1.Location = New System.Drawing.Point(16, 8)
    Me.Label1.Name = "Label1"
    Me.Label1.Size = New System.Drawing.Size(136, 24)
    Me.Label1.TabIndex = 0
    Me.Label1.Text = "Computer Score"
    Me.Label1.TextAlign = System.Drawing.ContentAlignment.TopCenter
    '
    'GroupBox1
    '
    Me.GroupBox1.BackColor = System.Drawing.Color.Blue
    Me.GroupBox1.Controls.AddRange(New System.Windows.Forms.Control() {Me.btnExit,
Me.btnNew})
    Me.GroupBox1.Location = New System.Drawing.Point(72, 392)
    Me.GroupBox1.Name = "GroupBox1"
    Me.GroupBox1.Size = New System.Drawing.Size(288, 56)
    Me.GroupBox1.TabIndex = 9
    Me.GroupBox1.TabStop = False
    '
    'btnExit
    '
    Me.btnExit.BackColor = System.Drawing.SystemColors.Control
    Me.btnExit.Location = New System.Drawing.Point(160, 16)
    Me.btnExit.Name = "btnExit"
    Me.btnExit.Size = New System.Drawing.Size(96, 24)
    Me.btnExit.TabIndex = 1
    Me.btnExit.Text = "Exit"
```

```
    '
    'btnNew
    '
    Me.btnNew.BackColor = System.Drawing.SystemColors.Control
    Me.btnNew.Location = New System.Drawing.Point(32, 16)
    Me.btnNew.Name = "btnNew"
    Me.btnNew.Size = New System.Drawing.Size(96, 24)
    Me.btnNew.TabIndex = 0
    Me.btnNew.Text = "New Game"
    '
    'timRemove
    '
    Me.timRemove.Interval = 1000
    '
    'Form1
    '
    Me.AutoScaleDimensions = New System.Drawing.SizeF(5.0!, 13.0!)
    Me.ClientSize = New System.Drawing.Size(440, 455)
    Me.Controls.AddRange(New System.Windows.Forms.Control() {Me.GroupBox1,
Me.grpInfo, Me.btn4, Me.btn3, Me.btn2, Me.btn1, Me.lblMessage, Me.picBall,
Me.pnlBalls})
    Me.FormBorderStyle = System.Windows.Forms.FormBorderStyle.FixedSingle
    Me.KeyPreview = True
    Me.Name = "Form1"
    Me.StartPosition = System.Windows.Forms.FormStartPosition.CenterScreen
    Me.Text = "Even Wins"
    Me.grpInfo.ResumeLayout(False)
    Me.GroupBox1.ResumeLayout(False)
    Me.ResumeLayout(False)

  End Sub

#End Region
  Dim picMarker(20) As PictureBox
  Dim GameOver As Boolean
  Dim Message As String
  Dim A As Integer, B As Integer
  Dim E As Integer, L As Integer
  Dim E1 As Integer, L1 As Integer
  Dim R(1, 5) As Integer, M As Integer, P As Integer
  Dim NumberToRemove As Integer
  Dim ComputersTurn As Boolean
  Dim LastOne As Boolean
  Dim MyRandom As New Random

  Private Sub Form1_Load(ByVal sender As System.Object, ByVal e As System.EventArgs)
Handles MyBase.Load
    Dim I As Integer, Border As Integer
    Dim Lf As Integer, T As Integer, W As Integer, H As Integer
    'create 21 picture boxes, with 5 pixels border
    'seven boxes in each row
    Border = 5
    W = Int((pnlBalls.ClientSize.Width - 8 * Border) / 7)
    H = Int((pnlBalls.ClientSize.Height - 4 * Border) / 3)
    Lf = Border
    T = Border
    For I = 0 To 20
      picMarker(I) = New PictureBox()
```

```
      picMarker(I).SizeMode = PictureBoxSizeMode.StretchImage
      picMarker(I).Left = Lf
      picMarker(I).Top = T
      picMarker(I).Width = W
      picMarker(I).Height = H
      pnlBalls.Controls.Add(picMarker(I))
      Lf = Lf + W + Border
      If Lf >= pnlBalls.Width - W Then
        Lf = Border
        T = T + H + Border
      End If
    Next
    'Variables to help teach computer
    For I = 0 To 5
      R(1, I) = 4
      R(0, I) = 4
    Next I
    lblMessage.Text = "Take turns with the computer removing beach balls (1 to 4).
You win if you finish with an even number of beach balls."
    lblMessage.Text = lblMessage.Text + ControlChars.CrLf + ">>Click New Game To
Start<<"
    btnNew.Focus()
  End Sub


  Private Sub btnNew_Click(ByVal sender As System.Object, ByVal e As
System.EventArgs) Handles btnNew.Click
    Dim I As Integer
    'Start new game
    GameOver = False
    lblMessage.Text = ""
    btnNew.Enabled = False
    btnExit.Text = "Stop"
    lblComputer.Text = "0"
    lblScore.Text = "0"
    Message = ""
    P = MyRandom.Next(7) * 2 + 9
    For I = 0 To 20
      picMarker(I).Visible = False
    Next I
    For I = 0 To P - 1
      picMarker(I).Image = picBall.Image
      picMarker(I).Visible = True
    Next I
    'A is your markers, B is computer
    A = 0
    B = 0
    Call ComputerTurn()
  End Sub


  Private Sub btnExit_Click(ByVal sender As System.Object, ByVal e As
System.EventArgs) Handles btnExit.Click
    'Either exit or stop current game
    If btnExit.Text = "Exit" Then
      Me.Close()
    Else
      btn1.Visible = False
```

```
      btn2.Visible = False
      btn3.Visible = False
      btn4.Visible = False
      btnExit.Text = "Exit"
      btnNew.Enabled = True
      If Not (GameOver) Then lblMessage.Text = ControlChars.CrLf + "Game Stopped"
      btnNew.Focus()
    End If
  End Sub

  Private Sub ComputerTurn()
    ComputersTurn = True
    'Computer choice - check for win
    E1 = E : L1 = L
    E = (A / 2 - Int(A / 2)) * 2
    L = Int((P / 6 - Int(P / 6)) * 6 + 0.5)
    If R(E, L) >= P Then
      'Took last one - game over
      LastOne = True
      R(E, L) = P
      M = P
      B = B + P
    Else
      LastOne = False
      M = R(E, L)
      B = B + M
    End If
    lblMessage.Text = ControlChars.CrLf + "Computer takes" + Str(M) + " beach
ball(s)."
    Call RemoveMarkers(M)
  End Sub


  Private Sub btn1_Click(ByVal sender As System.Object, ByVal e As System.EventArgs)
Handles btn1.Click
    Call YourTurn(1)
  End Sub

  Private Sub btn2_Click(ByVal sender As System.Object, ByVal e As System.EventArgs)
Handles btn2.Click
    Call YourTurn(2)
  End Sub

  Private Sub btn3_Click(ByVal sender As System.Object, ByVal e As System.EventArgs)
Handles btn3.Click
    Call YourTurn(3)
  End Sub

  Private Sub btn4_Click(ByVal sender As System.Object, ByVal e As System.EventArgs)
Handles btn4.Click
    Call YourTurn(4)
  End Sub

  Private Sub YourTurn(ByVal M As Integer)
    ComputersTurn = False
    btn1.Visible = False
    btn2.Visible = False
    btn3.Visible = False
```

```
      btn4.Visible = False
      lblMessage.Text = ControlChars.CrLf + "You removed" + Str(M) + " beach ball(s)."
      A = A + M
      Call RemoveMarkers(M)
  End Sub

  Private Sub RemoveMarkers(ByVal N As Integer)
      'Remove N markers
      NumberToRemove = N
      timRemove.Enabled = True
  End Sub

  Private Sub FinishTurn()
      Dim Imax As Integer
      If ComputersTurn Then
        lblComputer.Text = Format(B, "0")
        lblComputer.Refresh()
        If LastOne Then
          Call FindWinner()
          Exit Sub
        Else
          lblMessage.Text = lblMessage.Text + ControlChars.CrLf + "There are" + Str(P)
+ " remaining - Your move."
          lblMessage.Refresh()
          Imax = 4
          If P < Imax Then Imax = P
          btn1.Visible = True
          If Imax > 1 Then
            btn2.Visible = True
          End If
          If Imax > 2 Then
            btn3.Visible = True
          End If
          If Imax > 3 Then
            btn4.Visible = True
          End If
        End If
      Else
        lblScore.Text = Format(A, "0")
        lblScore.Refresh()
        'If none remaining, see who won - else continue
        If P = 0 Then
          Call FindWinner()
          Exit Sub
        Else
          Message = ControlChars.CrLf
          Call ComputerTurn()
        End If
      End If
  End Sub

  Private Sub FindWinner()
      GameOver = True
      If (B / 2) = Int(B / 2) Then
        'Computer wins
        lblMessage.Text = lblMessage.Text + ControlChars.CrLf + "Game Over. Computer
Wins!!!"
        lblMessage.Refresh()
```

```
      Else
        'You win
        lblMessage.Text = lblMessage.Text + ControlChars.CrLf + "Game Over. You
Win!!!"
        lblMessage.Refresh()
        'Computer knowledge gained by you winning
        If R(E, L) = 1 Then
          If R(E1, L1) <> 1 Then
            R(E1, L1) = R(E1, L1) - 1
          End If
        Else
          R(E, L) = R(E, L) - 1
        End If
      End If
      btnExit.PerformClick()
    End Sub



    Private Sub timRemove_Tick(ByVal sender As System.Object, ByVal e As
System.EventArgs) Handles timRemove.Tick
      picMarker(P - 1).Visible = False
      picMarker(P - 1).Refresh()
      P = P - 1
      Beep()
      timRemove.Enabled = False
      NumberToRemove = NumberToRemove - 1
      If NumberToRemove > 0 Then
        timRemove.Enabled = True
      Else
        Call FinishTurn()
      End If
    End Sub

    Private Sub Form1_KeyPress(ByVal sender As Object, ByVal e As
System.Windows.Forms.KeyPressEventArgs) Handles MyBase.KeyPress
      Select Case e.KeyChar
        Case "1"
          Call YourTurn(1)
        Case "2"
          Call YourTurn(2)
        Case "3"
          Call YourTurn(3)
        Case "4"
          Call YourTurn(4)
      End Select
    End Sub
End Class
```

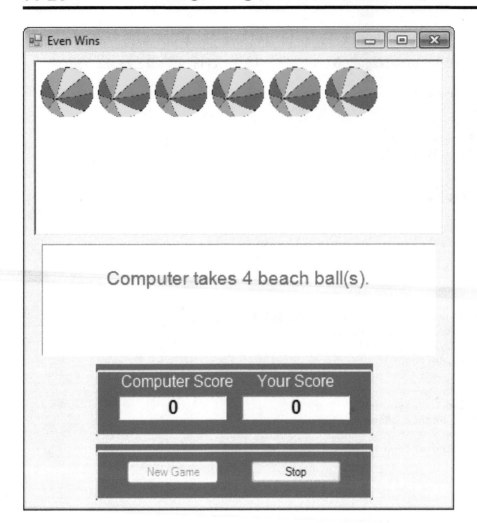

EVEN WINS – VISUAL C# SOURCE CODE

```csharp
#region Using directives

using System;
using System.Collections.Generic;
using System.ComponentModel;
using System.Data;
using System.Drawing;
using System.Windows.Forms;

#endregion

namespace Even
{
    partial class Form1 : Form
    {
        public Form1()
        {
            InitializeComponent();
        }
        PictureBox[] picMarker = new PictureBox[21];
        bool gameOver;
        int a, b, e, l, e1, l1, m, p;
        int[,] r = new int[2, 6];
        int numberToRemove;
        bool computersTurn;
        bool lastOne;
        Random myRandom = new Random();

        private void Form1_Load(object sender, EventArgs e)
        {
            int i, border;
            int lf, t, w, h;
            // create 21 picture boxes, with 5 pixels border
            // seven boxes in each row
            border = 5;
            w = (int) ((pnlBalls.ClientSize.Width - 8 * border) / 7);
            h = (int) ((pnlBalls.ClientSize.Height - 4 * border) / 3);
            lf = border;
            t = border;
            for (i = 0; i < 21; i++)
            {
                picMarker[i] = new PictureBox();
                picMarker[i].SizeMode = PictureBoxSizeMode.StretchImage;
                picMarker[i].Left = lf;
                picMarker[i].Top = t;
                picMarker[i].Width = w;
                picMarker[i].Height = h;
                pnlBalls.Controls.Add(picMarker[i]);
                lf = lf + w + border;
                if (lf >= pnlBalls.Width - w)
                {
                    lf = border;
                    t = t + h + border;
                }
            }
            // Variables to help teach computer
```

```
        for (i = 0; i < 6; i++)
        {
            r[1, i] = 4;
            r[0, i] = 4;
        }
        lblMessage.Text = "Take turns with the computer removing beach balls (1
to 4). You win if you finish with an even number of beach balls.";
        lblMessage.Text = lblMessage.Text + "\r\n>>Click New Game To Start<<";
        btnNew.Focus();
    }

    private void btnNew_Click(object sender, EventArgs e)
    {
        int i;
        // Start new game
        gameOver = false;
        lblMessage.Text = "";
        btnNew.Enabled = false;
        btnExit.Text = "Stop";
        lblComputer.Text = "0";
        lblScore.Text = "0";
        p = myRandom.Next(7) * 2 + 9;
        for (i = 0; i < 21; i++)
        {
            picMarker[i].Visible = false;
        }
        for (i = 0; i < p; i++)
        {
            picMarker[i].Image = picBall.Image;
            picMarker[i].Visible = true;
        }
        // A is your markers, B is computer
        a = 0;
        b = 0;
        ComputerTurn();
    }

    private void btnExit_Click(object sender, EventArgs e)
    {
        // Either exit or stop current game
        if (btnExit.Text == "Exit")
        {
            this.Close();
        }
        else
        {
            btn1.Visible = false;
            btn2.Visible = false;
            btn3.Visible = false;
            btn4.Visible = false;
            btnExit.Text = "Exit";
            btnNew.Enabled = true;
            if (!gameOver)
            {
                lblMessage.Text = "\r\nGame Stopped";
            }
            btnNew.Focus();
        }
```

```csharp
}

private void btn1_Click(object sender, EventArgs e)
{
    YourTurn(1);
}

private void btn2_Click(object sender, EventArgs e)
{
    YourTurn(2);
}

private void btn3_Click(object sender, EventArgs e)
{
    YourTurn(3);
}

private void btn4_Click(object sender, EventArgs e)
{
    YourTurn(4);
}

private void Form1_KeyPress(object sender, KeyPressEventArgs e)
{
    switch (e.KeyChar)
    {
        case '1':
            YourTurn(1);
            break;
        case '2':
            YourTurn(2);
            break;
        case '3':
            YourTurn(3);
            break;
        case '4':
            YourTurn(4);
            break;
    }
}

private void timRemove_Tick(object sender, EventArgs e)
{
    picMarker[p - 1].Visible = false;
    picMarker[p - 1].Refresh();
    p = p - 1;
    Console.Beep();
    timRemove.Enabled = false;
    numberToRemove = numberToRemove - 1;
    if (numberToRemove > 0)
    {
        timRemove.Enabled = true;
    }
    else
    {
        FinishTurn();
    }
}
```

```csharp
private void ComputerTurn()
{
    computersTurn = true;
    // Computer choice - check for win
    e1 = e; l1 = l;
    e = a % 2;
    l = p % 6;
    if (r[e, l] >= p)
    {
        // Took last one - game over
        lastOne = true;
        r[e, l] = p;
        m = p;
        b = b + p;
    }
    else
    {
        lastOne = false;
        m = r[e, l];
        b = b + m;
    }
    lblMessage.Text = "\r\nComputer takes " + Convert.ToString(m) + " beach ball(s).";
    RemoveMarkers(m);
}


private void YourTurn(int m)
{
    computersTurn = false;
    btn1.Visible = false;
    btn2.Visible = false;
    btn3.Visible = false;
    btn4.Visible = false;
    lblMessage.Text = "You removed " + Convert.ToString(m) + " beach ball(s).";
    a = a + m;
    RemoveMarkers(m);
}

private void RemoveMarkers(int n)
{
    // Remove N markers
    numberToRemove = n;
    timRemove.Enabled = true;
}

private void FinishTurn()
{
    int iMax;
    if (computersTurn)
    {
        lblComputer.Text = Convert.ToString(b);
        lblComputer.Refresh();
        if (lastOne)
        {
```

```
            FindWinner();
            return;
        }
        else
        {
            lblMessage.Text = lblMessage.Text + "\r\nThere are " +
Convert.ToString(p) + " remaining - Your move.";
            lblMessage.Refresh();
            iMax = 4;
            if (p < iMax)
            {
                iMax = p;
            }
            btn1.Visible = true;
            if (iMax > 1)
            {
                btn2.Visible = true;
            }
            if (iMax > 2)
            {
                btn3.Visible = true;
            }
            if (iMax > 3)
            {
                btn4.Visible = true;
            }
        }
    }
    else
    {
        lblScore.Text = Convert.ToString(a);
        lblScore.Refresh();
        // If none remaining, see who won - else continue
        if (p == 0)
        {
            FindWinner();
            return;
        }
        else
        {
            ComputerTurn();
        }
    }
}

private void FindWinner()
{
    gameOver = true;
    if (b % 2 == 0)
    {
        // Computer wins
        lblMessage.Text = lblMessage.Text + "\r\nGame Over. Computer
Wins!!!";
        lblMessage.Refresh();
    }
    else
    {
        // You win
```

```
        lblMessage.Text = lblMessage.Text + "\r\nGame Over. You Win!!!";
        lblMessage.Refresh();
        // Computer knowledge gained by you winning
        if (r[e, l] == 1)
        {
            if (r[e1, l1] != 1)
            {
                r[e1, l1] = r[e1, l1] - 1;
            }
        }
        else
        {
            r[e, l] = r[e, l] - 1;
        }
    }
    btnExit.PerformClick();
}

    }
}
```

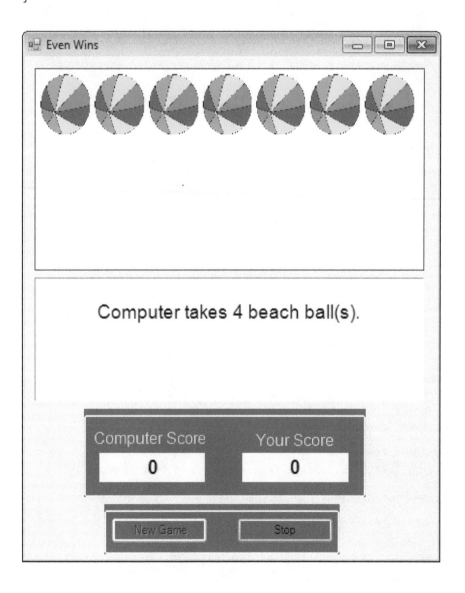

EVEN WINS – JAVA SOURCE CODE

```java
/*
 * Even Wins
 * Original Author: Eric Peters of Digital Equipment Corporation
 * BASIC COMPUTER GAMES,  Edited by David H. Ahl, Published in 1978
 * Ported with Permission to Java by Philip Conrod
 * © Biblebyte Books, 2010 - Find more at http://www.biblebytebooks.com
 */

import java.util.Random;

public class Even
{


        public static void main(String[] args)
        {

                boolean gameOver;
                int a, b;
                int e = 0, l = 0;
                int e1, l1;
                int m, p;
                int r[][] = new int[2][6];
                int numberToRemove;
                Random jRandom = new Random();

                System.out.println("Even Wins\n");
                System.out.println("Take turns with the computer removing markers (1 to 4).");
                System.out.println("You win if you finish with an even number of markers.\n");
                // Variables to help teach computer
                for (int i = 0; i < 6; i++)
                {
                        r[1][i] = 4;
                        r[0][i] = 4;
                }

                // Start new game loop
                do
                {
                        gameOver = false;
                        // number of markers, an odd number
                        p = (jRandom.nextInt(9) + 4) * 2 +1;
                        // a is your score, b is computer score
                        a = 0;
                        b = 0;
                        // Start alternating turn loop
                        do
                        {
                                System.out.println("\nComputer's turn:");
                                drawMarkers(p, a, b);
                                // computers choice and check for win
                                e1 = e;
```

```java
l1 = l;
e = (a / 2 - (int) (a / 2)) * 2;
l = (int) ((p / 6 - (int) (p / 6)) * 6 + 0.5);
if (r[e][l] >= p)
{
        //  took last one, game over
        gameOver = true;
        r[e][l] = p;
        m = p;
        b += p;
}
else
{
        gameOver = false;
        m = r[e][l];
        b += m;
}
System.out.println("I take " + m + " markers.");
p -= m;
if (!gameOver)
{
        System.out.println("\nYour turn:");
        // your turn
        drawMarkers(p, a, b);
        if (p > 4)
        {
                numberToRemove = 4;
        }
        else
        {
                numberToRemove = p;
        }
        do
        {
                m = Keyin.inInt("How many markers do you want
to remove (1 to " + numberToRemove + ")?");
        }
        while (m <= 0 || m > numberToRemove);
        a += m;
        p -= m;
        if (p == 0)
        {
                gameOver = true;
        }
}
}
while (!gameOver);
System.out.println("Game is over. I have " + b + " markers. You have " + a
+ " markers.");

// find winner
if ((float) (b)/ 2 == (int) (b / 2))
{
        System.out.println("I won!!!");
}
else
{
```

```
                                System.out.println("You won!!!");
                                //  computer knowledge gained by you winning
                                if (r[e][l] == 1)
                                {
                                        if (r[e1][l1] != 1)
                                        {
                                                r[e1][l1]--;
                                        }
                                }
                                else
                                {
                                        r[e][l]--;
                                }
                        }
                }
                while (Keyin.inString("\nPlay again? (enter a y for yes)").equals("y"));
        }

        private static void drawMarkers(int N, int A, int B)
        {
                System.out.println("There are " + N + " markers remaining:");
                for (int i = 0; i < N; i++)
                {
                        System.out.print("* ");
                }
                System.out.println();
                System.out.println("I have " + B + " markers.");
                System.out.println("You have " + A + " markers.");
        }

}
```

EVEN WINS – ORIGINAL BASIC SOURCE CODE

```
1 PRINT TAB(31);"EVEN WINS"
2 PRINT TAB(15);"CREATIVE COMPUTING  MORRISTOWN, NEW JERSEY"
3 PRINT:PRINT
4 Y1=0
10 M1=0
20 DIM M(20),Y(20)
30 PRINT "    THIS IS A TWO PERSON GAME CALLED 'EVEN WINS.'"
40 PRINT "TO PLAY THE GAME, THE PLAYERS NEED 27 MARBLES OR"
50 PRINT "OTHER OBJECTS ON A TABLE."
60 PRINT
70 PRINT
80 PRINT "    THE 2 PLAYERS ALTERNATE TURNS, WITH EACH PLAYER"
90 PRINT "REMOVING FROM 1 TO 4 MARBLES ON EACH MOVE.  THE GAME"
100 PRINT "ENDS WHEN THERE ARE NO MARBLES LEFT, AND THE WINNER"
110 PRINT "IS THE ONE WITH AN EVEN NUMBER OF MARBLES."
120 PRINT
130 PRINT
140 PRINT "    THE ONLY RULES ARE THAT (1) YOU MUST ALTERNATE TURNS,"
150 PRINT "(2) YOU MUST TAKE BETWEEN 1 AND 4 MARBLES EACH TURN,"
160 PRINT "AND (3) YOU CANNOT SKIP A TURN."
170 PRINT
180 PRINT
190 PRINT
200 PRINT "    TYPE A '1' IF YOU WANT TO GO FIRST, AND TYPE"
210 PRINT "A '0' IF YOU WANT ME TO GO FIRST."
220 INPUT C
225 PRINT
230 IF C=0 THEN 250
240 GOTO 1060
250 T=27
260 M=2
270 PRINT:PRINT "TOTAL=";T:PRINT
280 M1=M1+M
290 T=T-M
300 PRINT "I PICK UP";M;"MARBLES."
310 IF T=0 THEN 880
320 PRINT:PRINT "TOTAL=";T
330 PRINT
340 PRINT "    AND WHAT IS YOUR NEXT MOVE, MY TOTAL IS";M1
350 INPUT Y
360 PRINT
370 IF Y<1 THEN 1160
380 IF Y>4 THEN 1160
390 IF Y<=T THEN 430
400 PRINT "    YOU HAVE TRIED TO TAKE MORE MARBLES THAN THERE ARE"
410 PRINT "LEFT.  TRY AGAIN."
420 GOTO 350
430 Y1=Y1+Y
440 T=T-Y
450 IF T=0 THEN 880
460 PRINT "TOTAL=";T
470 PRINT
480 PRINT "YOUR TOTAL IS";Y1
```

```
490 IF T<.5 THEN 880
500 R=T-6*INT(T/6)
510 IF INT(Y1/2)=Y1/2 THEN 700
520 IF T<4.2 THEN 580
530 IF R>3.4 THEN 620
540 M=R+1
550 M1=M1+M
560 T=T-M
570 GOTO 300
580 M=T
590 T=T-M
600 GOTO 830
610 REM    250 IS WHERE I WIN.
620 IF R<4.7 THEN 660
630 IF R>3.5 THEN 660
640 M=1
650 GOTO 670
660 M=4
670 T=T-M
680 M1=M1+M
690 GOTO 300
700 REM    I AM READY TO ENCODE THE STRAT FOR WHEN OPP TOT IS EVEN
710 IF R<1.5 THEN 1020
720 IF R>5.3 THEN 1020
730 M=R-1
740 M1=M1+M
750 T=T-M
760 IF T<.2 THEN 790
770 REM    IS # ZERO HERE
780 GOTO 300
790 REM    IS = ZERO HERE
800 PRINT "I PICK UP";M;"MARBLES."
810 PRINT
820 GOTO 880
830 REM    THIS IS WHERE I WIN
840 PRINT "I PICK UP";M;"MARBLES."
850 PRINT
860 PRINT "TOTAL = 0"
870 M1=M1+M
880 PRINT "THAT IS ALL OF THE MARBLES."
890 PRINT
900 PRINT " MY TOTAL IS";M1;", YOUR TOTAL IS";Y1
910 PRINT
920 IF INT(M1/2)=M1/2 THEN 950
930 PRINT "    YOU WON.  DO YOU WANT TO PLAY"
940 GOTO 960
950 PRINT "    I WON.  DO YOU WANT TO PLAY"
960 PRINT "AGAIN?  TYPE 1 FOR YES AND 0 FOR NO."
970 INPUT A1
980 IF A1=0 THEN 1030
990 M1=0
1000 Y1=0
1010 GOTO 200
1020 GOTO 640
1030 PRINT
1040 PRINT "OK.  SEE YOU LATER."
```

```
1050 GOTO 1230
1060 T=27
1070 PRINT
1080 PRINT
1090 PRINT
1100 PRINT "TOTAL=";T
1110 PRINT
1120 PRINT
1130 PRINT "WHAT IS YOUR FIRST MOVE";
1140 INPUT Y
1150 GOTO 360
1160 PRINT
1170 PRINT "THE NUMBER OF MARBLES YOU TAKE MUST BE A POSITIVE"
1180 PRINT "INTEGER BETWEEN 1 AND 4."
1190 PRINT
1200 PRINT "    WHAT IS YOUR NEXT MOVE?"
1210 PRINT
1220 GOTO 350
1230 END
```

MUGWUMP (Original Author: Bob Albrecht of Peoples Computer Company)
BASIC COMPUTER GAMES, Edited by David H. Ahl, Published in 1978

The objective in this game is to find the four Mugwumps hiding on various squares of a 10 x 10 grid. After guessing a location, the computer gives you distance clues on how far you are from each Mugwump.

At the beginning of each game, a blank grid is shown. Choose a square to guess the location of a Mugwump. To choose a square, you are asked to enter the row (0 to 9) and column (0 to 9) of the selected square. After your guess, you are told how far (the famous Pythagorean triangle formula is used) you are from each remaining Mugwump. Use this information for your next guess. The program tells you how many Mugwumps are remaining and how many guesses you have taken. The game ends when all the Mugwumps have been found.

Playing the game with aid of graph paper and a compass should allow you to find all the Mugwumps in six or seven moves using triangulation similar to old Loran radio navigation (do some research to find out what this is).

MUGWUMP – SMALL BASIC SOURCE CODE

```smallbasic
'
' Mugwump
' Original Author: Bob Albrecht of Peoples Computer Company
' BASIC COMPUTER GAMES,  Edited by David H. Ahl, Published in 1978
' Ported with Permission to Small Basic by Philip Conrod
' © Biblebyte Books, 2010
'
TextWindow.Title = "Mugwump"
TextWindow.WriteLine("Find the four Mugwumps hidden on a 10 x 10
grid.")
TextWindow.WriteLine("After each guess, you are told how far you
are from each Mugwump.")
TextWindow.WriteLine("")

'  Start new game loop
GameLoop:
  remaining = 4
  tries = 0
  '  hide mugwumps
  for i = 0 to 9
    for j = 0 To 9
      map[i][j] = 0
    EndFor
  EndFor
  for i = 0 To 3
    HideHim:
      for j = 0 to 1
        p[i][j] = Math.GetRandomNumber(10) - 1
      endfor
      If (map[p[i][0]][p[i][1]] <> 0) Then
        Goto HideHim
      EndIf
      map[p[i][0]][p[i][1]] = 1
  EndFor
  for i = 0 To 3
    map[p[i][0]][p[i][1]] = 0
  EndFor
  '  Next turn loop
  While(remaining > 0)
    ' draw current game board grid
    TextWindow.WriteLine("Current grid (O-Guess, X-Last Guess, M-
Mugwump):")
    TextWindow.WriteLine("  0 1 2 3 4 5 6 7 8 9")
    for i = 0 To 9
```

```
        TextWindow.Write((i) + "|")
        For j = 0 To 9
          if (map[i][j] = 0) Then
            TextWindow.Write(" |")
          elseif (map[i][j] = 1) Then
            TextWindow.Write("O|")
          elseif (map[i][j] = 2) Then
            TextWindow.Write("X|")
            map[i][j] = 1
          Else
               TextWindow.Write("M|")
          EndIf
        EndFor
        TextWindow.WriteLine("")
      EndFor
GetInput:
TextWindow.Write("What row? ")
m = TextWindow.ReadNumber()
TextWindow.Write("What column? ")
n = TextWindow.ReadNumber()
if (m < 0 or m > 9 or n <0 Or n > 9) then
  Goto GetInput
EndIf
if (map[m][n] = 1) Then
  TextWindow.WriteLine("You already looked there!")
elseif (map[m][n] = 2) Then
  TextWindow.WriteLine("You already looked there!")
elseif (map[m][n] = 3) Then
  TextWindow.WriteLine("You already found this Mugwump!")
Else
  tries = tries + 1
  found = "false"
  for i = 0 to 3
    if (p[i][0] <> -1) then
      if (p[i][0] <> m or p[i][1] <> n) Then
        map[m][n] = 2
        d = Math.SquareRoot((p[i][0] - m) * (p[i][0] - m) +
(p[i][1] - n) * (p[i][1] - n))
        TextWindow.WriteLine("You are " + d + " units from
Mugwump " + (i + 1))
      Else
        found = "true"
      p[i][0] = -1
        TextWindow.WriteLine("You found Mugwump " + (i + 1) +
"!")
        remaining = remaining - 1
```

```
        EndIf
      Endif
    if (found = "true") then
        map[m][n] = 3
      EndIf
    EndFor
  endif


  EndWhile



TextWindow.Write("Play again? (enter a y for yes) ")
Answer = TextWindow.Read()
If (Answer = "y") Then
  Goto GameLoop
EndIf
```

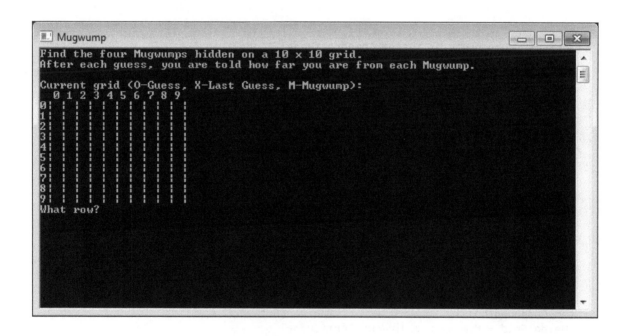

MUGWUMP – VISUAL BASIC SOURCE CODE

```vb
Public Class Form1
    Inherits System.Windows.Forms.Form

#Region " Windows Form Designer generated code "

    Public Sub New()
        MyBase.New()

        'This call is required by the Windows Form Designer.
        InitializeComponent()

        'Add any initialization after the InitializeComponent() call

    End Sub

    'Form overrides dispose to clean up the component list.
    Protected Overloads Overrides Sub Dispose(ByVal disposing As Boolean)
        If disposing Then
            If Not (components Is Nothing) Then
                components.Dispose()
            End If
        End If
        MyBase.Dispose(disposing)
    End Sub

    'Required by the Windows Form Designer
    Private components As System.ComponentModel.IContainer

    'NOTE: The following procedure is required by the Windows Form Designer
    'It can be modified using the Windows Form Designer.
    'Do not modify it using the code editor.
    Friend WithEvents pnlGrid As System.Windows.Forms.Panel
    Friend WithEvents lblMessage As System.Windows.Forms.Label
    Friend WithEvents pnlInfo As System.Windows.Forms.Panel
    Friend WithEvents Label1 As System.Windows.Forms.Label
    Friend WithEvents Label2 As System.Windows.Forms.Label
    Friend WithEvents lblMugwumps As System.Windows.Forms.Label
    Friend WithEvents lblGuesses As System.Windows.Forms.Label
    Friend WithEvents Panel1 As System.Windows.Forms.Panel
    Friend WithEvents btnNew As System.Windows.Forms.Button
    Friend WithEvents btnExit As System.Windows.Forms.Button
    Friend WithEvents picMugwump As System.Windows.Forms.PictureBox
    <System.Diagnostics.DebuggerStepThrough()> Private Sub InitializeComponent()
        Dim resources As System.ComponentModel.ComponentResourceManager = New
System.ComponentModel.ComponentResourceManager(GetType(Form1))
        Me.pnlGrid = New System.Windows.Forms.Panel
        Me.lblMessage = New System.Windows.Forms.Label
        Me.pnlInfo = New System.Windows.Forms.Panel
        Me.lblGuesses = New System.Windows.Forms.Label
        Me.lblMugwumps = New System.Windows.Forms.Label
        Me.Label2 = New System.Windows.Forms.Label
        Me.Label1 = New System.Windows.Forms.Label
        Me.Panel1 = New System.Windows.Forms.Panel
        Me.btnExit = New System.Windows.Forms.Button
        Me.btnNew = New System.Windows.Forms.Button
        Me.picMugwump = New System.Windows.Forms.PictureBox
```

```
        Me.pnlInfo.SuspendLayout()
        Me.Panel1.SuspendLayout()
        CType(Me.picMugwump, System.ComponentModel.ISupportInitialize).BeginInit()
        Me.SuspendLayout()
        '
        'pnlGrid
        '
        Me.pnlGrid.BackColor = System.Drawing.Color.White
        Me.pnlGrid.Location = New System.Drawing.Point(10, 8)
        Me.pnlGrid.Margin = New System.Windows.Forms.Padding(4, 3, 4, 3)
        Me.pnlGrid.Name = "pnlGrid"
        Me.pnlGrid.Size = New System.Drawing.Size(334, 328)
        Me.pnlGrid.TabIndex = 0
        '
        'lblMessage
        '
        Me.lblMessage.BackColor = System.Drawing.Color.FromArgb(CType(CType(255, Byte),
Integer), CType(CType(255, Byte), Integer), CType(CType(192, Byte), Integer))
        Me.lblMessage.BorderStyle = System.Windows.Forms.BorderStyle.Fixed3D
        Me.lblMessage.Font = New System.Drawing.Font("Arial", 11.25!,
System.Drawing.FontStyle.Regular, System.Drawing.GraphicsUnit.Point, CType(0, Byte))
        Me.lblMessage.ForeColor = System.Drawing.Color.FromArgb(CType(CType(0, Byte),
Integer), CType(CType(0, Byte), Integer), CType(CType(192, Byte), Integer))
        Me.lblMessage.Location = New System.Drawing.Point(364, 8)
        Me.lblMessage.Margin = New System.Windows.Forms.Padding(4, 0, 4, 0)
        Me.lblMessage.Name = "lblMessage"
        Me.lblMessage.Size = New System.Drawing.Size(278, 160)
        Me.lblMessage.TabIndex = 1
        Me.lblMessage.TextAlign = System.Drawing.ContentAlignment.MiddleCenter
        '
        'pnlInfo
        '
        Me.pnlInfo.BackColor = System.Drawing.Color.Magenta
        Me.pnlInfo.Controls.Add(Me.lblGuesses)
        Me.pnlInfo.Controls.Add(Me.lblMugwumps)
        Me.pnlInfo.Controls.Add(Me.Label2)
        Me.pnlInfo.Controls.Add(Me.Label1)
        Me.pnlInfo.Location = New System.Drawing.Point(374, 176)
        Me.pnlInfo.Margin = New System.Windows.Forms.Padding(4, 3, 4, 3)
        Me.pnlInfo.Name = "pnlInfo"
        Me.pnlInfo.Size = New System.Drawing.Size(259, 88)
        Me.pnlInfo.TabIndex = 2
        '
        'lblGuesses
        '
        Me.lblGuesses.BackColor = System.Drawing.Color.White
        Me.lblGuesses.BorderStyle = System.Windows.Forms.BorderStyle.Fixed3D
        Me.lblGuesses.Font = New System.Drawing.Font("Arial", 14.25!,
System.Drawing.FontStyle.Bold, System.Drawing.GraphicsUnit.Point, CType(0, Byte))
        Me.lblGuesses.Location = New System.Drawing.Point(134, 48)
        Me.lblGuesses.Margin = New System.Windows.Forms.Padding(4, 0, 4, 0)
        Me.lblGuesses.Name = "lblGuesses"
        Me.lblGuesses.Size = New System.Drawing.Size(106, 32)
        Me.lblGuesses.TabIndex = 3
        Me.lblGuesses.Text = "0"
        Me.lblGuesses.TextAlign = System.Drawing.ContentAlignment.MiddleCenter
        '
        'lblMugwumps
```

```
'
    Me.lblMugwumps.BackColor = System.Drawing.Color.White
    Me.lblMugwumps.BorderStyle = System.Windows.Forms.BorderStyle.Fixed3D
    Me.lblMugwumps.Font = New System.Drawing.Font("Arial", 14.25!,
System.Drawing.FontStyle.Bold, System.Drawing.GraphicsUnit.Point, CType(0, Byte))
    Me.lblMugwumps.Location = New System.Drawing.Point(134, 8)
    Me.lblMugwumps.Margin = New System.Windows.Forms.Padding(4, 0, 4, 0)
    Me.lblMugwumps.Name = "lblMugwumps"
    Me.lblMugwumps.Size = New System.Drawing.Size(106, 32)
    Me.lblMugwumps.TabIndex = 2
    Me.lblMugwumps.Text = "0"
    Me.lblMugwumps.TextAlign = System.Drawing.ContentAlignment.MiddleCenter
    '
    'Label2
    '
    Me.Label2.Font = New System.Drawing.Font("Arial", 9.75!,
System.Drawing.FontStyle.Regular, System.Drawing.GraphicsUnit.Point, CType(0, Byte))
    Me.Label2.Location = New System.Drawing.Point(19, 48)
    Me.Label2.Margin = New System.Windows.Forms.Padding(4, 0, 4, 0)
    Me.Label2.Name = "Label2"
    Me.Label2.Size = New System.Drawing.Size(106, 32)
    Me.Label2.TabIndex = 1
    Me.Label2.Text = "Guesses Taken"
    Me.Label2.TextAlign = System.Drawing.ContentAlignment.MiddleCenter
    '
    'Label1
    '
    Me.Label1.Font = New System.Drawing.Font("Arial", 9.75!,
System.Drawing.FontStyle.Regular, System.Drawing.GraphicsUnit.Point, CType(0, Byte))
    Me.Label1.Location = New System.Drawing.Point(10, 8)
    Me.Label1.Margin = New System.Windows.Forms.Padding(4, 0, 4, 0)
    Me.Label1.Name = "Label1"
    Me.Label1.Size = New System.Drawing.Size(125, 32)
    Me.Label1.TabIndex = 0
    Me.Label1.Text = "Mugwumps Remaining"
    Me.Label1.TextAlign = System.Drawing.ContentAlignment.MiddleCenter
    '
    'Panel1
    '
    Me.Panel1.BackColor = System.Drawing.Color.Magenta
    Me.Panel1.Controls.Add(Me.btnExit)
    Me.Panel1.Controls.Add(Me.btnNew)
    Me.Panel1.Location = New System.Drawing.Point(374, 272)
    Me.Panel1.Margin = New System.Windows.Forms.Padding(4, 3, 4, 3)
    Me.Panel1.Name = "Panel1"
    Me.Panel1.Size = New System.Drawing.Size(259, 56)
    Me.Panel1.TabIndex = 3
    '
    'btnExit
    '
    Me.btnExit.BackColor = System.Drawing.SystemColors.Control
    Me.btnExit.Location = New System.Drawing.Point(134, 16)
    Me.btnExit.Margin = New System.Windows.Forms.Padding(4, 3, 4, 3)
    Me.btnExit.Name = "btnExit"
    Me.btnExit.Size = New System.Drawing.Size(106, 32)
    Me.btnExit.TabIndex = 1
    Me.btnExit.Text = "Exit"
    Me.btnExit.UseVisualStyleBackColor = False
```

```
    '
    'btnNew
    '
    Me.btnNew.BackColor = System.Drawing.SystemColors.Control
    Me.btnNew.Location = New System.Drawing.Point(10, 16)
    Me.btnNew.Margin = New System.Windows.Forms.Padding(4, 3, 4, 3)
    Me.btnNew.Name = "btnNew"
    Me.btnNew.Size = New System.Drawing.Size(106, 32)
    Me.btnNew.TabIndex = 0
    Me.btnNew.Text = "New Game"
    Me.btnNew.UseVisualStyleBackColor = False
    '
    'picMugwump
    '
    Me.picMugwump.Image = CType(resources.GetObject("picMugwump.Image"),
System.Drawing.Image)
    Me.picMugwump.Location = New System.Drawing.Point(364, 320)
    Me.picMugwump.Margin = New System.Windows.Forms.Padding(4, 3, 4, 3)
    Me.picMugwump.Name = "picMugwump"
    Me.picMugwump.Size = New System.Drawing.Size(29, 16)
    Me.picMugwump.SizeMode = System.Windows.Forms.PictureBoxSizeMode.StretchImage
    Me.picMugwump.TabIndex = 0
    Me.picMugwump.TabStop = False
    Me.picMugwump.Visible = False
    '
    'Form1
    '
    Me.AutoScaleDimensions = New System.Drawing.SizeF(6.0!, 13.0!)
    Me.ClientSize = New System.Drawing.Size(655, 350)
    Me.Controls.Add(Me.Panel1)
    Me.Controls.Add(Me.pnlInfo)
    Me.Controls.Add(Me.lblMessage)
    Me.Controls.Add(Me.pnlGrid)
    Me.Controls.Add(Me.picMugwump)
    Me.FormBorderStyle = System.Windows.Forms.FormBorderStyle.FixedSingle
    Me.Margin = New System.Windows.Forms.Padding(4, 3, 4, 3)
    Me.Name = "Form1"
    Me.StartPosition = System.Windows.Forms.FormStartPosition.CenterScreen
    Me.Text = "Mugwump"
    Me.pnlInfo.ResumeLayout(False)
    Me.Panel1.ResumeLayout(False)
    CType(Me.picMugwump, System.ComponentModel.ISupportInitialize).EndInit()
    Me.ResumeLayout(False)

    End Sub

#End Region

    Dim GameOver As Boolean
    Dim P(4, 2) As Integer, Map(9, 9) As Integer
    Dim Tries As Integer
    Dim Remaining As Integer

    Dim MyMap As Graphics
    Dim GridBorder As Integer
    Dim GridDelta As Integer
    Dim MyRandom As New Random
```

```
   Private Sub Form1_Load(ByVal sender As Object, ByVal e As System.EventArgs)
Handles MyBase.Load
     MyMap = pnlGrid.CreateGraphics
     'Find grid dimensions
     GridBorder = 10
     GridDelta = CInt((pnlGrid.ClientSize.Width - 2 * GridBorder) / 10)
     lblMessage.Text = "Find the four Mugwumps hidden on a 10 x 10 grid. After each
guess, you are told how far you are from each Mugwump."
     lblMessage.Text = lblMessage.Text + ControlChars.CrLf + ControlChars.CrLf +
">Click New Game To Start<"
     btnNew.Focus()
   End Sub

   Private Sub pnlGrid_Paint(ByVal sender As Object, ByVal e As
System.Windows.Forms.PaintEventArgs) Handles pnlGrid.Paint
     Dim I As Integer, J As Integer
     For I = 0 To 10
       MyMap.DrawLine(Pens.Black, GridBorder, GridBorder + I * GridDelta, GridBorder
+ 10 * GridDelta, GridBorder + I * GridDelta)
       MyMap.DrawLine(Pens.Black, GridBorder + I * GridDelta, GridBorder, GridBorder
+ I * GridDelta, GridBorder + 10 * GridDelta)
     Next I
     'draw guesses and mugwumps
     For I = 0 To 9
       For J = 0 To 9
         If Map(I, J) = 1 Then
           MyMap.FillRectangle(Brushes.LightBlue, GridBorder + I * GridDelta + 1,
GridBorder + (9 - J) * GridDelta + 1, GridDelta - 1, GridDelta - 1)
         ElseIf Map(I, J) = -1 Then
           MyMap.DrawImage(picMugwump.Image, GridBorder + I * GridDelta, GridBorder +
(9 - J) * GridDelta, GridDelta, GridDelta)
         End If
       Next J
     Next I
   End Sub

   Private Sub btnNew_Click(ByVal sender As System.Object, ByVal e As
System.EventArgs) Handles btnNew.Click
     Dim I As Integer, J As Integer
     'Start new game
     GameOver = False
     lblMessage.Text = ""
     btnNew.Enabled = False
     btnExit.Text = "Stop"
     Remaining = 4
     Tries = 0
     lblMugwumps.Text = "4"
     lblGuesses.Text = "10"
     MyMap.Clear(pnlGrid.BackColor)
     For I = 0 To 9
       For J = 0 To 9
         Map(I, J) = 0
       Next J
     Next I
     For I = 1 To 4
       Do
         For J = 1 To 2
```

```
        P(I, J) = MyRandom.Next(10)
      Next J
    Loop Until Map(P(I, 1), P(I, 2)) = 0
    Map(P(I, 1), P(I, 2)) = 1
  Next I
  For I = 1 To 4
    Map(P(I, 1), P(I, 2)) = 0
  Next I
  pnlGrid_Paint(Nothing, Nothing)
  lblMessage.Text = "Four Mugwumps are now in hiding." + ControlChars.CrLf +
"Click where you might think one is."
  lblMessage.Refresh()
End Sub

  Private Sub btnExit_Click(ByVal sender As System.Object, ByVal e As
System.EventArgs) Handles btnExit.Click
    'Either exit or stop current game
    If btnExit.Text = "Exit" Then
      Me.Close()
    Else
      btnExit.Text = "Exit"
      btnNew.Enabled = True
      If Not (GameOver) Then lblMessage.Text = "Game Stopped"
      btnNew.Focus()
    End If
  End Sub

  Private Sub pnlGrid_MouseDown(ByVal sender As Object, ByVal e As
System.Windows.Forms.MouseEventArgs) Handles pnlGrid.MouseDown
    Dim I As Integer
    Dim M As Integer, N As Integer
    Dim D As Single
    Dim Found As Boolean
    If btnExit.Text = "Exit" Then Exit Sub
    If e.X < GridBorder Or e.X > GridBorder + 10 * GridDelta Then Exit Sub
    If e.Y < GridBorder Or e.Y > GridBorder + 10 * GridDelta Then Exit Sub
    'Find column
    For M = 0 To 9
      If e.X >= GridBorder + M * GridDelta And e.X <= GridBorder + (M + 1) *
GridDelta Then Exit For
    Next M
    'Find row
    For N = 9 To 0 Step -1
      If e.Y >= GridBorder + (9 - N) * GridDelta And e.Y <= GridBorder + (10 - N) *
GridDelta Then Exit For
    Next N
    If Map(M, N) <> 0 Then Exit Sub
    Beep()
    Map(M, N) = 1
    Tries = Tries + 1
    lblGuesses.Text = Format(Tries, "0")
    lblGuesses.Refresh()
    lblMessage.Text = ""
    Found = False
    For I = 1 To 4
      If P(I, 1) <> -1 Then
        If P(I, 1) <> M Or P(I, 2) <> N Then
          D = Math.Sqrt((P(I, 1) - M) ^ 2 + (P(I, 2) - N) ^ 2)
```

```
        lblMessage.Text = lblMessage.Text + "You are " + Format(D, "0.0") + "
units from Mugwump" + Str(I) + ControlChars.CrLf
      Else
        Found = True
        P(I, 1) = -1
        Map(M, N) = -1
        lblMessage.Text = lblMessage.Text + "You found Mugwump" + Str(I) +
ControlChars.CrLf
        Remaining = Remaining - 1
        lblMugwumps.Text = Format(Remaining, "0")
        lblMugwumps.Refresh()
      End If
    End If
  Next I
  If Found Then
    'draw mugwump in column M, row N - use cute picture
    MyMap.DrawImage(picMugwump.Image, GridBorder + M * GridDelta, GridBorder + (9
- N) * GridDelta, GridDelta, GridDelta)
  Else
    MyMap.FillRectangle(Brushes.LightBlue, GridBorder + M * GridDelta + 1,
GridBorder + (9 - N) * GridDelta + 1, GridDelta - 1, GridDelta - 1)
  End If
  If Remaining = 0 Then
    GameOver = True
    lblMessage.Text = lblMessage.Text + ControlChars.CrLf + "You found all 4
Mugwumps!" + ControlChars.CrLf + "It took you" + Str(Tries) + " guesses."
    btnExit.PerformClick()
  End If
  End Sub
End Class
```

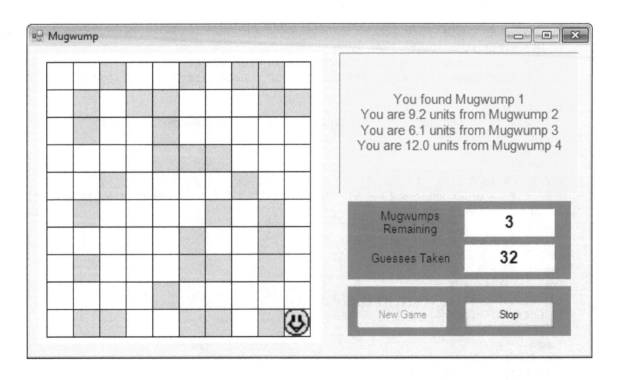

MUGWUMP – VISUAL C# SOURCE CODE

```csharp
#region Using directives

using System;
using System.Collections.Generic;
using System.ComponentModel;
using System.Data;
using System.Drawing;
using System.Windows.Forms;

#endregion

namespace Mugwump
{
    partial class Form1 : Form
    {
        public Form1()
        {
            InitializeComponent();
        }
        bool gameOver;
        int[,] p = new int[5, 3];
        int[,] map = new int[10, 10];
        int tries, remaining, gridBorder, gridDelta;
        Graphics myMap;
        Random myRandom = new Random();

        private void Form1_Load(object sender, EventArgs e)
        {
            myMap = pnlGrid.CreateGraphics();
            // Find grid dimensions
            gridBorder = 10;
            gridDelta = (int) ((pnlGrid.ClientSize.Width - 2 * gridBorder) / 10);
            lblMessage.Text = "Find the four Mugwumps hidden on a 10 x 10 grid.
After each guess, you are told how far you are from each Mugwump.";
            lblMessage.Text = lblMessage.Text + "\r\n\r\n>Click New Game To Start<";
            btnNew.Focus();
        }

        private void pnlGrid_Paint(object sender, PaintEventArgs e)
        {
            int i, j;
            for (i = 0; i < 11; i++)
            {
                myMap.DrawLine(Pens.Black, gridBorder, gridBorder + i * gridDelta,
gridBorder + 10 * gridDelta, gridBorder + i * gridDelta);
                myMap.DrawLine(Pens.Black, gridBorder + i * gridDelta, gridBorder,
gridBorder + i * gridDelta, gridBorder + 10 * gridDelta);
            }
            // draw guesses and mugwumps
            for (i = 0; i < 10; i++)
            {
                for (j = 0; j < 10; j++)
                {
                    if (map[i, j] == 1)
```

```
                {
                    myMap.FillRectangle(Brushes.LightBlue, gridBorder + i *
gridDelta + 1, gridBorder + (9 - j) * gridDelta + 1, gridDelta - 1, gridDelta - 1);
                }
                else if (map[i, j] == -1)
                {
                    myMap.DrawImage(picMugwump.Image, gridBorder + i *
gridDelta, gridBorder + (9 - j) * gridDelta, gridDelta, gridDelta);
                }
            }
        }
    }

    private void btnNew_Click(object sender, EventArgs e)
    {
        int i, j;
        // Start new game
        gameOver = false;
        lblMessage.Text = "";
        btnNew.Enabled = false;
        btnExit.Text = "Stop";
        remaining = 4;
        tries = 0;
        lblMugwumps.Text = "4";
        lblGuesses.Text = "0";
        myMap.Clear(pnlGrid.BackColor);
        for (i = 0; i < 10; i++)
        {
            for (j = 0; j < 10; j++)
            {
                map[i, j] = 0;
            }
        }
        for (i = 1; i < 5; i++)
        {
            do
            {
                for (j = 1; j < 3; j++)
                {
                    p[i, j] = myRandom.Next(10);
                }
            }
            while (map[p[i, 1], p[i, 2]] != 0);
            map[p[i, 1], p[i, 2]] = 1;
        }
        for (i = 1; i < 5; i++)
        {
            map[p[i, 1], p[i, 2]] = 0;
        }
        pnlGrid_Paint(null, null);
        lblMessage.Text = "Four Mugwumps are now in hiding.\r\nClick where you
might think one is.";
        lblMessage.Refresh();
    }

    private void btnExit_Click(object sender, EventArgs e)
    {
        // Either exit or stop current game
```

```csharp
            if (btnExit.Text == "Exit")
            {
                this.Close();
            }
            else
            {
                btnExit.Text = "Exit";
                btnNew.Enabled = true;
                if (!gameOver)
                {
                    lblMessage.Text = "Game Stopped";
                }
                btnNew.Focus();
            }
        }

        private void pnlGrid_MouseDown(object sender, MouseEventArgs e)
        {
            int i, m, n;
            double d;
            bool found;
            if (btnExit.Text == "Exit")
            {
                return;
            }
            if (e.X < gridBorder || e.X > gridBorder + 10 * gridDelta)
            {
                return;
            }
            if (e.Y < gridBorder || e.Y > gridBorder + 10 * gridDelta)
            {
                return;
            }
            // Find column
            for (m = 0; m < 10; m++)
            {
                if (e.X >= gridBorder + m * gridDelta && e.X <= gridBorder + (m + 1)
* gridDelta)
                    break;
            }
            // Find row
            for (n = 9; n >=0; n--)
            {
                if (e.Y >= gridBorder + (9 - n) * gridDelta && e.Y <= gridBorder +
(10 - n) * gridDelta)
                    break;
            }
            if (map[m, n] != 0)
            {
                return;
            }
            Console.Beep();
            map[m, n] = 1;
            tries++;
            lblGuesses.Text = Convert.ToString(tries);
            lblGuesses.Refresh();
            lblMessage.Text = "";
            found = false;
```

```
        for (i = 1; i < 5; i++)
        {
            if (p[i, 1] != -1)
            {
                if (p[i, 1] != m || p[i, 2] != n)
                {
                    d = Math.Sqrt((p[i, 1] - m) * (p[i, 1] - m) + (p[i, 2] - n)
* (p[i, 2] - n));
                    lblMessage.Text = lblMessage.Text + "You are " +
String.Format("{0:f1}", d) + " units from Mugwump " + Convert.ToString(i) + "\r\n";
                }
                else
                {
                    found = true;
                    p[i, 1] = -1;
                    map[m, n] = -1;
                    lblMessage.Text = lblMessage.Text + "You found Mugwump " +
Convert.ToString(i) + "\r\n";
                    remaining--;
                    lblMugwumps.Text = Convert.ToString(remaining);
                    lblMugwumps.Refresh();
                }
            }
        }
        if (found)
        {
            // draw mugwump in column M, row N - use cute picture
            myMap.DrawImage(picMugwump.Image, gridBorder + m * gridDelta,
gridBorder + (9 - n) * gridDelta, gridDelta, gridDelta);
        }
        else
        {
            myMap.FillRectangle(Brushes.LightBlue, gridBorder + m * gridDelta +
1, gridBorder + (9 - n) * gridDelta + 1, gridDelta - 1, gridDelta - 1);
        }
        if (remaining == 0)
        {
            gameOver = true;
            lblMessage.Text = lblMessage.Text + "\r\nYou found all 4
Mugwumps!\r\n" + "It took you " + Convert.ToString(tries) + " guesses.";
            btnExit.PerformClick();
        }
    }

    }
}
```

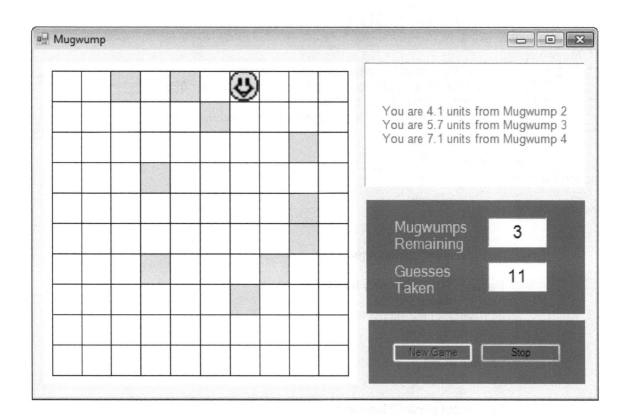

MUGWUMP - JAVA SOURCE CODE

```java
/*
 * Mugwump
 * Original Author: Bob Albrecht of Peoples Computer Company
 * BASIC COMPUTER GAMES, Edited by David H. Ahl, Published in 1978
 * Ported with Permission to Small Basic by Philip Conrod
 * © Biblebyte Books, 2010 - Find more at http://www.biblebytebooks.com
 */

import java.util.Random;
import java.text.*;

public class Mugwump
{

        public static void main(String[] args)
        {
                Random jRandom = new Random();
                int p[][] = new int[4][2];
                int map[][] = new int[10][10];
                int remaining, tries;
                int m, n;
                boolean found;


                System.out.println("Mugwumps\n");
                System.out.println("Find the four Mugwumps hidden on a 10 x 10 grid.");
                System.out.println("After each guess, you are told how far you are from each
Mugwump.\n");

                // Start new game loop
                do
                {
                        remaining = 4;
                        tries = 0;
                        // hide mugwumps
                        for (int i = 0; i < 10; i++)
                        {
                                for (int j = 0; j < 10; j++)
                                {
                                        map[i][j] = 0;
                                }
                        }
                        for (int i = 0; i <4; i++)
                        {
                                do
                                {
                                        for (int j = 0; j <2; j++)
                                        {
                                                p[i][j] = jRandom.nextInt(10);
                                        }
                                }
                                while (map[p[i][0]][p[i][1]] != 0);
                                map[p[i][0]][p[i][1]] = 1;
                        }
```

```
        for (int i = 0; i < 4; i++)
        {
                map[p[i][0]][p[i][1]] = 0;
        }
        // Next turn loop
        do
        {
                // draw current game board grid
                System.out.println("Current grid (O-Guess, X-Last Guess, M-
Mugwump):");
                System.out.println("  0 1 2 3 4 5 6 7 8 9");
                for (int i = 0; i < 10; i++)
                {
                        System.out.print((i) + "|");
                        for (int j = 0; j < 10; j++)
                        {
                                switch (map[i][j])
                                {
                                        case 0:
                                        System.out.print(" |");
                                        break;
                                        case 1:
                                        System.out.print("O|");
                                        break;
                                        case 2:
                                        System.out.print("X|");
                                        map[i][j] = 1;
                                        break;
                                        case 3:
                                        System.out.print("M|");
                                        break;
                                }
                        }
                System.out.println();
                }
                System.out.println("\n" + remaining + " Mugwumps are now in
hiding. Where do you think one is?");
                do
                {
                        m = Keyin.inInt("What row?");
                        n = Keyin.inInt("What column?");
                }
                while (m < 0 || m > 9 || n <0 || n > 9);
                switch (map[m][n])
                {
                        case 1:
                        System.out.println("You already looked there!");
                        break;
                        case 2:
                        System.out.println("You already looked there!");
                        break;
                        case 3:
                        System.out.println("You already found this Mugwump!");
                        break;
                        case 0:
                        tries++;
```

```
                                        found = false;
                                        for (int i = 0; i < 4; i++)
                                        {
                                                if (p[i][0] != -1)
                                                {
                                                        if (p[i][0] != m || p[i][1] != n)
                                                        {
                                                                map[m][n] = 2;
                                                                double d = Math.sqrt((p[i][0] - m) *
(p[i][0] - m) + (p[i][1] - n) * (p[i][1] - n));
                                                                System.out.println("You are " +
new DecimalFormat("0.0").format(d) + " units from Mugwump " + (i + 1));
                                                        }
                                                        else
                                                        {
                                                                found = true;
                                                                p[i][0] = -1;
                                                                System.out.println("You found
Mugwump " + (i + 1) + "!");
                                                                remaining--;
                                                        }
                                                }
                                                if (found)
                                                {
                                                        map[m][n] = 3;
                                                }
                                        }
                                }
                                while (remaining > 0);
                                System.out.println("You found all the Mugwumps with " + tries + " tries!
Good job!");

                        }
                        while (Keyin.inString("\nPlay again? (enter a y for yes)").equals("y"));
                }

}
```

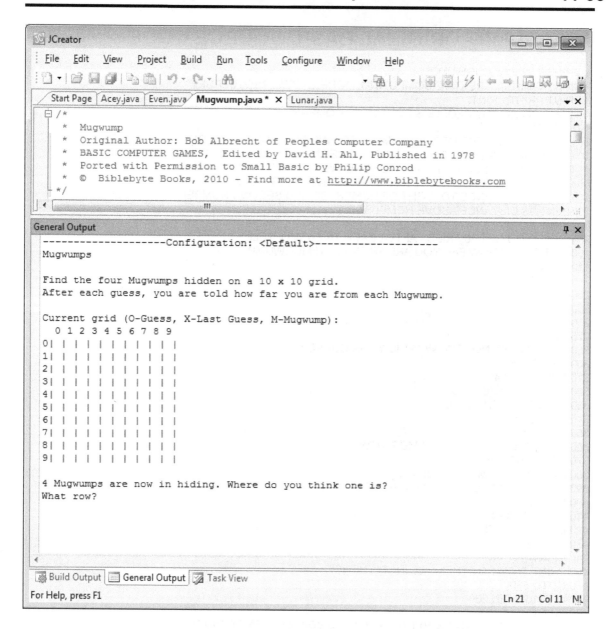

MUGWUMP - ORIGINAL BASIC SOURCE CODE

```
1 PRINT TAB(33);"MUGWUMP"
2 PRINT TAB(15);"CREATIVE COMPUTING  MORRISTOWN, NEW JERSEY"
3 PRINT:PRINT:PRINT
4 REM    COURTESY PEOPLE'S COMPUTER COMPANY
10 DIM P(4,2)
20 PRINT "THE OBJECT OF THIS GAME IS TO FIND FOUR MUGWUMPS"
30 PRINT "HIDDEN ON A 10 BY 10 GRID.  HOMEBASE IS POSITION 0,0."
40 PRINT "ANY GUESS YOU MAKE MUST BE TWO NUMBERS WITH EACH"
50 PRINT "NUMBER BETWEEN 0 AND 9, INCLUSIVE.  FIRST NUMBER"
60 PRINT "IS DISTANCE TO RIGHT OF HOMEBASE AND SECOND NUMBER"
70 PRINT "IS DISTANCE ABOVE HOMEBASE."
80 PRINT
90 PRINT "YOU GET 10 TRIES.  AFTER EACH TRY, I WILL TELL"
100 PRINT "YOU HOW FAR YOU ARE FROM EACH MUGWUMP."
110 PRINT
240 GOSUB 1000
250 T=0
260 T=T+1
270 PRINT
275 PRINT
290 PRINT "TURN NO.";T;"-- WHAT IS YOUR GUESS";
300 INPUT M,N
310 FOR I=1 TO 4
320 IF P(I,1)=-1 THEN 400
330 IF P(I,1)<>M THEN 380
340 IF P(I,2)<>N THEN 380
350 P(I,1)=-1
360 PRINT "YOU HAVE FOUND MUGWUMP";I
370 GOTO 400
380 D=SQR((P(I,1)-M)^2+(P(I,2)-N)^2)
390 PRINT "YOU ARE";(INT(D*10))/10;"UNITS FROM MUGWUMP";I
400 NEXT I
410 FOR J=1 TO 4
420 IF P(J,1)<>-1 THEN 470
430 NEXT J
440 PRINT
450 PRINT "YOU GOT THEM ALL IN";T;"TURNS!"
460 GOTO 580
470 IF T<10 THEN 260
480 PRINT
490 PRINT "SORRY, THAT'S 10 TRIES.  HERE IS WHERE THEY'RE HIDING:"
540 FOR I=1 TO 4
550 IF P(I,1)=-1 THEN 570
560 PRINT "MUGWUMP";I;"IS AT (";P(I,1);",";P(I,2);")"
570 NEXT I
580 PRINT
600 PRINT "THAT WAS FUN! LET'S PLAY AGAIN......."
610 PRINT "FOUR MORE MUGWUMPS ARE NOW IN HIDING."
630 GOTO 240
1000 FOR J=1 TO 2
1010 FOR I=1 TO 4
1020 P(I,J)=INT(10*RND(1))
1030 NEXT I
1040 NEXT J
1050 RETURN
1099 END
```

Appendix I. Small Basic Colors

Color	Name	RGB Value
	AliceBlue	#F0F8FF
	AntiqueWhite	#FAEBD7
	Aqua	#00FFFF
	Aquamarine	#7FFFD4
	Azure	#F0FFFF
	Beige	#F5F5DC
	Bisque	#FFE4C4
	Black	#000000
	BlanchedAlmond	#FFEBCD
	Blue	#0000FF
	BlueViolet	#8A2BE2
	Brown	#A52A2A
	BurlyWood	#DEB887
	CadetBlue	#5F9EA0
	Chartreuse	#7FFF00
	Chocolate	#D2691E
	Coral	#FF7F50
	CornflowerBlue	#6495ED

	Color	Hex
	Cornsilk	#FFF8DC
	Crimson	#DC143C
	Cyan	#00FFFF
	DarkBlue	#00008B
	DarkCyan	#008B8B
	DarkGoldenrod	#B8860B
	DarkGray / DarkGrey[†]	#A9A9A9
	DarkGreen	#006400
	DarkKhaki	#BDB76B
	DarkMagenta	#8B008B
	DarkOliveGreen	#556B2F
	DarkOrange	#FF8C00
	DarkOrchid	#9932CC
	DarkRed	#8B0000
	DarkSalmon	#E9967A
	DarkSeaGreen	#8FBC8F
	DarkSlateBlue	#483D8B
	DarkSlateGray / DarkSlateGrey[†]	#2F4F4F
	DarkTurquoise	#00CED1
	DarkViolet	#9400D3
	DeepPink	#FF1493

	Color	Hex
	DeepSkyBlue	#00BFFF
	DimGray / DimGrey[†]	#696969
	DodgerBlue	#1E90FF
	FireBrick	#B22222
	FloralWhite	#FFFAF0
	ForestGreen	#228B22
	Fuchsia	#FF00FF
	Gainsboro	#DCDCDC
	GhostWhite	#F8F8FF
	Gold	#FFD700
	Goldenrod	#DAA520
	Gray / Grey[†]	#808080
	Green	#008000
	GreenYellow	#ADFF2F
	Honeydew	#F0FFF0
	HotPink	#FF69B4
	IndianRed	#CD5C5C
	Indigo	#4B0082
	Ivory	#FFFFF0
	Khaki	#F0E68C
	Lavender	#E6E6FA

	Color	Hex
	LavenderBlush	#FFF0F5
	LawnGreen	#7CFC00
	LemonChiffon	#FFFACD
	LightBlue	#ADD8E6
	LightCoral	#F08080
	LightCyan	#E0FFFF
	LightGoldenrodYellow	#FAFAD2
	LightGreen	#90EE90
	LightGray† / LightGrey	#D3D3D3
	LightPink	#FFB6C1
	LightSalmon	#FFA07A
	LightSeaGreen	#20B2AA
	LightSkyBlue	#87CEFA
	LightSlateGray / LightSlateGrey†	#778899
	LightSteelBlue	#B0C4DE
	LightYellow	#FFFFE0
	Lime	#00FF00
	LimeGreen	#32CD32
	Linen	#FAF0E6
	Magenta	#FF00FF
	Maroon	#800000

	MediumAquamarine	#66CDAA
	MediumBlue	#0000CD
	MediumOrchid	#BA55D3
	MediumPurple	#9370DB
	MediumSeaGreen	#3CB371
	MediumSlateBlue	#7B68EE
	MediumSpringGreen	#00FA9A
	MediumTurquoise	#48D1CC
	MediumVioletRed	#C71585
	MidnightBlue	#191970
	MintCream	#F5FFFA
	MistyRose	#FFE4E1
	Moccasin	#FFE4B5
	NavajoWhite	#FFDEAD
	Navy	#000080
	OldLace	#FDF5E6
	Olive	#808000
	OliveDrab	#6B8E23
	Orange	#FFA500
	OrangeRed	#FF4500
	Orchid	#DA70D6

	PaleGoldenrod	#EEE8AA
	PaleGreen	#98FB98
	PaleTurquoise	#AFEEEE
	PaleVioletRed	#DB7093
	PapayaWhip	#FFEFD5
	PeachPuff	#FFDAB9
	Peru	#CD853F
	Pink	#FFC0CB
	Plum	#DDA0DD
	PowderBlue	#B0E0E6
	Purple	#800080
	Red	#FF0000
	RosyBrown	#BC8F8F
	RoyalBlue	#4169E1
	SaddleBrown	#8B4513
	Salmon	#FA8072
	SandyBrown	#F4A460
	SeaGreen	#2E8B57
	Seashell	#FFF5EE
	Sienna	#A0522D
	Silver	#C0C0C0

	SkyBlue	#87CEEB
	SlateBlue	#6A5ACD
	SlateGray / SlateGrey⁺	#708090
	Snow	#FFFAFA
	SpringGreen	#00FF7F
	SteelBlue	#4682B4
	Tan	#D2B48C
	Teal	#008080
	Thistle	#D8BFD8
	Tomato	#FF6347
	Turquoise	#40E0D0
	Violet	#EE82EE
	Wheat	#F5DEB3
	White	#FFFFFF
	WhiteSmoke	#F5F5F5
	Yellow	#FFFF00
	YellowGreen	#9ACD32

We publish several Self-Study or Instructor-Led Computer Programming Tutorials for Microsoft® Small Basic:

Small Basic For Kids is an illustrated introduction to computer programming that provides an interactive, self-paced tutorial to the new Small Basic programming environment. The book consists of 30 short lessons that explain how to create and run a Small Basic program. Elementary students learn about program design and many elements of the Small Basic language. Numerous examples are used to demonstrate every step in the building process. The tutorial also includes two complete games (Hangman and Pizza Zapper) for students to build and try. Designed for kids ages 8 and up.

The Beginning Microsoft Small Basic Programming Tutorial is a self-study first semester "beginner" programming tutorial consisting of 11 chapters explaining (in simple, easy-to-follow terms) how to write Microsoft Small Basic programs. Numerous examples are used to demonstrate every step in the building process. The last chapter of this tutorial shows you how four different Small Basic games could port to Visual Basic, Visual C# and Java. This beginning level self-paced tutorial can be used at home or at school. The tutorial is simple enough for kids ages 10 and above yet engaging enough for beginning adults.

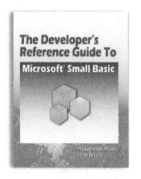

Programming Games with Microsoft Small Basic is a self-paced second semester "intermediate" level programming tutorial consisting of 10 chapters explaining (in simple, easy-to-follow terms) how to write video games in Microsoft Small Basic. The games built are non-violent, family-friendly, and teach logical thinking skills. Students will learn how to program the following Small Basic video games: Safecracker, Tic Tac Toe, Match Game, Pizza Delivery, Moon Landing, and Leap Frog. This intermediate level self-paced tutorial can be used at home or school. The tutorial is simple enough for kids yet engaging enough for beginning adults.

Programming Home Projects with Microsoft Small Basic is a self-paced programming tutorial explains (in simple, easy-to-follow terms) how to build Small Basic Windows applications. Students learn about program design, Small Basic objects, many elements of the Small Basic language, and how to debug and distribute finished programs. Sequential file input and output is also introduced.. The projects built include a Dual-Mode Stopwatch, Flash Card Math Quiz, Multiple Choice Exam, Blackjack Card Game, Weight Monitor, Home Inventory Manager and a Snowball Toss Game.

The Developer's Reference Guide to Microsoft Small Basic
While developing all the different Microsoft Small Basic tutorials we found it necessary to write The Developer's Reference Guide to Microsoft Small Basic. The Developer's Reference Guide to Microsoft Small Basic is over 500 pages long and includes over 100 Small Basic programming examples for you to learn from and include in your own Microsoft Small Basic programs. It is a detailed reference guide for new developers.

David Ahl's Small Basic Computer Adventures is a Microsoft Small Basic re-make of the classic *Basic Computer Games* programming *book* originally written by David H. Ahl. This new book includes the following classic adventure simulations; Marco Polo, Westward Ho!, The Longest Automobile Race, The Orient Express, Amelia Earhart: Around the World Flight, Tour de France, Subway Scavenger, Hong Kong Hustle, and Voyage to Neptune. Learn how to program these classic computer simulations in Microsoft Small Basic. This "intermediate" level self-paced tutorial can be used at home or school.

Basic Computer Games - Small Basic Edition is a re-make of the classic BASIC COMPUTER GAMES book originally edited by David H. Ahl. It contains 100 of the original text based BASIC games that inspired a whole generation of programmers. Now these classic BASIC games have been re-written in Microsoft Small Basic for a new generation to enjoy! The new Small Basic games look and act like the original text based games. The book includes all the original spaghetti code GOTO commands and it will make you appreciate the structured programming techniques found in our other tutorials.

We also publish several Self-Study or Instructor-Led Computer Programming Tutorials for Microsoft® Visual Basic® Express and Visual C#® Express:

Visual Basic® Express For Kids is a beginning programming tutorial consisting of 10 chapters explaining (in simple, easy-to-follow terms) how to build a Visual Basic Express Windows application. Students learn about project design, the Visual Basic Express toolbox, and many elements of the BASIC language. The tutorial also includes several detailed computer projects for students to build and try. These projects include a number guessing game, a card game, an allowance calculator, a drawing program, a state capitals game, Tic-Tac-Toe and even a simple video game. Designed for kids ages 12 and up.

Beginning Visual Basic® Express is a semester long self-paced "beginner" programming tutorial consisting of 10 chapters explaining (in simple, easy-to-follow terms) how to build a Visual Basic Express Windows application. The tutorial includes several detailed computer projects for students to build and try. These projects include a number guessing game, card game, allowance calculator, drawing program, state capitals game, and a couple of video games like Pong. We also include several college prep bonus projects including a loan calculator, portfolio manager, and checkbook balancer. Designed for students age 15 and up.

Programming Games with Visual Basic® Express is a semester long "intermediate" programming tutorial consisting of 10 chapters explaining (in simple, easy-to-follow terms) how to build Visual Basic Video Games. The games built are non-violent, family-friendly, and teach logical thinking skills. Students will learn how to program the following Visual Basic video games: Safecracker, Tic Tac Toe, Match Game, Pizza Delivery, Moon Landing, and Leap Frog. This intermediate level self-paced tutorial can be used at home or school. The tutorial is simple enough for kids yet engaging enough for beginning adults.

Programming Home Projects with Visual Basic® Express is a semester long self-paced programming tutorial explains (in simple, easy-to-follow terms) how to build a Visual Basic Express Windows project. Students learn about project design, the Visual Basic Express toolbox, many elements of the Visual Basic language, and how to debug and distribute finished projects. The projects built include a Dual-Mode Stopwatch, Flash Card Math Quiz, Multiple Choice Exam, Blackjack Card Game, Weight Monitor, Home Inventory Manager and a Snowball Toss Game.

Visual C#® Express For Kids is a beginning programming tutorial consisting of 10 chapters explaining (in simple, easy-to-follow terms) how to build a Visual C# Express Windows application. Students learn about project design, the Visual C# Express toolbox, and many elements of the C# language. Numerous examples are used to demonstrate every step in the building process. The projects include a number guessing game, a card game, an allowance calculator, a drawing program, a state capitals game, Tic-Tac-Toe and even a simple video game. Designed for kids ages 12 and up.

Beginning Visual C#® Express is a semester long "beginning" programming tutorial consisting of 10 chapters explaining (in simple, easy-to-follow terms) how to build a C# Express Windows application. The tutorial includes several detailed computer projects for students to build and try. These projects include a number guessing game, card game, allowance calculator, drawing program, state capitals game, and a couple of video games like Pong. We also include several college prep bonus projects including a loan calculator, portfolio manager, and checkbook balancer. Designed for students age 15 and up.

Programming Games with Visual C#® Express is a semester long "intermediate" programming tutorial consisting of 10 chapters explaining (in simple, easy-to-follow terms) how to build a Visual C# Video Games. The games built are non-violent, family-friendly and teach logical thinking skills. Students will learn how to program the following Visual C# video games: Safecracker, Tic Tac Toe, Match Game, Pizza Delivery, Moon Landing, and Leap Frog. This intermediate level self-paced tutorial can be used at home or school. The tutorial is simple enough for kids yet engaging enough for beginning adults.

Programming Home Projects with Visual C#® Express is a semester long self-paced programming tutorial explains (in simple, easy-to-follow terms) how to build a Visual C# Express Windows project. Students learn about project design, the Visual C# Express toolbox, many elements of the Visual C# language, and how to debug and distribute finished projects. The projects built include a Dual-Mode Stopwatch, Flash Card Math Quiz, Multiple Choice Exam, Blackjack Card Game, Weight Monitor, Home Inventory Manager and a Snowball Toss Game.

We also publish several Self-Study or Instructor-Led Computer Programming Tutorials for Oracle® Java® :

Java™ For Kids is a beginning programming tutorial consisting of 10 chapters explaining (in simple, easy-to-follow terms) how to build a Java application. Students learn about project design, object-oriented programming, console applications, graphics applications and many elements of the Java language. Numerous examples are used to demonstrate every step in the building process. The projects include a number guessing game, a card game, an allowance calculator, a state capitals game, Tic-Tac-Toe, a simple drawing program, and even a basic video game. Designed for kids ages 12 and up.

Beginning Java™ is a semester long "beginning" programming tutorial consisting of 10 chapters explaining (in simple, easy-to-follow terms) how to build a Java application. The tutorial includes several detailed computer projects for students to build and try. These projects include a number guessing game, card game, allowance calculator, drawing program, state capitals game, and a couple of video games like Pong. We also include several college prep bonus projects including a loan calculator, portfolio manager, and checkbook balancer. Designed for students age 15 and up.

Learn Java™ GUI Applications is a 9 lesson Tutorial covering object-oriented programming concepts, using a integrated development environment to create and test Java projects, building and distributing GUI applications, understanding and using the Swing control library, exception handling, sequential file access, graphics, multimedia, advanced topics such as printing, and help system authoring. Our **Beginning Java** tutorial is a pre-requisite for this tutorial.

Programming Games with Java™ is a semester long "intermediate" programming tutorial consisting of 10 chapters explaining (in simple, easy-to-follow terms) how to build a Visual C# Video Games. The games built are non-violent, family-friendly and teach logical thinking skills. Students will learn how to program the following Visual C# video games: Safecracker, Tic Tac Toe, Match Game, Pizza Delivery, Moon Landing, and Leap Frog. This intermediate level self-paced tutorial can be used at home or school. The tutorial is simple enough for kids yet engaging enough for beginning adults. Our **Beginning Java** and **Learn Java GUI Applications** tutorials are required pre-requisites for this tutorial.

Programming Home Projects with Java™ is a Java GUI Swing tutorial covering object-oriented programming concepts. It explains (in simple, easy-to-follow terms) how to build Java GUI project to use around the home. Students learn about project design, the Java Swing controls, many elements of the Java language, and how to distribute finished projects. The projects built include a Dual-Mode Stopwatch, Flash Card Math Quiz, Multiple Choice Exam, Blackjack Card Game, Weight Monitor, Home Inventory Manager and a Snowball Toss Game. Our **Beginning Java** and **Learn Java GUI Applications** tutorials are pre-requisites for this tutorial.

We also publish several advanced Honors Level Self-Study or Instructor-Led "College-Prep" and College Level Computer Programming Tutorials for Microsoft® Visual Basic® Professional Edition and Visual C#® Professional Edition:

LEARN VISUAL BASIC PROFESSIONAL EDITION is a comprehensive college prep programming tutorial covering object-oriented programming, the Visual Basic integrated development environment, building and distributing Windows applications using the Windows Installer, exception handling, sequential file access, graphics, multimedia, advanced topics such as web access, printing, and HTML help system authoring. The tutorial also introduces database applications (using ADO .NET) and web applications (using ASP.NET).

VISUAL BASIC AND DATABASES PROFESSIONAL EDITION is a tutorial that provides a detailed introduction to using Visual Basic for accessing and maintaining databases for desktop applications. Topics covered include: database structure, database design, Visual Basic project building, ADO .NET data objects (connection, data adapter, command, data table), data bound controls, proper interface design, structured query language (SQL), creating databases using Access, SQL Server and ADOX, and database reports. Actual projects developed include a book tracking system, a sales invoicing program, a home inventory system and a daily weather monitor.

LEARN VISUAL C# PROFESSIONAL EDITION is a comprehensive college prep computer programming tutorial covering object-oriented programming, the Visual C# integrated development environment and toolbox, building and distributing Windows applications (using the Windows Installer), exception handling, sequential file input and output, graphics, multimedia effects (animation and sounds), advanced topics such as web access, printing, and HTML help system authoring. The tutorial also introduces database applications (using ADO .NET) and web applications (using ASP.NET).

VISUAL C# AND DATABASES PROFESSIONAL EDITION is a tutorial that provides a detailed introduction to using Visual C# for accessing and maintaining databases for desktop applications. Topics covered include: database structure, database design, Visual C# project building, ADO .NET data objects (connection, data adapter, command, data table), data bound controls, proper interface design, structured query language (SQL), creating databases using Access, SQL Server and ADOX, and database reports. Actual projects developed include a books tracking system, a sales invoicing program, a home inventory system and a daily weather monitor.